Legal Education for Wellbeing

This book aims to assist legal educators and law schools in integrating wellbeing within the design and delivery of the legal curriculum. It also encourages the evaluation of wellbeing-related initiatives, to develop an evidence-based, sustainable approach to its inclusion.

The contributions to this volume each focus upon different aspects of wellbeing and the curriculum, including the applications of vulnerability and social identity theory, the role of transitions and inductions, the implementation and evaluation of law school wellbeing initiatives, reflections on both the Socratic method and assessment, the results of a longitudinal student study and a consideration of the legal profession's perspective. They contain both theoretical and empirical evidence to support the development of wellbeing-informed teaching and learning and foster positive interactions and experiences for both staff and students. Taken together, and coupled with international perspectives, they provide evidence and examples to support a holistic approach to wellbeing in legal education which moves beyond simply ameliorating damaging impacts and instead identifies meaningful routes to fostering positive wellbeing.

This volume will be of interest to legal academics and others with an interest in legal education, including legal professionals and law students. It will also appeal to those who have an interest in integrating wellbeing into the curriculum within higher education. This book was originally published as a special issue of *The Law Teacher.*

Emma Jones is Senior Lecturer of Law at the University of Sheffield's School of Law. Her research focuses on the role of wellbeing and emotions in legal education and the legal profession. She is Chair of the Association of Law Teachers and an International Bar Association Wellbeing Commissioner.

Caroline Strevens is Professor of Legal Education at the University of Portsmouth's School of Law. Her research focuses on the wellbeing of law staff and students including investigating how principles of positive psychology may influence or promote flourishing.

Legal Education for Wellbeing

Design, Delivery and Evaluation

Edited by

Emma Jones and Caroline Strevens

Routledge
Taylor & Francis Group
LONDON AND NEW YORK

First published 2025
by Routledge
4 Park Square, Milton Park, Abingdon, Oxon OX14 4RN

and by Routledge
605 Third Avenue, New York, NY 10158

Routledge is an imprint of the Taylor & Francis Group, an informa business

British Library Cataloguing in Publication Data
A catalogue record for this book is available from the British Library

ISBN13: 978-1-032-77633-0 (hbk)
ISBN13: 978-1-032-77677-4 (pbk)
ISBN13: 978-1-003-48430-1 (ebk)

DOI: 10.4324/9781003484301

Typeset in Myriad Pro
by Newgen Publishing UK

Publisher's Note
The publisher accepts responsibility for any inconsistencies that may have arisen during the conversion of this book from journal articles to book chapters, namely the inclusion of journal terminology.

Contents

Citation Information

The chapters in this book were originally published in *The Law Teacher*, volume 56, issue 1 (2022). When citing this material, please use the original page numbering for each article, as follows:

Introduction

Legal education for wellbeing: design, delivery and evaluation
Emma Jones and Caroline Strevens
The Law Teacher, volume 56, issue 1 (2022), pp. 1–4

Chapter 1

Law-students wellbeing and vulnerability
Graham Ferris
The Law Teacher, volume 56, issue 1 (2022), pp. 5–19

Chapter 2

"I was able to ask for help when I became stressed rather than sitting alone and struggling": psychology and law students' views of the impact of identity and community on mental wellbeing
Michael Fay and Yvonne Skipper
The Law Teacher, volume 56, issue 1 (2022), pp. 20–36

Chapter 3

"Make glorious mistakes!" Fostering growth and wellbeing in HE transition
Stella Coyle and Hannah Gibbons-Jones
The Law Teacher, volume 56, issue 1 (2022), pp. 37–53

Chapter 4

Is using the term wellbeing with students a mistake? Evaluating a wellbeing intervention in a UK Law School - suggestions for repositioning strategies to address the impact of deficit-discourse
Denise Meyer and Caroline Strevens
The Law Teacher, volume 56, issue 1 (2022), pp. 54–66

Chapter 5

Influences on students' interest in a legal career, satisfaction with law school, & psychological distress: trends in New Zealand
Valerie Sotardi, Lynne Taylor, Erik Brogt, Ursula Cheer and Natalie Baird
The Law Teacher, volume 56, issue 1 (2022), pp. 67–89

Chapter 6

"Hell is other people": rethinking the Socratic method for quiet law students
Rachel Spencer
The Law Teacher, volume 56, issue 1 (2022), pp. 90–104

Chapter 7

Feeling feedback: screencasting assessment feedback for tutor and student well-being
Alison Turnbull
The Law Teacher, volume 56, issue 1 (2022), pp. 105–118

Chapter 8

The role of employer/educator collaboration in improving the wellbeing of lawyers
Nigel Jones
The Law Teacher, volume 56, issue 1 (2022), pp. 119–129

Chapter 9

Harnessing the winds of change
Anne Macduff and Vivien Holmes
The Law Teacher, volume 56, issue 1 (2022), pp. 130–144

Notes on Contributors

Natalie Baird, Faculty of Law, University of Canterbury, Christchurch, New Zealand.

Erik Brogt, Academic Quality, University of Canterbury, Christchurch, New Zealand.

Ursula Cheer, Faculty of Law, University of Canterbury, Christchurch, New Zealand.

Stella Coyle, Keele University School of Law, Keele, Staffordshire, UK.

Michael Fay, School of Law, Keele University, Newcastle-under-Lyme, UK.

Graham Ferris, Nottingham Law School, Nottingham Trent University, Nottingham, UK.

Hannah Gibbons-Jones, Keele University School of Law, Keele, Staffordshire, UK.

Vivien Holmes, ANU College of Law, Australian National University, Australia.

Emma Jones, School of Law, University of Sheffield, UK.

Nigel Jones, City Mental Health Alliance, UK.

Anne Macduff, ANU College of Law, Australian National University, Australia.

Denise Meyer, Director of Student Wellbeing, Canterbury Christ Church University, Canterbury, Kent, England.

Yvonne Skipper, School of Education, Glasgow University, Glasgow, UK.

Valerie Sotardi, School of Educational Studies and Leadership, University of Canterbury, Christchurch, New Zealand.

Rachel Spencer, Faculty of Law, Monash University, Monash Law Clinics, Melbourne, Australia.

Caroline Strevens, Faculty of Business and Law, Portsmouth School of Law, University of Portsmouth, Portsmouth, England.

Lynne Taylor, Faculty of Law, University of Canterbury, Christchurch, New Zealand.

Alison Turnbull, Law School, Birmingham City University, Birmingham, UK.

Introduction – Legal education for wellbeing: design, delivery and evaluation

Emma Jones and Caroline Strevens

Over the past five or so years, it has become almost trite to refer to the significant wellbeing issues which arise within higher education among both the student body generally and law students in particular.[1] In the UK, the increasing acknowledgement of these issues is demonstrated by the publication of the Universities UK Step Change: Mentally Healthy Universities Framework and the University Mental Health Charter.[2] Both of these advocate a "whole university" approach to wellbeing, viewing wellbeing as fundamental to all aspects of university life, not just those traditionally viewed as pastoral in nature.

The starting point for this volume is that it is vital for law schools to adjust to this "whole university" approach in the way they design, deliver and evaluate their teaching, foster learning, interact with their students and facilitate their students' experience. Whilst mental health, wellbeing and other pastoral services have a crucial role to play in higher education, they are not sufficient on their own. Neither are generic central policies and processes for recognition of wellbeing as a curricular matter. An effective "whole university" approach also requires each individual school and department to consider how to acknowledge the value of wellbeing and integrate it into the curriculum in an evidence-based and sustainable manner appropriate to their discipline.

For law schools in particular, there is a rich body of international evidence demonstrating that the culture, norms and approaches common in legal studies can be potentially harmful to student wellbeing.[3] As a result there is a strong ethical imperative upon them to address their role in this as part of implementing such a "whole university" approach.[4] Given the bi-directional relationship between wellbeing and

---

[1] The Insight Network, "University Student Mental Health Survey 2018" (The Insight Network, March 2009) <https://uploads-ssl.webflow.com/561110743bc7e45e78292140/5c7d4b5d314d163fecdc3706_Mental%20Health%20Report%202018.pdf> accessed 19 January 2022. For an interesting analysis of trends in the general population, see Lucy Foulkes, *Losing Our Minds: What Mental Health Really Is and What It Isn't* (The Bodley Head 2021) 13–27.

[2] Universities UK, *Step Change: Mentally Healthy Universities* (Universities UK 2021) <www.universitiesuk.ac.uk/sites/default/files/field/downloads/2021-07/uuk-stepchange-mhu.pdf#page=12> accessed 17 January 2022; Gareth Hughes and Leigh Spanner, "The University Mental Health Charter" (Student Minds 2019).

[3] Kennon S Sheldon and Lawrence S Krieger, "Understanding the Negative Effects of Legal Education on Law Students: A Longitudinal Test of Self-Determination Theory" (2007) 33 Personality and Social Psychology Bulletin 883; Norm Kelk and others, *Courting the Blues: Attitudes towards Depression in Australian Law Students and Lawyers* (Brain & Mind Research Institute 2009); Caroline Strevens and Clare Wilson, "Law Student Wellbeing in the UK: A Call for Curriculum Intervention" (2016) 11(1) Journal of Commonwealth Law and Legal Education 44; Emma Jones, Rajvinder Samra and Mathijs Lucassen, "The World at Their Fingertips? The Mental Wellbeing of Online, Distance-Based Law Students" (2019) 53 The Law Teacher 49.

[4] Nigel J Duncan, Caroline Strevens and Rachael Field, "Resilience and Student Wellbeing in Higher Education: A Theoretical Basis for Establishing Law School Responsibilities for Helping Our Students to Thrive" (2020) 1(1) European Journal of Legal Education 83.

teaching and learning, there are also sound pragmatic reasons for such an approach. Student retention, progression and attainment are all potentially affected by law schools' approach to wellbeing. As Houghton and Anderson explain:

> Mental wellbeing is core to the curriculum in the way we teach and what we teach. It is not solely the responsibility of support services, rather we have a collective responsibility to promote the wellbeing of our students. Maximising their success in higher education is dependent on ensuring our own and our colleagues' wellbeing too.[5]

The chapters included in this volume each consider different aspects of student wellbeing within law schools, with a particular focus upon its use within the curriculum. Graham Ferris begins this volume by discussing the use of vulnerability theory as a heuristic for understanding student wellbeing. This is valuable both in providing a theoretical grounding, and as a reminder that wellbeing should not be over-individualised.[6] It is affected by a range of cultural and structural factors (including curriculum design) which influence the levels of resilience of individuals. The contribution of Michael Fay and Yvonne Skipper complements this by considering the relevance of social identity theory[7] and exploring it in relation to the sense of identity and belonging experienced by both law and psychology students. The comparisons between disciplines echo previous literature on law school wellbeing in drawing out the potential significance of competitive and adversarial norms and a lack of social connectedness within legal education.[8]

The chapter by Stella Coyle and Hannah Gibbons-Jones also focuses upon issues of identity and community, examining student transitions into the law school. Their discussion of a bespoke module, designed to orientate students and foster a sense of belonging, suggests practical ways in which legal educators can intentionally use curriculum design to promote better wellbeing. It also addresses the concerns within the wider literature that wellbeing may decline relatively swiftly upon law students' entry to law school.[9]

Although there is often an (understandable) focus on this initial transition, the entirety of a law degree can be characterised as a series of transitions. This includes adjusting to changes in years, modules, accommodation and motivations (amongst other factors).[10] The piece by Caroline Strevens and Denise Meyer recognises this by discussing a range of initiatives implemented at a UK law school, with the aim of improving student wellbeing and psychological resilience during the student journey. It focuses upon reframing narratives around wellbeing away from a deficit-led model through the use of student co-creation, employing carefully evidenced methodology

[5]Ann-Marie Houghton and Jill Anderson, "Embedding Mental Wellbeing in the Curriculum: Maximising Success in Higher Education" (Higher Education Authority 2017, 5) <www.advance-he.ac.uk/knowledge-hub/embedding-mental-wellbeing-curriculum-maximising-success-higher-education> accessed 19 January 2022.

[6]Christine Parker, "The Moral Panic over Psychological Wellbeing in the Legal Profession: A Personal or Political Ethical Response" (2014) 37 UNSWLJ 1103.

[7]H Tajfel and JC Turner, "An Integrative Theory of Intergroup Conflict"' in William G Austin and Stephen Worchel (eds), *The Social Psychology of Intergroup Relations* (Brooks/Cole 1979).

[8]See, for example, Adele Bergin and Kenneth Pakenham, "Law Student Stress: Relationships Between Academic Demands, Social Isolation, Career Pressure, Study/Life Imbalance and Adjustment Outcomes in Law Students" (2015) 22 Psychiatry, Psychology and Law 388.

[9]Molly Townes O'Brien, Stephen Tang and Kath Hall, "No Time to Lose: Negative Impact on Law Student Wellbeing May Begin in Year One" (2011) 2(2) The International Journal of the First Year in Higher Education 49.

[10]Eilidh Cage and others, "Student Mental Health and Transitions into, through and out of University: Student and Staff Perspectives" (2021) 45(8) Journal of Further and Higher Education 1076.

and a range of practical initiatives. The contribution by Valerie Sotardi, Lynne Taylor, Erik Brogt, Ursula Cheer and Natalie Baird takes a similarly broad perspective, investigating cross-sectional and longitudinal trends relating to law students at three New Zealand universities, across their three years of study. This chapter highlights again the potential for psychological distress amongst this population. It also emphasises the importance of promoting academic self-efficacy amongst students and considering academic support and assessment workload as important focuses for programme-level changes.

The piece by Rachel Spencer has a strong pedagogic focus, reflecting upon the impact of the Socratic method of teaching with quiet law students, and proposing instead an approach emphasising compassion, contemplation, active listening and emotional intelligence. It not only expounds a strong pedagogic rationale for this, but also demonstrates the importance of reflection in the work of legal educators, ably demonstrated by Spencer's reflective writing.

Given its pedagogic significance and strong inter-relationship with wellbeing, it was seen as important to include the topic of assessment within the volume.[11] As well as its significance being highlighted by Sotardi and others, assessment is also the focus of Alison Turnbull's contribution. She explores the impacts of feedback upon the wellbeing of both law students and tutors and considers the use of audiovisual feedback (via screencasting) and its potential in terms of relational and affective aspects.

The penultimate chapter in this volume introduces a somewhat different perspective, that of employers within the legal profession. The role of employability and its legitimacy as an aim of the law degree are highly contested.[12] Nevertheless, within the neoliberal university there are undoubtedly marketing, reputational and metric-driven impetuses for law schools to foster links with the legal profession. Nigel Jones' piece considers whether greater collaboration between legal educators and the legal profession could potentially assist in promoting better wellbeing for both students and lawyers, providing insights into the work on wellbeing currently being carried out by employers.

The final chapter, by Anne Macduff and Vivien Holmes, reports on the piloting of a "Wellbeing in the Curriculum Tool" at an Australian law school. Discussion of this tool is valuable in its own right, suggesting a potential way forward for those legal educators seeking to acknowledge wellbeing within the curriculum. However, more broadly, it also highlights the important role of legal educators in facilitating change and the need for rigorous evaluation of initiatives, to ensure they are evidence-based and sustainable.

Taken as a whole, the chapters in this volume illustrate the huge variety of ways in which wellbeing can be explored and integrated into the curriculum by law schools. The theoretical engagements, empirical studies and discussions within the contributions demonstrate the importance and value of so doing. They also emphasise the particular significance of three words in the title of this issue, namely, design, delivery and evaluation. The reference to "design" emphasises the need for a carefully planned, intentional approach. For wellbeing to become an accepted part of the curriculum requires the use of well-thought-out, pedagogically sound approaches that can be explained and justified both to students and institutionally. While a lone dedicated

---

[11] Michaela C Pascoe, Sarah E Hetrick and Alexandra G Parker, "The Impact of Stress on Students in Secondary School and Higher Education" (2020) 25 International Journal of Adolescence and Youth 104; N Šimic and I Manenica, "Exam Experience and Some Reactions to Exam Stress" (2012) 38 Human Physiology 67.

[12] Anthony Bradney, *Conversations, Choices and Chances: The Liberal Law School in the Twenty-First Century* (Hart Publishing 2003).

legal educator can undoubtedly make a difference, law schools need to think about designing a wellbeing-infused curriculum across all their programmes and modules. Doing less risks characterising wellbeing as an individual enthusiasm, a topic only relevant in very limited capacities or as a disposable adjunct to the work of teaching and learning.

The reference to "delivery" encapsulates pedagogic considerations around how best to implement a focus upon wellbeing in practice. This is likely to involve the adjustment of teaching materials and techniques, and individual legal educators undergoing additional training or upskilling themselves in other ways. Given that doing these tasks will undoubtedly demand time and effort on the part of those individuals, it is crucial that their wellbeing is also taken into account. There is already evidence of wellbeing issues amongst legal academics, so a challenge for law schools is to facilitate delivery in a manner which does not seek to prioritise student wellbeing at the expense of staff wellbeing.[13] Finally when referring to delivery, it seems an opportune moment to mention the Covid-19 global pandemic. This is referred to in a number of contributions within this special edition, with planned initiatives and projects having to be altered and adapted at very short notice. As an extreme example of disruption within law schools, it illustrates the need for delivery to be adaptable and flexible enough to withstand sudden change.

The final word, "evaluation", is perhaps the least explored within legal education literature generally, but is arguably key to integrating wellbeing into the curriculum in the long term. Appropriate evaluation enables law schools to evidence the value of wellbeing-related approaches and initiatives. It encourages legal educators to become "reflective practitioners" and leads to a continuous cycle of improvement.[14] As we move towards a post-pandemic law school, sharing evaluations of work done around wellbeing and the curriculum is vital to enable challenges to be overcome and successes to be replicated. We hope that this volume contributes to this process, so that in the future law school students (and staff) can not only survive, but also thrive.

Disclosure statement

No potential conflict of interest was reported by the authors.

ORCID

Emma Jones http://orcid.org/0000-0003-0172-4484
Caroline Strevens http://orcid.org/0000-0001-9016-839X

[13] Richard Collier, "Blackstone's Tower Revisited: Legal Academic Wellbeing, Marketization and the Post-Pandemic Law School" (2021) 2 Amicus Curiae: The Journal of the Society for Advanced Legal Studies 474.
[14] Donald A Schon, *The Reflective Practitioner: How Practitioners Think in Action* (Basic Books 1983).

OPEN ACCESS

Law-students wellbeing and vulnerability

Graham Ferris

ABSTRACT

There is compelling evidence that law students in the UK, USA, and Australia are subject to low levels of wellbeing. There is also compelling evidence that university students in the UK are also subject to low levels of wellbeing. Low wellbeing is produced by difficulties responding to stressors and life events, or low resilience. Therefore, law students are a sub-group of a larger group of young people with low resilience, however, law students have lower self-reported wellbeing than the overall student group. The trend for student well-being is downwards. Vulnerability theory offers a theoretically coherent heuristic that can enable us to think constructively about the problems of law students and students generally and to generate ideas for potentially beneficial courses of action. With such widespread phenomena, for law students across three continents and over many years, it is unrealistic to posit individualistic explanations as causes. Resilience, and consequent well-being, is not best understood as a characteristic of individuals but as generated or degraded by life histories, family and community resources, institutional supports or stressors, and social factors. We need to look at institutional and cultural factors if our response is to be coherent and effective. We need to seek a responsive law school in a responsive university in a responsive state.

Low levels of law student wellbeing

Poor wellbeing of law students was first identified as a problem in the USA.[1] An important early study uncovered the problem accidently, when law students were used as a control group for the students of primary interest to the investigators who were medical students.[2] In a recent UK study a similar effect occurred when research impelled by concern over the wellbeing of veterinary students and other students studying medical degrees (veterinary medicine, medicine, dentistry and pharmacy) used law students as a control group, and discovered lower wellbeing, higher levels of psychological distress, and higher levels of depression amongst the law students than the various types of medical students.[3] The law

[1]In this article I use "wellbeing" as a convenient word to capture self-reported wellbeing, positive affect, low negative affect, low levels of psychological distress including anxiety and depression, and good "mental health" in a broad sense. These categories are not synonyms. I touch on problems of technical usages of the word "wellbeing" below.

[2]Stephen B Shanfield and G Andrew H Benjamin, 'Psychiatric Distress in Law Students' (1985) 35 Journal of Legal Education 65.

[3]Elisa G Lewis and Jacqueline M Cardwell, 'A comparative study of mental health and wellbeing among UK students on professional degree programmes' (2019) 43 Journal of Further and Higher Education 1226, 1229-1231; Elisa G Lewis and Jacqueline M Cardwell, 'The big five personality traits, perfectionism and their association with mental health among UK students on professional degree programmes' (2020) 8:54 BMC Psychology available at <https://doi.org/10.1186/s40359-020-00423-3> accessed 13 August 2020.

students were chosen as comparators because they were studying a vocational subject and had similarly high academic credentials to the medical students.[4] A striking feature of each of these studies is the results were viewed as *prima facie* counter-intuitive, as law students were not seen as a vulnerable group of people.

This assumption that law students are not a vulnerable group, because they are a privileged and successful group, is one reason for selecting a vulnerability approach to this area of research. Vulnerability is universal, everyone is vulnerable.[5] However, a second reason is that vulnerability theory tells us to look at wider institutional and structural forces in order to understand vulnerability. Vulnerability makes us susceptible to events that degrade wellbeing, but these events are mediated by sources of resilience originating in our life histories and lived social contexts. Universities are important parts of that potentially supportive or degrading lived social context, and experience of university education becomes an important part of students' life histories. Law students are a sub-category of university students, and there is significant evidence that the wellbeing of university students is on a downward trajectory in the UK.[6] As Poppy Brown summarized[7]

> We might expect students in higher education to have better mental health than the general population. Strong social networks and better employment prospects are two of the many benefits of going to university. Yet survey data repeatedly show that, on average, students are less happy and more anxious than non-students, including other young people.

Our evidence is not as good as we could wish, and we are better talking about risk factors than causes,[8] in part because of the difficulty of discerning the direction of causation in social systems[9] and in part due to the intractability of systems as complex and unpredictable as educational systems,[10] but also because so much research assumes the benign

---

4 Entry requirements of at least AAA at A-level, Lewis and Cardwell, 'A comparative study' (n 3), 1227.

5 Martha Albertson Fineman, 'The Vulnerable Subject: Anchoring equality in the Human Condition' (2008) 20 Yale Journal of Law and Feminism 1, 1.

6 Royal College of Psychiatrists, *Mental health of students in higher education* (2011) College Report CR166; Ahmed K Ibrahim, Shona J Kelly, Clive E Adams, and Chris Glazebrook, 'A systematic review of studies of depression prevalence in university students' (2013) 47 Journal of Psychiatric Research 391; Emma Broglia, Abigail Millings, and Michael Barkham, 'Challenges to addressing student mental health in embedded counselling services: a survey of UK higher and further education institutions', (2018) 46 British Journal of Guidance & Counselling 441; Lewis and Cardwell 'A comparative study (n 3) found all five groups of students had lower wellbeing and psychological distress than comparator groups. See: Wendy Larcombe, Sue Finch and Rachel Sore, 'Who's Distressed? Not Only Law Students: Psychological Distress Levels in University Students Across Diverse Fields of Study' (2015) 37 Sydney Law Review 243 and Wendy Larcombe, Sue Finch, Rachel Sore, Christina M Murray, Sandra Kentish, Raoul A Mulder, Parshia Lee-Stecum, Chi Baik, Orania Tokatlidis and David A Williams, 'Prevalence and socio-demographic correlates of psychological distress among students at an Australian university' (2014) 41 Studies in Higher Education 1074. Sue Hubble and Paul Bolton, *Support for students with mental health issues in higher education in England* (House of Commons Library, Briefing Paper 8593, 2 March 2020) available at: https://researchbriefings.files.parliament.uk/documents/CBP-8593/CBP-8593.pdf accessed 24 August 2020.

7 Poppy Brown, *The invisible problem? Improving students' mental health* (2016) HEPI report 88, 7.:

8 Royal College of Psychiatrists (n 6), 14, [13] and 27.

9 Is low wellbeing a cohort effect: Jean M Twenge, 'The Age of Anxiety? Birth Cohort Change in Anxiety and Neuroticism, 1952-1993 (2000) 79 Journal of Personality and Social Psychology 1007, Larcombe et al (n 8); or is low wellbeing a characteristic of those choosing legal study: Susan Diacoff, 'Asking Leopards to Change Their Spots: Should Lawyers Change – A Critique of Solutions to Problems with Professionalism by Reference to Empirically-Derived Attorney Personality Attributes' (1998) 11 Georgetown Journal of Legal Ethics 547; or is low wellbeing produced by Law Schools: G Andrew H Benjamin, Alfred Kaszniak, Bruce Sales and Stephen B Shanfield, 'The Role of Legal Education in Producing Psychological Distress Among Law Students and Lawyers' (1986) American Bar Foundation Research Journal225. Probably all three at once.

10 Mervyn King and John Kay, *Radical Uncertainty: Decision-making for an unknowable future* (The Bridge Street Press 2020), any system that responds to information about itself is radically unpredictable, see: Robert J Shiller, *Narrative Economics: How Stories Go Viral and Drive Major Economic Events* (Princeton University Press 2020).

nature of educational systems. There can be little doubt that we are looking at problems that require both a law school and an university level response as three is evidence of problems at both levels.[11] We may be looking at problems that require a broader sectoral, cultural, economic, or political response.[12]

Awareness of the risk of a negative effect on wellbeing from legal education is long standing and situational. There is a good review of the sources that establish this in *Emotions in the Law School*.[13] The sources on student wellbeing demonstrate that contemporary low wellbeing levels among law students is part of a larger phenomenon of low wellbeing among students in higher education. Neither problem is one that individual students can be expected to solve through acquisition of resilience skills. Indeed, resilience is not something an individual can learn through hard work and application, but the product of external resources such as money, cultural capital, social networks, health care through time as well as lived life history:

> Resilience is not something we are born with. Instead, it is accrued over the course of our lifetimes within an array of social structures and institutions over which individuals may have little, if any control.[14]

This insight is the third and final reason for choosing to look at this problem through the lens of vulnerability theory.[15] The theory avoids the individualized approach that can shift responsibility for resilience onto the students, and even deteriorate into victim blaming. If law school and university education has negative impacts upon law students then our focus for reform should be upon law schools and universities and not upon those individuals and groups who suffer most from any deleterious effects.

The literature is not univocal on risk factors or putative causal factors of poor wellbeing. Law students are not a uniform group of people and we need to think about the differences between them as well as the commonalities. There are specific difficulties facing international law students who are far from home and may be unable to access their support networks and who are at high risk of social isolation.[16] Victims of sexual or physical or emotional abuse face consequential distress and far higher risk of further abuse.[17] People who worry about debt levels, and those who work long hours to alleviate debt problems and support themselves whilst studying are at greater risk.[18]

---

[11]Larcombe et al (n 8), Emma Jones, *Emotions in the Law School: Transforming Legal Education Though the Passions* (Routledge 2020 pp 225-146. Mark Dooris, Alan Farrier, Sharon Doherty, Maxine Holt, Robert Monk and Susan Powell, 'The UK Healthy Universities Self-Review Tool: Whole System Impact' (2018) 33 Health Promotion International 448. Available at: https://academic.oup.com/heapro/article/33/3/448/2732587 accessed 12 August 2020.

[12]For the potential negative role of technological culture that would require a strong political and economic response, see: Shoshana Zuboff, *The Age of Surveillance Capitalism: The Fight for a Human Future at the New Frontier of Power* (Profile Books 2019) chapter 16.

[13]Jones 'Emotions' (n 11).

[14]Martha Albertson Fineman, 'Equality and Difference - The Restrained State' (2015) 66 Alabama Law Review 609, 623.

[15]Fineman, 'The Vulnerable Subject (2008) (n 5).

[16]Mental health of Students (n 6), 11, 14 [12], 17, 28; Coroners Court of Victoria, Coroner warns of barriers to mental health support for international students 14 January 2019 available at: https://www.coronerscourt.vic.gov.au/coroner-warns-barriers-mental-health-support-international-students accessed 13 august 2020; Tracey Shelton, Erwin Renaldi, and Bang Xiao, 'World Suicide Prevention Day: How international students are vulnerable to mental health issues', ABC News, 9 September 2019, available at: https://www.abc.net.au/news/2019-09-10/suicide-prevention-day-pressures-facing-international-students/11476938 accessed 13 august 2020. Contra: Larcombe et al, 'Prevalence' (n 6), 1088.

[17]Mental Health of Students (n 6), 29-30.

[18]Mental health of Students (n 6), 27-28.

People who drink a lot of alcohol or use non-prescribed drugs are at greater risk.[19] Law schools and universities need to respond to the specific characteristics of students as well as attempting to do no harm, and to build wellbeing across the student cohort as the one common characteristic all law students of an institution have is that they are law students at that institution.

The context

There are a lot of students engaged in higher education, in Nottingham around 66,000 across the city's two established universities in 2018/19.[20] The Augar review noted that[21] "The proportion of English young people entering HE has risen from below 20% in 1990 to almost 50% today". It is generally accepted that UK higher education has shifted from an elite to a mass system over the last 30 to 40 years.

There are a lot of law students in the UK, around 74,000 undergraduates and 20,500 post-graduates in 2018/19. Most of the undergraduates are UK citizens (c 60,000), and about half the postgraduate law students are home students (c 11,500). That means there are significant numbers of non-UK undergraduates and relatively large numbers of non-UK postgraduate students. In fact, non-UK students are a majority amongst postgraduate research students (1,145 as against 1,040 UK students).[22]

In 2015/16 some 6,452 solicitors were admitted to the roll.[23] In 2015/16 1,300 people were called to the Bar.[24] In 2014/15 some 57,325 students were enrolled full time to study law as a first degree.[25] If we assume a three year degree programme, deduct an estimated number of students as presumably engaged in legal study in Scotland, and divide by three then around 17,500 law students would have graduated in 2014/15.[26] It seems reasonable to conclude that *most* of those students would not be joining the solicitors or barristers professions.[27]

The Augar review noted that[28] "Undergraduate teaching after 2012 became a profitable activity and the sector responded as it was meant to by recruiting more students, improving student support and developing facilities". Thus, on the supply side selling university education has produced a surplus, and subjects like law and business in particular, with high student demand and low demands for specialist equipment,

[19] Mental health of Students (n 6), 25-27.

[20] HESA <https://www.hesa.ac.uk/data-and-analysis/students/whos-in-he> accessed 6 August 2020, figures for University of Nottingham and Nottingham Trent University. The University of Law also offers undergraduate and postgraduate law in Nottingham, and some further education colleges offer undergraduate level education.

[21] Philip Augar, Sir Ivor Crewe, Jacqueline de Rojas, Edward Peck, Beverley Robinson, and Baroness Alison Wolf, *Independent panel report to the Review of Post-18 Education and Funding* (Department for Education 2019), 63.:

[22] HESA https://www.hesa.ac.uk/data-and-analysis/students/what-study accessed 6 August 2020.

[23] SRA Annual review 2015/16 https://www.sra.org.uk/globalassets/documents/sra/research/annual-review-2015-16.pdf?version=4a1aca accessed 6 August 2020.

[24] Bar Standards Board https://www.barstandardsboard.org.uk/news-publications/research-and-statistics/statistics-about-the-bar/call-to-the-bar-and-tenancy.html accessed 6 August 2020.

[25] HESA https://www.hesa.ac.uk/data-and-analysis/students/whos-in-he accessed 6 August 2020.

[26] (57,325 x 0.08) divided by 3 = 17,579.

[27] Of course, those graduating would not be the same as the people enrolled or called to the bar in the same year. However, 2015/16 is the most recent year for which annual numbers for admission to the roll seem to be available, and also the earliest year for student numbers in the HESA tables available online. There is no reason to suppose a higher proportion of law graduates have entered the two senior legal professions post 2014/15. The calculation also leaves out those who were admitted to the roll with overseas qualifications (c 500) or via CILEx (237) or qualified for either profession after completing a Graduate Diploma in Law.

[28] Augar et al (n 21), 63.:

have been cash-cows for universities.[29] These economic factors combined with government policy explain those high numbers of students in higher education and in legal education.

In public discourse much is made of the graduate premium,[30] which draws attention to the privileges associated with higher education. In part this emphasis suits a rhetoric around the funding of higher education through conditional student fees linked to the private gains from higher education, as opposed to an emphasis on the public gains from higher education which had been associated with direct state funding of institutions.[31] It will be argued here that students in higher education are vulnerable, both because everyone is vulnerable and because the resources supporting their resilience are inadequate as demonstrated by their self-reported low wellbeing. Further, that it is important to recognize that inadequacies in resilience are social and institutional, and not personal failings or lack in the skill sets of students in higher education. Otherwise, resilience becomes individualized and a lack of resources becomes framed as a personal failing.[32] Finally, the wellbeing studies show that law students are caught up in this more general malaise but are suffering even higher levels of distress due to peculiarities of legal education, or of those choosing to study law, or both.

Vulnerability

Professor Fineman has developed a theoretically grounded heuristic around the concept of vulnerability.[33] It can be thought of as an alternative to the heuristic of the social contract as a foundational concept for justice theory.[34] Instead of basing justice on self-interested cooperation and reciprocation Fineman bases justice on shared vulnerability and mutual dependancy. The autonomy and self-reliance of the social contractors is mythical and excludes those who at any particular time are dependant.[35] The social contract heuristic systematically distorts theories of justice as it refuses to recognize the need and fact of social reproduction across time.[36] Vulnerability makes our humanity

[29]Jonathan Moules, UK universities use business schools as cash cows, Financial Times, 25 April 2015.

[30]Tej Nathwani, Dan Cook, Gianna Boero, Robin Naylor and Jeremy Smith, *The Return To A Degree: new evidence on the birth cohort studies and the labour force survey* (HESA 2019) available at: https://www.hesa.ac.uk/files/Return_to_a_degree_main_report.pdf accessed 6 August 2020. An earlier and more optimistic estimate is: Ian Walker and Yu Zhu, *The Impact of University Degrees on the Lifecycle of Earnings: Some Further Analysis* (Department for Business Innovation and Skills 2013), BIS research Paper 112. Law (alongside medicine and economics) is reputed to lead to large returns, see: Study International Staff, 'These are the degrees with the highest ROI in the UK' 10 March 2020 available at: https://www.studyinternational.com/news/financial-returns-degrees/ accessed 6 August 2020, note the potentially self-interested optimism of the study international source.

[31]Dawn Holland, Iana Liadze, Cinzia Rienzo and David Wilkinson, *The relationship between graduates and economic growth across countries* (Department for Business Innovation and Skills 2013), BIS research Paper 110. Ourania Filippakou and Gareth Williams (Eds), *Higher Education As a Public Good: Critical Perspectives on Theory, Policy and Practice* (Peter Lang 2013).

[32]Fineman, (n 14).

[33]Fineman, 'The Vulnerable Subject' (2008) (n 5), 9. Martha Albertson Fineman, 'Equality, Autonomy, and the Vulnerable Subject in Law and Politics' in Martha Albertson Fineman and Anna Grear (eds), *Vulnerability: Reflections on a new ethical foundation for law and politics* (Ashgate 2013) 20.

[34]Peter Laslett (ed), John Locke, *Two Treatises on Government*, (first published 1689, Cambridge University Press 1988); John Rawls, *A Theory of Justice* (Revd ed, Oxford University Press 1999).

[35]Martha Albertson Fineman, *The Autonomy Myth: A Theory of Dependency* (The New Press 2004).

[36]A problem Rawls tried to address (inadequately) through his just savings principle: Rawls (n 30) 251-262.

the basis for justice rather than our ability to contribute to society. Society is a response to our vulnerability, and organized social power, the state, exists and is justified by its ability to respond to our vulnerability.

The shift from contractual to vulnerability heuristics has profound consequences. Social contract theories have a strong propensity to view the state as a threat to those interests that pre-date the social contract. The resulting theories of justice tend to be one-sided in concern with the need to limit state power to do harm.[37] Vulnerability theory places demands upon the state to respond actively to vulnerability, it generates a more balanced view of the relationship of state power and justice, similar to that described by Voltaire[38] "That wise Government where the Prince is all powerful to do good, and, at the same time, is restrained from committing evil". Vulnerability demands a responsive state that is "all powerful" to respond to vulnerability and support the resilience of its citizens.

Thus, vulnerability justifies a responsive state. At this point it is important to recognize that although vulnerability is universal it is also particular because we do not all face the world with the same resources. Some of us are healthy and others subject to disabling conditions, some of us are well connected and others of us are outsiders to those circles that bestow honour and respect, some of us have adequate shelter and others of us live in inadequate housing. We are all vulnerable but how well we can recover from events that expose our vulnerability is widely variable and dependant on the assets we have access to. Resilience in vulnerability theory is a function of those resources a person can call upon and not an internal individual characteristic.[39] Some resources are entirely external to the individual body (wealth), some are embodied through lived experiences (material environment, medical care, social and cultural experiences).

The resources a person may be able to call upon are various. Fineman lists five types: physical (i.e. material e.g. money, housing, transport); human (i.e. embodied e.g. education, health, character); social (i.e. membership of organizations or groups e.g. family, professional associations, social networks); ecological or environmental (i.e. natural and constructed world e.g. clean water, access to parks or woodland or rural environments, clean air); existential (i.e. sources of meaning e.g. culture and art, systems of meaning such as religion, caring for others, vocation).[40] All of these assets, including human, are produced through the actions of social institutions, they are not given at birth but are constructed[41] "while vulnerability is both inevitable and universal, it is also socially constructed in its particularities". Even health is produced through the interaction of the organism and the environment, in obvious ways such as the skeletal deformities arising from a chronic lack of vitamin D,[42] to the more subtle effects of maternal nutrition on the health outcomes and personality of the unborn child,[43] or the effects of low status upon both morbidity and mortality.[44] Resilience is a function of resources and those

[37]Most obvious in Robert Nozick, *Anarchy, State and Utopia* (Basic Books 1974).
[38]Voltaire, *Letters on England* (first published 1733), Letter VIII On the Parliament available at: https://www.gutenberg.org/files/2445/2445-h/2445-h.htm accessed 7 August 2020.:
[39]Fineman and Grear, 'Equality' (n 33) 21-24.
[40]Martha Albertson Fineman, 'Vulnerability and Inevitable Inequality' (2017) 4 Oslo Law Review 133, 146.
[41]Fineman, 'The Vulnerable Subject (2008) (n 5), 10, n 27.:
[42]Roy Porter, *The Greatest Benefit to Mankind: A Medical History of Humanity from Antiquity to the Present* (Harper Collins 1997), 554-555.
[43]David J P Barker, 'The developmental origins of well-being' in Felicia A Huppert, Nick Baylis and Barry Keverne (eds), *The science of well-being* (Oxford University Press 2005).
[44]Michael Marmot, *Status Syndrome: How Your Social Standing Directly Affects Your Health* (Bloomsbury Paperbacks 2012).

with more resources have a far higher chance of withstanding and recovering from adverse events. It is because law students are stereotypically seen as having assets, such as education, family support, youth and health, money, and the chance for a good life that they are not usually considered vulnerable. Outside of vulnerability theory vulnerability is usually used as a term to describe populations with few assets that support their resilience, and it can have stigmatizing effect.[45]

Which brings us to how we should approach the question of law student wellbeing, or its absence, if we take an approach informed by the vulnerability heuristic. We start with the structures, the social institutions within which law students find themselves. Hence, this article has already noted the context of UK higher education, the university and the law school, and the legal services market. We noted in passing that mass higher education was funded through conditional loans and this funding mechanism was justified by the graduate premium. Several potential issues are raised by this context which challenge lazy stereotypes.

Contrary to stereotypes there will be many law students who have asset deficiencies, due to being far from home in the case of overseas students, because of limited social networks and access to information for first generation university students, and because professional recruitment is not capable of absorbing the numbers of students graduating with law degrees. We cannot know whether these issues are going to impact on wellbeing without significant and sophisticated research. We do know that there are clearly identifiable aspects of the structure of contemporary legal education that are likely to impact negatively upon law students. Vulnerability theory sensitizes us to the importance of institutional construction of particular vulnerabilities, the subject matter of inquiry is not the individual law student, but how the resilience of law students is being supported or undermined by their situation.

Vulnerability theory is not the only theory that could be used. Christine Parker made a similar attempt to recognize the value issues implicit in much wellbeing discourse and shift focus from individual students to institutional causes.[46] Parker used a heuristic of "moral panic" developed by Stanley Cohen to try and unearth the forces that were pushing the discourse towards an individual deficiency model.[47] However, the problem, as argued at the beginning of this article, is real, not manufactured, and most of the people who are engaged in the discourse are not seeking to discipline students as "folk devils" but to support law students and lawyers. For these reasons Cohen's concept does not fit the problem it was applied to. Vulnerability theory is both more radical, cutting at it does at the foundational assumptions of neo-liberalism, and more flexible in application.

There are other theories current that could be called into service, such as a theory of justice based upon capabilities as developed by Sen and Nussbaum.[48] I have used a range of theorists over my research career drawn from history, philosophy, education, English, social psychology, psychology, and economics as well as law and jurisprudence.

[45]Fineman, 'The Vulnerable Subject (2008) (n 5), 8.

[46]Christine Parker, 'The 'moral panic' over psychological wellbeing in the legal profession: a personal or political ethical response' (2014) 37 University of New South Wales Law Journal 1103. Although I would argue that the vital imperative is value discourse not value advocacy.

[47]Stanley Cohen, *Folk Devils and Moral Panics: The Creation of the Mods and Rockers* (first published 1973, Routledge 2011).

[48]Amartya Sen, *The Idea of Justice* (Allen Lane 2009) Martha C Nussbaum, *Creating Capabilities: The Human Development Approach* (Harvard University Press 2011).

We need theory to identify causes, to search out potential actions to address problems, and to provide us with a theory of change.[49] Failure to find a workable theory will render our good intentions vulnerable to misdirected effort. Medical and therapeutic discourses have been concerned with causes of resilience in individuals and groups for many years,[50] but their focus upon pathology makes them a poorer fit than vulnerability theory for analysis of student wellbeing. Vulnerability theory developed from feminist jurisprudence offers a powerful resource to all those concerned with law student wellbeing in the modern university.

Fineman in effect follows Hobbes by starting from an over-riding concern with human vulnerability and each developed an argument for an active state.[51] For some theorists, such as Robert Nozick, redistributive action by the state is presumptively unjust,[52] and Fineman clearly and consistently argues for state action by the responsive state that would, inter alia, have redistributive consequences. Therefore, in accepting vulnerability theory as our conceptual frame we are accepting the theoretical justifiability of a strong state with redistributive powers which will be deployed to counter act imbalances in those assets that generate resilience in its citizens, which Fineman calls the responsive state.

Wellbeing

Wellbeing as a technical term is a key concept in two partially overlapping discourses, one originating in economics and one originating in psychology.[53] Wellbeing is usually measured using subjective self-report questionnaires. The economics literature tends to use questionnaires that ask about life satisfaction. The economics literature has a focus on the relationship between wellbeing and material resources.[54] The emphasis on the importance of resources, physical assets, aligns easily with vulnerability theory.[55] The psychology questionnaires tend to assess more sophisticated qualities of a person's affective experience using constructs like anxiety, stress, positive or negative affect, intrinsic or extrinsic motivation, and depression. Both literatures attempt to find out about how people experience their lives.

---

[49]Ken Robinson and Lou Aronica, *Creative Schools: Revolutionizing Education from the Ground Up* (Penguin 2016) loc 133.

[50]Drue H. Barrett, Leonard W. Ortmann, Angus Dawson, Carla Saenz, Andreas Reis and Gail Bolan (eds), *Public Health Ethics: Cases Spanning the Globe* (Springer 2016), Michael Rutter, 'Resilience Concepts and findings: implications for family therapy' (1999) 21 Journal of Family Therapy 119.

[51]Thomas Hobbes, *Leviathan* (first published 1651, Penguin 1985), chapter XIII. Indeed, see Michael Oakeshott, 'Introduction to Leviathan' in Michael Oakeshott, *Rationalism in politics and other essays* (Liberty Fund 1991), 227: " ... the unity of the history of political philosophy lies in a pervading sense of human life as a predicament and ... ".

[52]Nozick 'Anarchy' (n 37). Although note he does permit redistribution by state action for the purpose of rectification of past injustices at 152-153.

[53]See: Angus Deaton, *The Great Escape: Health, Wealth, and the Origins of Inequality* (Princeton University Pres 2013); Martin Seligman, *Flourish: A New Understanding of Happiness and Wellbeing: The practical guide to using positive psychology to make you happier and healthier* (Nicholas Brealey Publishing 2011); Graham Ferris, 'The Promise and Perils of Positive Psychology' available at: <http://irep.ntu.ac.uk/id/eprint/30325/> accessed 7 August 2020.

[54]Richard Easterlin, 'Does Economic Growth Improve the Human Lot? Some Empirical Evidence' in Paul A David and Melvin W Reder (eds) *Nations and Households in Economic Growth Essays in Honor of Moses Abramovitz* (Academic Press 1974) 147.

[55]That the relationship is non-linear (more things does not lead to more happiness) is known as the Easterlin paradox. The emphasis on various types of asset and their inter-relationships mean the phenomenon does not seem paradoxical in vulnerability theory.

Wellbeing in the psychology literature has a focus on positive aspects of lived experience. In this article poor wellbeing is treated as synonymous with self-reported distress, but in the psychology literature the two terms are not part of a single scale. The focus on "wellbeing" rather than distress or mental ill-health (pathology) in psychology is intended to: avoid stigma, make people more willing to discuss feelings and behaviours, emphasize that affective states are located on a range or spectrum, and to help identify interventions that are generally applicable.[56]

It is possible to identify sources of wellbeing and a convenient summary of research findings is the collection of pieces *The science of well-being*.[57] The science is congruent with vulnerability theory if we simply transpose sources of wellbeing with sources of resilience.[58] Wellbeing is supported by exercise,[59] adequate maternal diet and health,[60] social activity,[61] nutrition,[62] access to natural environments for leisure,[63] material resources,[64] and meaningful work.[65] These are all easily assimilated to the sources or assets for resilience identified by vulnerability theory. The sole important divergence is around the role and importance of styles or habits of thought,[66] vulnerability theory does not identify positive thinking, for example, as a source of resilience unless it is a feature of some existential asset.

Thus, approaching issues of student wellbeing through the concept of "wellbeing" as it is used in positive psychology literatures should align easily with vulnerability theory and help to avoid any tendency to pathologise or individualize inappropriately student wellbeing. However, there are three other significant factors at work that we need to acknowledge, and which render positive psychology alone an inadequate approach to law student wellbeing. First, is a broad approach to the world that I will term the neo-liberal world view. Second, is a tendency towards the medicalization of social problems which itself seems to be a feature of the neo-liberal world view. Third, is the institutional practice around student support services.

The neo-liberal world view is based on a set of heuristics, including the social contract approach to justice. There is a clear impulse in neo-liberalism to assign social inequalities to individual failings.[67] Starting with an unexamined concept of autonomy and self-reliance neo-liberal theory views dependence as dysfunction and as justifying social disciplining.[68] Neo-liberal heuristics direct attention to the alleged failings of individuals as a universal cause of poverty, crime, lack of social mobility, and unhealthy behaviours. Vulnerability theory was developed to counter-act this damaging refusal to attend to systemic causes of social phenomena.

---

[56]This precis is based on accounts of positive psychology, see: Martin E P Seligman, and Mihaly Csikszentmihalyi, 'Positive psychology: An introduction' (2000) 55 American Psychologist 5.
[57]Felicia A Huppert, Nick Baylis and Barry Keverne, *The science of well-being* (Oxford University Press 2005).
[58]Although vulnerability theory has no view on brain structure or chemistry, or evolutionary insights into wellbeing.
[59]Stuart JH Biddle and Panteleimon Ekkekakis in Huppert et al (n 57).
[60]David JP Barker, in Huppert et al (n 57).
[61]John F Helliwell and Robert D Putnam in Huppert et al (n 57).
[62]Bernard Gesch in Huppert et al (n 57).
[63]George W Burns in Huppert et al (n 57).
[64]Robert H Frank; and John Galtung, both in Huppert et al (n 57).
[65]Susan Verducci and Howard Gardner in Huppert et al (n 57).
[66]Barbara L Fredrickson; and Martin EP Seligman, Acacia C Parks and Tracy Steen both in Huppert et al (n 57)
[67]Lawrence M Mead, *Beyond Entitlement: The social obligations of citizenship* (Free Press 1986).
[68]Fineman, *Autonomy Myth* (n 35), 33-44.

Medicalization is an aspect of this neo-liberal impulse to place responsibility for their own disadvantage on individuals who suffer disadvantage. At its worst it has fuelled mass mortality in the USA as opioid prescription to members of groups suffering from the effects of social and economic dislocation reached epidemic levels.[69]

Universities predominantly respond to student distress, poor student wellbeing, by offering individualized support or referral to mental health services. The models for this support seem to be tripartite: counselling; pastoral support; and skills enhancement.[70] In practice student support tends towards addressing the problems (or deficiencies) of the individual, although they do not have to do so.[71] It is in the operations of student support services that the primary institutional response to student, including law student, wellbeing is often found.

These three factors converge around a common-sense view of student wellbeing as a mental health issue. Individual students have problems and the law school should support them to overcome their problems by teaching them techniques to cope with life or offering time with someone who is able to help them overcome their problems. This may be well meaning and beneficent but it is deficient, because it fails to address the possibility that some of the problems are situated outside of the student.[72] A lack of training contracts is not counteracted by an arms race in CV drafting. A lack of community is not cured by working on one's social skills. A sense of meaninglessness from chasing opportunities for social mobility that are rapidly disappearing is not resolved by developing a positive attitude to repeated rejection.[73] Vulnerability theory tells us to seek the sources of degraded resilience in the social institutions that should support resilience, not in the internalized self-blame of the victims of failing social systems.

Wellbeing discourse naturally leads to institutional analysis. It is only institutional and theoretical blinkers that turn attention onto deficiencies of students. At this point I feel it is useful to make it plain that I am not attacking those who are addressing the problems of students within institutional structures such as student support services. Indeed, I owe my awareness of the problems around student wellbeing to student support staff whose keen and clear eyed analysis of a mounting crisis of student wellbeing alerted me to what I consider to be a serious issue for all law teachers, and which has informed my teaching and research activity profoundly. Nor, am I attacking those who work within institutional structures to address wellbeing problems through pastoral or curricula or teaching delivery.[74] I have developed my practice and published on this and it was a central concern in my PhD.[75] What I am arguing is unless we have an

[69] Anne Case and Angus Deaton, *Deaths of Despair and the Future of Capitalism* (Princeton University Press 2020).

[70] Broglia et al, 'Challenges' (n 6); Ruth Caleb, 'Supporting student mental health and wellbeing in higher education', Slide 10 available at: https://claud.org.uk/wp-content/uploads/2019/08/A-Ruth-Caleb-wellbeing.pdf accessed 14 August 2020; Gareth Hughes, *Be Well, Learn Well: Improve Your Wellbeing and Academic Performance* (Red Globe Press 2020).

[71] Working Group for the Promotion of Mental Wellbeing in Higher Education, *Student mental wellbeing in higher education: Good practice guide* (UK Universities 2015).

[72] A similar failure to incorporate consideration of situational and institutional factors into the disciplining of lawyers took place in *SRA v James* [2018] EWHC 3058 (Admin).

[73] Lee Elliot Major and Stephen Machin, *Social Mobility: And Its Enemies* (Pelican 2018).

[74] I am in sympathy with Carroll who sees much common ground amongst those concerned with student wellbeing, Claire Carroll, 'Alert but not alarmed: A response to Parker's critique of wellbeing scholarship in law' (2019) 29 Legal Education Review 1. Although I do not agree that psychological theories suffice for framing and informing our work, hence my advocacy of vulnerability theory.

[75] Graham Ferris, 'What is Entailed by a Student-Centred Approach to Legal Education?' (PhD by published works, Nottingham Trent University 2019) available at: http://irep.ntu.ac.uk/id/eprint/39047/ accessed 14 August 2020.

adequate theoretical approach to student wellbeing then we will find ourselves falling into responses structured by neo-liberal concepts, medicalization, and individualized responses because these are the materials that constitute common sense in current society.[76] We live in a culture where to arouse pity is to be stigmatized as inadequate and repulsive as witnessed by the use of the word "pathetic" as a term of contempt.

Responses to low levels of student wellbeing

There are several measures that academics can take to try and support wellbeing.[77] However, because our knowledge base is not wholly robust and causation is not clear given the complexity of different potentially causative factors in play, we need to proceed with some humility and adhere, so far as possible, to the principle of do no harm.[78] Academic and managerial vulnerability and fallibility are important to bear in mind, and in this area of institutional action there is good reason to think that student input into any reform process would be valuable and that the very recognition of a student voice might have a beneficial effect.[79]

At the level of the academic creating academic materials and delivering legal education the design of modules and courses with regard to the three human needs identified by self-determination theory seems sensible and unlikely to be harmful.[80] Those needs are a sense of competence, some autonomy or control, and a feeling of relatedness with others. It is possible to support these needs whilst delivering academic content, it need not impose new demands upon students. The recognition of these needs is congruent with awareness of student vulnerability.

Providing an alternative discourse to a crude neo-liberal discourse which values only external goods (money and power) and instrumentalizes the individual (who invests in their own human capital through education and training to facilitate adaptation to the market) seems worthwhile. Vulnerability theory juxtaposes a radically different common sense to that of the neo-liberal world view, reminding us of its unrealistic assumptions about humanity. There may be some truth in the neo-liberal worldview, but the unargued assumption of its veracity is clearly unjustified. Given the ascendancy of neo-liberalism a failure to engage in value discourse in the curriculum is not neutral but

[76]A concern shared and articulated by Parker 'moral panic' (n 46).

[77]See: Caroline Strevens and Rachael Field (eds), *Educating for Well-Being in Law: Positive Professional Identities and Practice* (Routledge 2019).

[78]It is not certain that improved student experience leads to improved student wellbeing, see: Wendy Larcombe, Letty Tumbaga, Ian Malkin, Pip Nicholson and Orania Tokatlidis, 'Does an Improved Experience of Law School Protect Students against Depression, Anxiety and Stress? An Empirical Study of Wellbeing and the Law School Experience of LLB and JD Students' (2013) 35 Sydney Law Review 407. However, it cannot be seen as a harmful response.

[79]Molly Townes O'Brien, 'Walking the walk: Using student-faculty dialogue to change an adversarial curriculum' (2011) 4 Journal of the Australasian Law Teachers Association 129; Chi Baik, Wendy Larcombe and Abi Brooker, 'How universities can enhance student mental wellbeing: the student perspective' (2019) 38 Higher Education Research & Development 674. Facilitating articulation of a student voice is not given any priority in the whole university approach taken in UK Universities, Stepchange: Mental health in Higher Education available at: https://www.universitiesuk.ac.uk/policy-and-analysis/stepchange/Pages/default.aspx accessed 24 August 2020. Sen has argued for the importance of voice for both justice and development, Sen, 'Idea of Justice' (n 48), 87; Amartya Sen, *Development as Freedom* (Oxford University Press 1999) 151-159.

[80]See: Graham Ferris and Rebecca Huxley-Binns, 'What Students Care About and Why We Should Care' in Paul Maharg and Caroline Maughan, *Affect and Legal Education: Emotion in Learning and Teaching the Law* (Ashgate 2011); Rebecca Huxley-Binns and Graham Ferris, 'Putting Theory into Practice: Designing a Curriculum According to Self-Determination Theory' (2013) 19 (3) The International Journal of Pedagogy and Curriculum; Carroll, 'Alert but not alarmed' (n 74).

surrender of the student to a highly contentious set of dominant values which if assumed in teaching are *de facto* presented as common sense and inevitable.[81] Engaging in value discourses provides tools through which students might constitute a more satisfactory sense of their identity and values, as Appiah argued[82] "[To] give people a conceptual vocabulary is to influence them; but to deprive them of it is to cripple them, not empower them". The black letter technical approach to law with its positivist foundation is insufficient, an example of "academicization" which not only does not advocate for values but attempts to decouple them from legal knowledge.[83]

One misleading characteristic of doctrinal, as opposed to humanistic or socio-legal, undergraduate legal education is it treats the law as a given from the point of view of lawyers. This perpetuates something of a myth – that lawyers do not advocate on behalf of their clients for legal change.[84] Whilst arguing within the confines of authority will always be a core legal skill it should not be presented as the sole legal skill. Coupled with an assumption of concern only with the individual client, the private lawyer not the cause lawyer,[85] advocacy of acceptance of the law can be alienating to students. Vulnerability theory tells us it is also inadequate, as it plays into acceptance of present power relations mediated through law as if they were natural rather than constituted by the state and legal system. We need to look beyond the individual to the group, the institutions, the state, and society.

Not all students want to enter legal practice. But for many students a law degree was chosen because of a perhaps uninformed belief of the pre-law-student that she aspired to become a legal professional. For such aspiring students the law degree is a source of information that can inform that aspiration and flesh it out. The student will identify with "the lawyer" and will incorporate some image of the lawyer into her self-identity.[86] This makes it desirable that law schools provide a range of potentially satisfying models of the legal professional, and that they do not only hold out the lawyer acting for private clients in a commercial or corporate practice as the ideal. As noted above there is the cause lawyer, or the lawyer who seeks to serve the community through legal aid practice.[87] There is the small firm lawyer in a practice that services a local community.[88] There is the specialist in negotiation or ADR who eschews the adversarial model of legal practice.[89] There is the in-house lawyer or public sector lawyer. There is the lawyer as trusted

---

[81] Parker, 'moral panic' (n 46) argues legal ethics is a necessary site for such discourse. In the UK and Singapore it might be jurisprudence that meets the need, see: Seow Hon Tan 'Teaching legal ideals through jurisprudence' (2009) 43 The Law Teacher 14. However, I would argue value discourse is not subject specific but should be present across private law and public law subjects.

[82] Kwame Anthony Appiah, *The Ethics of Identity* (Princeton University Press 2005) Loc 1067.:

[83] For "academicization" see: Stanley Fish, *Save the World on Your Own Time* (Oxford University Press 2012) who states at 19: "But neither the university as a collective nor its faculty should advocate personal, political, moral, or any other kind of views except academic views." I have argued that some substantive values should be advocated in law schools in Graham Ferris, *Uses of Values in Legal Education* (Intersentia 2015) chapter 3.

[84] Graham Ferris and Nick Johnson, 'Practical Nous as the Aim of Legal Education' (2013) 19 International Journal of Clinical Legal Education 271.

[85] See: Stuart A Scheingold and Austin Sarat, *Something to Believe In: Politics, Professionalism, and Cause Lawyering* (Stanford University Press 2004).

[86] I have argued at length for the importance of the student identity project for legal education in Ferris, 'What is Entailed' (n 75). See: Neil W Hamilton and Verna E Monson, 'Ethical Professional (Trans)Formation: Themes from Interviews about Professionalism with Exemplary Lawyers' (2012) 52 Santa Clara Law Review 921.

[87] Nicola Harris, Roxanna Dehaghani and Daniel Newman, 'Vulnerability, the future of the criminal defence profession, and the implications for teaching and learning' (2021) 55 The Law Teacher57.

[88] Lawrence S Krieger & Kennon M Sheldon, 'What Makes Lawyers Happy?: A Data-Driven Prescription to Redefine Professional Success' (2015) 83 George Washington Law Review 554

[89] Rachael M Field and James Duffy, 'Law student psychological distress, ADR and sweet-minded, sweet-eyed hope' (2012) 23 Australasian Dispute Resolution Journal 195.

advisor.[90] Courses can be taught that highlight these alternatives to the ideal of qualification at a magic circle firm or commercial litigation chambers sites of work associated with aggressive workplace masculinity.[91]

All of these suggestions share a common characteristic, they are reactions to assumptions in the curriculum about the characteristics of the ideal hyper-rational, masculine, autonomous, competitive, liberal subject. Being autonomous and competitive they neglect collective action. Being hyper-rational and autonomous they have no emotional needs and are happy if left at liberty to pursue their own pre-given ends. Being masculine they are primarily the recipients of care, not care givers. Neo-liberalism reduces all values to money and market choices. The law exists to sustain markets, not to impose collective values upon markets. Vulnerability theory rejects this world view and asserts the importance of social reproduction, of the vulnerable individual, and the need for collective responses to deficiencies in resilience. A legal curriculum that recognizes vulnerability as fundamental to law and justice would provide a counterbalance to the current pervasive drift towards neo-liberal paradigms.

Institutions need to do more than offering support to individual students. The numbers of students seeking support is putting unsustainable pressure on student support services, who in response are at risk of becoming primarily referral agencies.[92] It is clear that a more proactive response is required, although it is less clear what that response should be.[93] Academics and managers of law schools concerned with law student wellbeing need to identify shared concerns and potential alliances within their institutions which are part of the environment of students which can either support or degrade resilience.[94]

Finally, vulnerability theory tells us we need to be ready to challenge, alongside students and professional bodies, prevailing neo-liberal concepts and ideals because they are untrue and harmful. To look to these paradigms for the solutions to low levels of wellbeing is to try to escape from our hole by digging faster. Vulnerability theory provides a way to uncover harmful assumptions and identify the sources of potential workable solutions to problems of poor student wellbeing.

[90]Anthony T Kronman, *The Lost Lawyer: Failing ideals of the legal profession* (Harvard University Press 1993); Arthur L Liman, *Lawyer: A life of counsel and controversy* (Public Affairs 1998).

[91]Hilary Sommerlad, '"A pit to put women in": professionalism, work intensification, sexualisation and work–life balance in the legal profession in England and Wales' (2016) 23 International Journal of the Legal Profession 61; Margaret Thornton, 'Hypercompetitiveness or a Balanced Life? Gendered Discourses in the Globalisation of Australian Law Firms' (2014) 17 Legal Ethics 153; Richard Collier, 'Fatherhood, gender and the making of professional identity in large law firms: bringing men into the frame' (2018) 15 International Journal of Law in Context 68.

[92]Broglia et al, 'Challenges' (n 6).

[93]Universities UK, Stepchange (n 79); Mental Wellbeing in Higher Education Working Group, *Student Mental Wellbeing in Higher Education: Good Practice Guide* (Universities UK 2015); Mark Dooris et al, Healthy Universities (n 11); University of York, Student Mental Ill-health Task Group: Report to the Vice-Chancellor, March 2016 available at: https://www.york.ac.uk/media/studenthome/features/2016/Student%20Mental%20Ill-health%20Task%20Group%20Report%20Mar%202016.pdf accessed 24 August 2020; UK Healthy Universities Network available at: <https://healthyuniversities.ac.uk/> accessed 24 August 2020; Abi Brooker, Meredith McKague and Lisa Phillips, 'Implementing a Whole-of-Curriculum Approach to Student Wellbeing' (2019) 10 Student Success 55.

[94]There is a risk that a neo-liberal managerialist reform response can aggravate existing negative pressures on the wellbeing of academics rather than supporting the wellbeing of students, see the special edition of The Law Teacher (2021) 55(1) on Vulnerability and Academic Labour.

Conclusions

Vulnerability theory is a powerful heuristic that helps us to analyse the problems of student wellbeing as system problems and avoid an inappropriate contemporary tendency to seek the causes for problems in individual choices and character.

The theory helps us to see the problems of individual students, or of groups of students, as problems of institutional and social support rather than of individual inadequacy. It does not assume that either the problem or the solution lies at the institutional level. However, neither does it absolve the institution from taking action in the public sphere to call upon the state to provide those legal, regulatory, and financial supports necessary to building resilience and ultimately wellbeing among law students and indeed all students in higher education. For academics and for student support professionals vulnerability theory provides a way to respond to the problem of student wellbeing without endorsing an individualistic (and usually medical or moralistic) analytical frame. It identifies the key question as: "what do these students need (to give them resilience)" and rejects the question: "how is this student deficient (in resilience)?"

The problem of low student wellbeing is complex, and we urgently need more research to diagnose and ameliorate the situation. But to be effective that research needs to be informed by a theory that identifies which questions we need to ask, and vulnerability theory offers such a theory. The scholarship of teaching and learning can be called into aid in framing institutional responses, and especially those works which attempt to refocus higher education and legal education on questions of character.[95] It is clear that individual resilience is linked to a sense of meaningfulness in activities and life as reflected in vulnerability theory by identification of the category of existential assets of resilience.[96] Therefore, any constructive facilitation of student engagement with questions of meaning is likely to support wellbeing and serve as an asset for resilience, especially for those students who are young adults.[97]

However, it should not be thought only ethical or value discourses as such are likely to support resilience. As Perry explained many years ago the nature of value discourse has a strong cognitive element,[98] and it is fairly clearly tied to such accepted educational aims as the development of critical thinking.[99] Unfortunately, it seems that the task of getting students to "think like a lawyer" traditionally achieves the aim of "knock[ing] your ethics into temporary anaesthesia" in a manner that aggravates

---

[95]The "third apprenticeship" in William M. Sullivan, Anne Colby, Judith Welch Wegner, Lloyd Bond, and Lee S. Shulman, *Educating Lawyers: Preparation for the Profession of Law* (Jossey Bass 2007); although the issue goes beyond professional education as exemplified in Anthony T Kronman, *Education's End: Why Our Colleges and Universities Have Given Up on the Meaning of Life* (Yale University Press 2007). The importance and difficulty of the subject has been explored by the author in Graham Ferris, 'Values ethics and legal ethics: the QLD and LETR Recommendations 6, 7, 10, and 11 (2014) 48 The Law Teacher 20 and Graham Ferris, *Uses of Values in Legal Education* (Intersentia 2015).

[96]Fineman, n 40. Steven Southwick and Dennis Charney, *Resilience: The Science of Mastering Life's Greatest Challenges* (2nd ed, Cambridge University Press 2018) chapters 4, 5 and 11.

[97]Graham Ferris, 'What is entailed by a student-centred approach to legal education?' (DPhil thesis by publication, Nottingham Trent University 2020).

[98]William Perry Jr, *Forms of Ethical Intellectual Development in the College Years: A Scheme* (Jossey-Bass 1998).

[99]Richard Arum and Josipa Roksa, *Academically Adrift: Limited Learning on College Campuses* (University of Chicago Press 2011) and Richard Arum and Josipa Roksa, *Aspiring Adults Adrift: Tentative Transitions of College Graduates* (University of Chicago Press 2014); Martha C Nussbaum, *Not For Profit: Why Democracy Needs the Humanities* (Princeton University Press 2010) and Martha C Nussbaum, *Cultivating Humanity: Classical Defense of Reform in Liberal Education: A Classical Defense of Reform in Liberal Education* (Harvard University Press 1998).

value confusion.[100] It may well be that one element of legal education that needs more attention is the deconstruction of the ethical and power based aspects of law throughout the curriculum.[101]

Thus, the challenge is not to abandon rigour and consensus educational aims such as critical thinking, but to re-invigorate the higher education project as one of building up students as critical thinkers and citizens.[102] It is likely that re-connecting with the university as a source of public good,[103] a source of resilience for students, staff, and society is likely to be fruitful. Understanding why this beneficent aim is likely to face resistance, because of neo-liberal narratives that are in opposition to it, is the final gift of vulnerability theory to the task of supporting the wellbeing of our students in the modern law school, providing as it does both an analysis that explains the opposition and a counter narrative of the responsive university within a responsive state.

Disclosure statement

No potential conflict of interest was reported by the author(s).

[100]The expression comes from Karl Llewellyn, *The Bramble Bush: The Classic Lectures on the Law and Law School* (Oxford University Press 1996), 116.

[101]David Pace, *The Decoding the Disciplines Paradigm: Seven Steps to Increased Student Learning* (Indiana University Press 2017).

[102]Bill Readings, *The University in Ruins* (Harvard University 1996), 63-67; Anne Colby, Thomas Ehrlich, Elizabeth Beaumont and Jason Stephens, *Educating Citizens: Preparing America's Undergraduates for Lives of Moral and Civic Responsibility* (Jossey-Bass 2003).

[103]Ourania Filippakou and Gareth Williams (Eds), *Higher Education As a Public Good: Critical Perspectives on Theory, Policy and Practice* (Peter Lang Inc 2013).

"I was able to ask for help when I became stressed rather than sitting alone and struggling": psychology and law students' views of the impact of identity and community on mental wellbeing

Michael Fay and Yvonne Skipper

ABSTRACT

People derive a sense of self from membership of social groups. Universities consist of many different groups and provide a significant opportunity to explore how group memberships can affect mental wellbeing. A key university group is students' school of study, membership of which enables individuals to develop an academic identity. We argue that a strong sense of belonging, and thus academic identity, within the school community can lead to positive mental wellbeing. We focus on belonging within academic schools because the positive impact of group membership is likely to exist to a greater degree in an academic school than in other university communities. We conducted online focus groups with 21 undergraduate students studying either law or psychology at a research-intensive university. Our aim was to explore their academic identity and belonging within their academic school of study, and how these variables affected their mental wellbeing. Our thematic analysis indicates that students with strong identities, who feel a sense of belonging in their school community – particularly among peers – display greater help-seeking behaviours in difficult times. If peers are viewed negatively, students are less forthcoming when in need of support. Promoting peer support is therefore a way of improving student mental wellbeing.

Introduction

Mental wellbeing challenges appear endemic among the UK undergraduate population. One in four undergraduates suffers poor mental wellbeing during their degree.[1] Only 17% of students believe their life is highly worthwhile,[2] 50.3% report thoughts of self-harm, 42.8% display high levels of anxiety, and 33.9% experience serious psychological issues requiring professional help.[3] An

---

[1]YouGov, "One in Four Students Suffer from Mental Health Problems" (2016) <https://yougov.co.uk/topics/lifestyle/articles-reports/2016/08/09/quarter-britains-students-are-afflicted-mental-hea> accessed 14 January 2021.

[2]Jonathan Neves and Nick Hillman, *Student Academic Experience Survey* (Higher Education Policy Institute 2018) 51.

[3]Stephen Pereira and others, "University Student Mental Health Survey 2018" (The Insight Network 2019).

increasing number of students are disclosing mental wellbeing problems to their institutions, with mental health accounting for 17% of all disabilities disclosed by first-year students in 2015/2016 and 27.2% in 2019/2020, compared to 5% in 2006/2007.[4] Typically, institutional responses to poor mental wellbeing "encourage people to medicalize their emotional suffering" and a majority of people "think that their emotions are profoundly individual";[5] therefore interventions are typically offered at the individual level (i.e. counselling, medication).[6] However, our communities and cultural beliefs shape our thoughts, feelings and behaviours[7] and we therefore argue that mental wellbeing is more properly seen as a community issue. Research has shown that psychologically meaningful group memberships have a positive impact on mental wellbeing,[8] and community-based interventions may be a way for universities "to address the high levels of psychological distress being experienced" by community members.[9] Developing an understanding of how community, belonging and identity influence students' mental wellbeing is an important contribution to the literature. A "whole university approach" is a core pillar of the University Mental Health Charter, creating an increasing role for proactive, community-based interventions instead of relying solely on reactive services. The Charter marks an important step towards making student and staff mental health a university-wide priority and delivering improved mental health and wellbeing outcomes.[10]

We argue that a strong academic identity and sense of belonging within the academic community can lead to positive mental wellbeing. We focus on a sense of belonging within academic schools as every student will be a member of at least one school, whereas they may choose not to engage with extracurricular groups like sports clubs. The positive impact of group membership may exist to a greater degree within academic schools than in other communities. This is because the academic school community is a bounded group,[11] its members share experiences and values,[12] can

[4]Craig Thorley, "Not by Degrees: Improving Student Mental Health in the UK's Universities" (Institute for Public Policy Research 2017); UCAS, "Starting the Conversation: UCAS Report on Student Mental Health" (UCAS 2021).

[5]Allan V Horwitz, "An Overview of Sociological Perspectives on the Definitions, Causes, and Responses to Mental Health and Illness" in Teresa L Scheid and Tony N Brown (eds), *A Handbook for the Study of Mental Health: Social Contexts, Theories, and Systems* (2nd edn, CUP 2010) 19.

[6]An example of this focus is highlighted by the Institute for Public Policy Research, which reports that 94% of UK universities saw demand for counselling by students increase between 2012 and 2017, with 61% reporting an increase of over 25%: Craig Thorley, "Not by Degrees: Improving Student Mental Health in the UK's Universities" (Institute for Public Policy Research 2017). In 2019/2020, 42% of students accessed counselling support: Randstad, "A Degree of Uncertainty: Student Wellbeing in Higher Education" (Randstad NV 2020).

[7]Thorley (n 8).

[8]S Alexander Haslam, Stephen D Reicher and Mark Levine, "When Other People Are Heaven, When Other People Are Hell: How Social Identity Determines the Nature and Impact of Social Support" in Jolanda Jetten, Catherine Haslam and S Alexander Haslam (eds), *The Social Cure: Identity, Health and Well-Being* (Psychology Press 2012) 157–74; Catherine Haslam and others, *The New Psychology of Health: Unlocking the Social Cure* (Routledge 2018).

[9]James Duffy, Rachael Field and Melinda Shirley, "Engaging Law Students to Promote Psychological Health" (2011) 36 Alternative Law Journal 250.

[10]Gareth Hughes and Leigh Spanner, "The University Mental Health Charter" (Student Minds, Leeds 2019).

[11]See Virginie Cobigo, Lynn Martin and Rawad Mcheimech, "Understanding Community" (2016) 5(4) Canadian Journal of Disability Studies 181; Silvia Cristina Bettez and Kathy Hytten, "Community Building in Social Justice Work: A Critical Approach" (2013) 49 Educational Studies 45; Keren Lehavot, Kimberly F Balsam and Gemma D Ibrahim-Wells, "Redefining the American Quilt: Definitions and Experiences of Community among Ethnically Diverse Lesbian and Bisexual Women" (2009) 37 Journal of Community Psychology 439.

[12]See Guendalina Capece and Roberta Costa, "The New Neighbourhood in the Internet Era: Network Communities Serving Local Communities" (2013) 32 Behaviour & Information Technology 438.

effectively empathise with each other and offer support,[13] and are looking to join similar professional communities, which may create a sense of solidarity.[14] We suggest that when students have a strong academic identity and supportive peers they are likely to feel able to turn to them for help, which is likely to encourage help-seeking behaviours earlier rather than at the point of crisis. As peer support is a significant influence on remaining in higher education (HE), creating successful peer-to-peer communities is an important aspect of supporting positive mental health.[15] Indeed, a higher sense of belonging can reduce stress and improve wellbeing.[16]

In this paper, we use the term mental wellbeing to mean the extent to which an individual is able "to develop their potential, work productively and creatively, build strong and positive relationships with others, and contribute to their community".[17] This definition highlights how positive mental wellbeing is linked with being productive rather than a state of happiness. We consider this to be distinct from conceptualisations of mental health linked to diagnosable mental health conditions. It is possible for an individual to have mental health difficulties but also have good mental wellbeing. For example, a student may have a diagnosis of depression, but receive appropriate treatment and have a strong support network of friends and family. Although their diagnosis suggests they may have poor mental health, they may still experience positive mental wellbeing because of the support they can rely on. Likewise, an individual with no diagnosable mental illness may have poor mental wellbeing due to loneliness, isolation or stress. This paper focuses on mental wellbeing as it is something all students experience and can be supported without medical or clinical intervention.

Social identity

According to social identity theory (SIT) we derive a sense of identity from our group memberships.[18] Being part of a group provides us with a social sense of identity and fosters a sense of belonging. Meaningful group memberships also influence our well-being and are "associated with a vast array of both physical and psychological health outcomes".[19] However, membership of social groups can also be linked to negative health outcomes such as "stigma, discrimination and inequality".[20] Wellbeing is affected by the state and circumstances of the group with which people identify,[21] thus "wellbeing will be boosted or dampened to the extent that the group ... does well or badly".[22]

[13]See Esther Rothblum, "Where Is the 'Women's Community?' Voices of Lesbian, Bisexual, and Queer Women and Heterosexual Sisters" (2010) 20 Feminism & Psychology 454.

[14]Gillian Vogl, "Work as Community: Narratives of Solidarity and Teamwork in the Contemporary Workplace, Who Owns Them?" (2008) 14(4) Sociological Research Online 4.

[15]Liz Thomas, "Building Student Engagement and Belonging in Higher Education at a Time of Change" (Report from the What Works? Student Retention and Success Programme, 2012).

[16]Y Skipper and M Fay "The Relationship Between Sense of Belonging, Mental Wellbeing and Stress in Students of Law and Psychology in an English University" (forthcoming).

[17]Foresight Mental Capital and Wellbeing Project, "Mental Capital and Wellbeing: Making the Most of Ourselves in the 21st Century. Final Project Report" (Government Office for Science 2008) 10.

[18]H Tajfel and JC Turner, "An Integrative Theory of Intergroup Conflict" in WG Austin and S Worchel (eds), *The Social Psychology of Intergroup Relations* (Brooks/Cole 1979).

[19]Juliet RH Wakefield and others, "When Groups Help and When Groups Harm: Origins, Developments, and Future Directions of the 'Social Cure' Perspective of Group Dynamics" (2019) 13(3) Social and Personality Psychology Compass e12440 2.

[20]ibid.

[21]See n 8.

[22]Haslam and others (2018) (n 8) 250.

The collective success or poor performance of a group will increase or reduce wellbeing.[23] So too will others' value (or lack thereof) of that social identity.[24] When individuals have strong, positive social identities, they are likely to experience higher self-esteem, higher life satisfaction and less psychological distress.

Self-categorisation theory explains that when we define ourselves in terms of a specific social identity, we generally try to live up to the norms and values associated with that group.[25] People with a strong social identity are more likely to act in line with group norms.[26] Although some of these norms may be linked to healthy behaviours, some may lead to ill health or increase an individual's vulnerability to stress. For example, students may develop stronger drinking intentions[27] or engage in more binge drinking[28] if consumption of alcohol is a norm. Groups may also have anti-help-seeking norms because support is perceived as stigmatising within their community.[29] This suggests that groups can enhance or harm wellbeing dependent on their membership norms.

As well as providing a sense of identity and providing behavioural norms, feeling part of a group may lead people to feel able to access support, which can lead to more positive mental wellbeing. We are more likely to provide social support to people who share our social identity[30] and more likely to accept help from our communities.[31] However, while groups "can be an important source of strength when members are able to band together and work effectively at solving/reframing stressors", they "can exacerbate (and even create) stress if such processes fail to occur", leaving members feeling "distressed and incapable".[32]

Law students' identity

Law students – and younger lawyers – have a higher rate of distress than their non-law peers, and experience barriers to recognising and seeking help for their distress; for example, in Australia, 35% of law students experience high levels of psychological distress compared with 18% of medicine students and 13% of people aged between 18 and 34 in the general population.[33]

---

[23] Nyla Branscombe and Daniel Wann, "Collective Self-Esteem Consequences of Outgroup Derogation When a Valued Social Identity Is on Trial" (1994) 24 European Journal of Social Psychology 641; Daniel Wann and Nyla Branscombe, "Die-Hard and Fair-Weather Fans: Effects of Identification on BIRGing and CORFing Tendencies" (1990) 14 Journal of Sport & Social Issues 103.

[24] Kathleen A Ethier and Kay Deaux, "Negotiating Social Identity When Contexts Change: Maintaining Identification and Responding to Threat" (1994) 67 Journal of Personality and Social Psychology 243.

[25] John C Turner, "Towards a Cognitive Definition of the Social Group" in Henri Tajfel (ed), *Social Identity and Intergroup Relations* (Cambridge University Press 1982); John C Turner, *Social Influence* (Oxford University Press 1991).

[26] John C Turner, "Social Categorization and the Self-Concept: A Social Cognitive Theory of Group Behaviour" in Edward J Lawler (ed), *Advances in Group Processes*, vol 2 (JAI Press 1985).

[27] Andrew G Livingstone, Hollie Young and Antony S Manstead, "'We Drink, Therefore We Are': The Role of Group Identification and Norms in Sustaining and Challenging Heavy Drinking Culture" (2011) 14 Group Processes & Intergroup Relations 637.

[28] Jennifer L Howell and others, "Happy but Unhealthy: The Relationship between Social Ties and Health in an Emerging Network" (2014) 44 European Journal of Social Psychology 612.

[29] Michelle Kearns and others, "Understanding Help-Seeking amongst University Students: The Role of Group Identity, Stigma, and Exposure to Suicide and Help-Seeking" (2015) 6 Frontiers in Psychology 1462.

[30] Mark Levine and others, "Identity and Emergency Intervention: How Social Group Membership and Inclusiveness of Group Boundaries Shape Helping Behavior" (2005) 31 Personality and Social Psychology Bulletin 443; Juliet RH Wakefield and others, "The Impact of Adopting Ethnic or Civic Conceptions of National Belonging for Others' Treatment" (2011) 37 Personality and Social Psychology Bulletin 1599.

[31] S Alexander Haslam and others, "Social Identity, Health and Well-Being: An Emerging Agenda for Applied Psychology" (2009) 58 Applied Psychology 1.

[32] Wakefield and others (n 19) 5.

[33] See Duffy, Field and Shirley (n 9) 250.

One possible reason for this higher rate of distress is the way law students are trained to think. A law degree seeks to develop students' logical, analytical and rational capabilities. It tends to emphasise doctrinal content and linear thinking, while de-emphasising "creativity, personal values, reflexivity and interdisciplinary factors such as justice and social policy"; it also "promotes personality traits such as defensiveness, perfectionism and pessimism which can lead to unhappiness".[34] Law students are less likely to find their course intrinsically interesting and to say they are at university to learn, and are more likely to study law for external reasons (i.e. parental pressure); to believe future employers were concerned more with their grades than other personal or social characteristics; to view grades as the crucial indicator of their success; to view and assess friendships in terms of networking and career advancement; to dislike group work; and to be more concerned with their university's reputation.[35] These characteristics may have a significant impact on law students' likelihood of developing depression, particularly as they "may have ... less social connectedness than may be optimal for mental health".[36] Social connectedness can help to prevent depression,[37] but law students' competitiveness can interfere with their capacity and willingness to connect with peers beyond a merely instrumental level. These traits "may help to explain the disproportionate rate of depression in law students".[38]

During their first year of undergraduate study, law students move away from intrinsic values, like community service, and towards extrinsic values, like appearance and image. Sheldon and Krieger highlight this shift among US law students.[39] Although in the US law is studied at postgraduate level, the literature suggests that similar changes may occur in UK undergraduate law students. Law students feel less self-determined in their goals during undergraduate study and are more concerned with impressing others and less with their own interest and enjoyment.[40] Law school "may bring about some negative changes in student motivations and values", and there are "significant correlations" between such changes and the changes in student wellbeing.[41]

Psychology students' identity

Although a wealth of research has explored the experiences of law students, considerably less literature is devoted to subjects like psychology. Psychology students also often experience poor mental health. A study by the American Psychological Association found 87% of psychology graduate students experienced

[34]ibid.
[35]Massimiliano Tani and Prue Vines, "Law Students' Attitudes to Legal Education: Pointers to Depression in the Legal Academy and the Profession?" (2009) 19(1) Legal Education Review, Article 2.
[36]ibid 25.
[37]Keith L Williams and Renee V Galliher, "Predicting Depression and Self-Esteem from Social Connectedness, Support, and Competence" (2006) 25 Journal of Social and Clinical Psychology 855.
[38]Tani and Vines (n 35) 1.
[39]Kennon M Sheldon and Lawrence S Krieger, "Does Legal Education Have Undermining Effects on Law Students? Evaluating Changes in Motivation, Values, and Well-Being" (2004) 22 Behavioral Sciences and the Law 261.
[40]Tani and Vines (n 35). See also Caroline Strevens and Clare Wilson, "Law Student Wellbeing in the UK: A Call for Curriculum Intervention" (2016) 11 Journal of Commonwealth Law and Legal Education 44; Lydia Bleasdale and Sarah Humphreys, "Identity, Well-Being and Law Students" in Caroline Strevens and Rachael Field (eds), *Educating for Well-Being in Law* (Routledge 2019).
[41]Sheldon and Krieger (n 39) 284.

anxiety and 68% symptoms of depression.[42] One reason for this may be that psychology students generally score higher for neuroticism as a personality trait.[43] They also score highly for openness, potentially indicating their degree choice is a reflection of a desire to better understand the self. This is consistent with the perception of psychology as "me search" – research that is reflective of the researcher and their experiences.[44]

Psychology students aspire to join a broad range of careers. Only 20% of psychology students become professional psychologists.[45] In 2016, psychology graduates embarked on careers in human health (35%), education (22%), scientific research (7%) and office work (4%).[46] When a student aspires to become a "psychologist", there is a broad range of specialisms covering sport and exercise to education and forensics. This diversity might lead students to develop a more permeable social identity and feel a weaker sense of community as group members have different aspirations and trajectories. However, it is also possible that this diversity might lead to lower levels of career competition and lead students to feel a greater sense of community.

Psychology students may also have a strongly "other" orientated focus, with "helping others" as their dominant value.[47] This suggests psychology students are less likely to seek prestige or financial gain from prospective careers but rather seek to improve the lives of others. The finding is consistent with psychology students' lower scores for extraversion and higher scores for agreeableness.[48] Attributing a lower value to personal gain and prestige may help reduce conflict and create a more positive "learning together" environment, such as group-based projects and development of listening skills.[49] Furthermore, psychology courses typically involve the development of skills to promote positive interpersonal interactions.[50] The three top skills employers desire in psychologists are listening skills, an ability to work with others, and getting along well with others.[51]

In addition, as psychology is the scientific study of the mind and how it dictates and influences behaviour, students explicitly cover topics such as mental health, stress, social identity, empathy and helping behaviours. As part of their course, they are likely to learn more about mental health and how it can be improved. Furthermore, many psychology degrees involve first and second years participating in research studies conducted by third-year students, to help them better understand the research process. This also supports the third-year students to obtain

[42]C Willyard, "Need to Heal Thyself" (2012) 10(1) *Grad Psych Magazine* 28; see also Christina M Rummell, "An Exploratory Study of Psychology Graduate Student Workload, Health, and Program Satisfaction" (2015) 46 Professional Psychology, Research and Practice 391.

[43]Anna Vedel, "Big Five Personality Group Differences across Academic Majors: A Systematic Review" (2016) 92 Personality and Individual Differences 1.

[44]See Jill Bolte Taylor, *My Stroke of Insight* (Viking 2008).

[45]Quality Assurance Agency, Subject Benchmark Statement Psychology (QAA 2016).

[46]Lisa Coulthard, "BPS Careers Destinations (Phase 3) Survey 2016 Report" (British Psychological Society 2017).

[47]R Bromnick and A Horowitz, "Reframing Employability: Exploring Career-related Values in Psychology Undergraduates" (HEA STEM Annual Learning and Teaching Conference, University of Birmingham, Birmingham, UK, 17 April 2013).

[48]Vedel (n 43).

[49]Quality Assurance Agency (n 45).

[50]Quality Assurance Agency (n 45).

[51]R Eric Landrum and Renee Harrold, "What Employers Want from Psychology Graduates" (2003) 30 Teaching of Psychology 131.

larger samples for their projects, giving the work greater impact. This may help students to feel a stronger sense of community with students in other year groups. Furthermore, most psychology courses also include elements of psychological literacy, which involves applying psychological principles to issues in work, relationships and the community.[52] These skills may lead students to be better placed to support each other and therefore lead to better mental wellbeing.

Current research

The literature suggests that law students experience a student community that is competitive. Their developing academic identity also increases students' focus on external measures of success, such as image. This prevalence of competitiveness may create a less positive community. In contrast, psychology students may experience a more collegiate, positive community with less competition, and may be orientated towards helping others rather than personal gain.

We conducted online focus groups with 21 undergraduate students studying either law or psychology. Our aim was to explore their academic identity and sense of belonging within their academic school of study. The literature indicates that the development of these variables has a significant impact on student mental wellbeing,[53] therefore we sought to develop our understanding of students' perceptions of the building of communities and belonging within their school of study.

Method

Participants

Participants were 17 psychology students and four law students from one research-led university. The reason for the disparity in numbers is that we were able to offer credits to psychology students for participating in the study, but this option was not open to law students. Three participants were male, and 18 participants were female; 20 were home students and one was an international student. There were five focus groups in total; the make-up of focus groups is presented in Table 1. One group contained a mix of participants to explore whether responses from students on one course influenced responses by the other. There was no discernible effect on responses.

Materials and procedure

Participants were sent an open invitation via email to participate in one of five asynchronous online focus groups. This approach was chosen as it maximised opportunities for participation and discussion. The groups were organised and

---

[52]Julie A Hulme and Jacquelyn Cranney, "Psychological Literacy and Learning for Life" in Joerg Zumbach and others (eds), *International Handbook of Psychology Learning and Teaching* (Springer 2020); Jacquelyn Cranney, Lorayne Botwood and Sue Morris, *National Standards for Psychological Literacy and Global Citizenship: Outcomes of Undergraduate Psychology Education* (Office for Learning and Teaching 2012).

[53]Karen F Osterman, "Students' Need for Belonging in the School Community" (2000) 70 Review of Education Research 323; Carol Goodenow, "The Psychological Sense of School Membership among Adolescents: Scale Development and Educational Correlates" (1993) 30 Psychology in the Schools 79.

Table 1. Focus group make-up by gender and degree subject.

Focus group	Participants' gender	Degree subject
Group A	1 Male 5 Female	All Psychology
Group B	0 Male 4 Female	All Psychology
Group C	0 Male 3 Female	All Law
Group D	1 Male 3 Female	All Psychology
Group E	1 Male 3 Female	1 Law 3 Psychology

hosted by a neutral researcher to ensure participants did not feel pressured to participate and to allow for honest responses. Students registered by email and were allocated a group and provided the dates and times the group would be open. Groups were accessible to participants for a week. When the groups went live, participants read an information sheet, gave consent, created an anonymous username and logged in. They answered a series of questions and could return throughout the week to add any further thoughts and respond to comments from other participants. However, the majority of students logged in to complete the questions and did not engage in discussion. The questions participants were asked were organised around three main topic areas:

Academic identity

(1) Do you have a strong identity as a psychology/law student? Why/why not?
(2) How did your identity as a law/psychology student develop over time? Are there any key things/times/activities which helped you develop this identity?

Sense of community

(1) Do you personally feel a strong sense of community with the law/psychology school? Why/Why not?
(2) Do you feel that other people experience the law/psychology community in the same way you do? Why?
(3) What have staff in your school done to support or hinder a sense of community?
(4) Do you feel like the other students in your school are supportive and help create a sense of community or not? How?
(5) What important times or events during your degree have helped or hindered you in feeling a part of the law/psychology community?
(6) Do you feel part of the broader community of law/psychology professionals? How does your school currently facilitate this and how could they do this better?

Mental wellbeing

(1) How stressed and overloaded have you felt during your course?
(2) What have been some of the toughest times for you in terms of high stress or poor mental health, for example, first assessment results released? First exams, etc.?
(3) How did your school/tutors support your mental health during this time? How could your school/tutors do this better?
(4) Did your academic identity or sense of community affect your response to stressful times?

When the group closed, participants were sent a debrief which included links to sources of support.

Analytic method

An inductive thematic analysis was conducted to identify and analyse and report themes within the data.[54] Transcripts were read thoroughly by both researchers and the data coded and organised into themes or "coherent and meaningful pattern(s) in the data".[55] The transcripts were continually consulted to make sure all themes were fully explored, and our understandings were data-driven. Themes were continually reviewed by both researchers and refined to ensure the most accurate representation of the data.

Limitations

A key limitation of this study is the limited number of participants. Owing to the credit-bearing nature of participation for psychology students, we were able to recruit more strongly from that cohort than from law. A larger number of law students would deepen our understanding of the cohorts' experiences and lessen potential bias. A second limitation is the use of a random sample of students and more targeted recruitment of a representative sample would deepen our understanding of diverse students' experience.

Analysis

Results

Three main themes were identified across the five focus groups: *relationships, Subject Culture* and *sources of support.*

Relationships

The relationships between members of subject communities were important and recurring across the focus groups. Relationships with both staff and peers were central to the participants' perception of community. *Peer connections* and *staff connections* were identified as important sub-themes.

Peer connections. Participants expressed differing views of peer-to-peer relationships. There was a strong sense of a peer community for psychology participants:

> I can sense a strong community within the psychology school, everyone is very friendly for example in the psychology society and the large online psychology group chat . . . I have met nice people just in practical classes/seminar groups and/or just asking for directions in the building. (P3, Group E)

Psychology participants discussed how this community was developed from a shared interest in their subject: "everyone who took psychology obviously were interested in similar things as most other students so are able to support each other with work and so on" (P4, Group A). Participation in classes and extracurricular activities also helped to develop community:

> I feel that in classes in psychology such as seminars and lab classes there is encouragement to engage with people around you during activities rather than staying alone and working on tasks alone. Staff encourage this often and this therefore creates a sense of community because you are able to engage with the class as a community. (P4, Group E)

[54] Virginia Braun and Victoria Clarke, "Using Thematic Analysis in Psychology" (2006) 3 Qualitative Research in Psychology 77.

[55] Victoria Clarke and Virginia Braun, *Successful Qualitative Research: A Practical Guide for Beginners* (Sage 2013) 120.

> I find that seminar groups and practical classes are important times that help me feel involved and part of the psychology community. Also being part of the psychology society is a big help as then you are part of a group and get involved with activities outside classes. (P3, Group E)

The community's intellectual diversity was also a factor, as it made psychology "more interesting to learn and debate" because "everyone has different ideas and opinions" (P3, Group A). Assessments and group work were also important factors in developing peer-to-peer relationships and a sense of community: "assessments are good at creating a sense of community as students will help each other out" (P1, Group A); "I feel that working on tasks in groups is what helps to create a community" (P4, Group E).

Students who did not experience a sense of community in psychology appeared to be self-excluded: "I don't take part in psychology activities, really ... I just see this undergraduate degree as a gateway to what I want to do in the future" (P5, Group A), or felt that there was exclusion (e.g. cliques and closed society meetings): "I feel like it is classically clique-like. The psychology society holds meetings that aren't publicised so psychology students don't know about them and therefore cannot attend" (P4, Group D).

Law participants typically expressed a negative view of peer relationships. Although some students were described as helpful, participants felt a lack of community with their peers. There was concern about being in competition with each other: "I do feel that some students are extremely competitive" (P1, Group E); "I don't feel as close with my fellow students because at the end of the day we compete against each other for jobs and placements" (P3, Group C); "it'd be a lie to say if we all didn't feel like we were in competition with each other" (P2, Group C). Participants spoke of a need to ignore others' feelings in order to succeed:

> While some students are really kind and helpful, many students I have come into contact with are usually focused on themselves ... I feel the attitude of most students does make it very hard. It seems as though the message is that you have to disregard the feelings of others if you wish to succeed. (P1, Group C)

Responses demonstrated an adversarial and negative feeling about peer-to-peer engagements among law participants.

Staff connections. While psychology participants focused on relationships with peers in their responses, relationships with staff were also viewed positively: "I feel comfortable to approach my personal tutor, seminar tutor and practical class teachers" (P3, Group E). Approachability and active facilitation in teaching sessions were highlighted as positive staff contributions towards developing community:

> I feel that in classes in psychology such as seminars and lab classes there is encouragement to engage with people around you during activities rather than staying alone and working on tasks alone. Staff encourage this often and this therefore creates a sense of community because you are able to engage with the class as a community. (As above, P4, Group E)

Law participants focused strongly on positive relationships with staff and high levels of support: "The lecturers do nothing but support every student they come in contact with which will obviously help with a sense of community" (P3, Group C); "the staff have been very helpful" (P1, Group C). Law students appeared to experience a greater sense of community with staff while psychology students appeared to experience positive relationships with staff and peers.

Subject Culture

The culture of the academic school community was also a strong, recurring theme. Community culture was seen as influencing participants' academic identities. This theme can be broken down into the sub-themes *collaborative vs competitive participation* and *professional membership*.

Collaborative vs competitive participation. Psychology participants' developing academic identity was connected to a culture of collaborative participation. Deciding to go to university was an important milestone in the process: "I think making the choice to come to University really developed my identity as a psychology student" (P3, Group E). Time as a part of the community – including A-level study – enjoying the subject, taking an active role in the community (attending classes, extracurricular activities) and developing peer-to-peer relationships also played a significant role:

> I believe that it [my identity] is growing as my time at University continues. I'm being to see things from a psychological point of view and everything that I see I am seeing and analysing as a psychologist. As I've been learning about new topics, I'm being to see more clearly which route I want to take as a career and looking into volunteering to explore this more. (Original, P1, Group A)

> I used to study psychology at A-level so it built up from there. I am really interested in mental health and I have friends and family who have struggled with it so that's when I became really sure psychology was something I wanted to study. I think an identity developed when I got to Keele, and all my flatmates in the first year were studying psychology as well. Also, I am a student ambassador and I talk a lot to prospective students about studying psychology so that helped as well. (P2, Group A)

Psychology participants explained how their identity had developed over time due to participation in the learning community. Broader experiences (e.g. volunteering) and deeper immersion in the subject community (e.g. taking part in psychological research) were also highlighted as contributing to the development of participants' academic identity. Responses demonstrated intrinsic motivation as students were interested in and enjoyed studying the subject, as opposed to seeing it as a means to an end.

Law participants highlighted how networking with other law students with a strong academic identity helped develop their own identity: "after socialising more with students who definitely did have a strong identity as a law student, I would say my identity as a law student grew" (P1, Group E). Academic identity also developed when participants started thinking like a lawyer: "I have started to develop my thinking and have started to adapt to the processes of being involved in the legal world" (P1, Group C). However, law participants generally developed their academic identity through complying with the competitive norms of being a law student, rather than through collaborative participation in the learning community. Competition and success (both academic and personal, e.g. election to a society committee) were important elements of the community culture and in law participants' developing identities: "I believe I have a strong identity in law. This is because I have taken part in all competitions available from the school. I am on a first name basis with most staff and students. This is shown in my getting voted for the law society committee" (P3, Group C); "after the first set of exams...my identity as a law student started to grow. Doing well in the first set of exams increased my drive" (Original, P1, Group E).

Taking part in extracurricular activities involving competition or aspects of legal practice were also important: "I feel this [my identity] all began when my personal tutor kept giving me extracurricular activities to do such as being a client for the client interview" (P3, Group C); "I started to get more involved in the extracurricular activities the law school offered" (P1, Group E); "having to apply techniques learned in class to real circumstances has helped me to bridge the gap between merely learning the subject and using it in a practical way" (P1, Group C).

Professional membership. Both groups of participants felt they were "students" and had not yet developed an identity as part of the broader "professional" community of psychologists/lawyers. While participants recognised that there were some opportunities to begin developing connections, there was clearly felt to be a gap between "student" identity and community membership and "professional" identity and community membership: "I always feel there is a barrier between those who are students and professionals which is why the sense of broader community is hindered" (P4, Group E); "I feel there is a gap to be bridged between being a law student and being taken seriously as a legal professional" (P1, Group C).

Sources of support

A third theme was the sources of support participants described as available to them during challenging times. Understanding of stressors differed by subject and participants also articulated different sources of available support based on the types of relationships that existed within the learning community. This theme can be broken down into three sub-themes: *coping with challenging times*, *peer support* and *staff support*.

Coping with challenging times. Both groups of participants described experiencing stress during their time at university. Psychology participants discussed experiencing variable levels of stress and were generally reflective, self-aware and knew the root cause of their stress and when it was likely to happen. They identified specific periods of stress at particular times throughout their degree, such as when settling in to university. Assessments were seen as a significant source of stress: "I feel stressed when it comes to assignments, especially if they're all due at similar times because you finally finish one then have another to do straight after" (P1, Group A); "Exam time is definitely the most stressful for me" (P1, Group A); "Stressful times are usually around deadline period" (P2, Group A); "when exams have come round and big assignments I have become very stressed and overloaded" (P4, Group B).

The day assessment results are released was also recognised as being stressful: "Results day is also stressful as I find myself constantly checking my phone to see if they've been released" (P1, Group A); "my mental health suffered during the waiting times for exam results" (P3, Group B); "During exams and the release of results my mental health tends to be at an all time low" (P4, Group B).

Assessments were also identified as challenging by law participants. Participants explained that "achieving good grades" often meant ignoring their mental health, either by not practising self-care or by feeling unable to access support: "I tend to disregard my own health needs because I am too concerned about achieving good grades" (P1, Group C); "I knew who to go to in times of stress but very often didn't because I didn't feel like I had the time to" (P3, Group C). However, law participants generally described themselves as being "extremely" stressed and did not display as nuanced reflections on the times and experiences they found stressful beyond assessment.

Peer support. Psychology participants were generally very positive about the support received from their peers. Belonging to a community of peers sharing their experiences made an important contribution to positive mental wellbeing. Being able to seek empathetic support from others on the course – either in person or via social media – was seen as a key way to cope with stressful experiences: "during stressful times I felt comfortable to ask questions in the online group chat or to friends I met in classes which was helpful and nice to hear that other people felt the same" (P3, Group E); "I actually think the students are very supportive! Any time I've asked for help I've always been given it (via the psychology group chat, and in person in lectures and labs)" (P2, Group E).

There was significant focus on how social media "group chats" brought people together and provided an important source of support: "we have a large group chat that involves most people on the course I think and people are always willing to help each other on there" (P2, Group A).

Law participants expressed fears of being judged or treated differently by others on the degree course if they sought peer support:

> sometimes I would feel ashamed to admit weakness and reach out for help . . . It feels as though your peers view you differently knowing you have struggled during your legal study. (P1, Group C)

Participants' identity as law students also inhibited mental wellbeing, as group norms like competition appeared to undermine the potential for peer-to-peer support: "the message is that you have to disregard the feelings of others if you wish to succeed" (P1, Group C). Participants were wary of peer-to-peer support because other law students were not perceived as being forthcoming: "students do help but clearly hold things back to prevent you knowing everything they do. Keeping their edge" (P3, Group C). Furthermore, because of a perception that studying a law degree is "stressful", participants felt they were "just expected . . . to be able to deal with it" (P2, Group C).

Staff support. Staff also played a supportive role in the community by answering questions students had, delivering good quality teaching and by giving workshops on how to handle anxiety and stress. Psychology participants highlighted it was "really nice and reassuring knowing I have my tutor there for extra support and that I can go to them whenever I need" (P1, Group A).

For law participants, it seemed that belonging to a staff–student community contributed to positive mental wellbeing. There was a strong emphasis on staff support. Participants spoke very highly of the support they had received from their lecturers during stressful times: "My lecturers continually do everything they can to make the course less stressful" (P3, Group C); "[lecturers] are really wonderful and I haven't felt too burdensome when asking for help. Their open office hours are something to make the most of" (P1, Group C).

Discussion

The aim of this study was to explore how academic identity and a sense of belonging to a learning community can have a positive impact on students' mental wellbeing, and potential areas in which this impact may be improved.

Peer-to-peer relationships appeared to be an important indicator of positive mental health among participants. As identified in the themes *peer connections* and *staff connections*, there appeared to be a difference between the relationships developed by participants studying psychology and those studying law. Psychology participants appeared to benefit from a collegiate and supportive peer-to-peer community and spoke positively about their relationships with other psychology students. This appeared to have a positive impact on their mental wellbeing. The norms of law participants' academic identity, which focused on competition and success,[56] did not appear to aid in the development of a supportive peer-to-peer community. As identified in the theme *staff connections*, law participants spoke more positively about staff–student relations than about relationships with their peers, whom they viewed as competitors. This had a negative influence on mental wellbeing. This finding is in line with social identity theory and social cures[57] as students' group memberships appeared to affect their attitudes towards peers and staff. The two academic in-groups were different in their attitudes towards peers, and members reported different behaviours in line with their group norms.

The "social cure" perspective highlights the potentially transformative nature of the social support we receive from group members and how such support helps us cope with stress.[58] Building on this view, the results of our focus groups suggest that academic identity and community are important factors when undergraduate students are coping with challenging times. This is seen in the themes *coping with challenging times*, *peer support* and *staff support*. Psychology participants displayed a nuanced awareness of the times and reasons they may experience stress while law participants described themselves as being "extremely stressed". Psychology participants also drew notably more support from peers than was reported by law participants. Positive peer-to-peer relationships created an empathetic peer support network that psychology participants felt able to access through social media or in person. A strong academic identity and sense of belonging to the learning community appeared to be related to help-seeking behaviours likely to contribute to positive mental wellbeing, such as reaching out on group chats. However, groups "can be an important source of strength" when members feel "supported and capable", but "can exacerbate (and even create) stress" if they "feel distressed and incapable", and very different outcomes can occur if support is actively withheld.[59] This is similarly indicated in the apparent distinction between psychology and law participants' experience of peer relationships and support (see *peer connections* and *peer support*): law participants expressed a concern that even helpful peers would hold back so as to retain a competitive edge. This may suggest that students' membership of a school of study can be influential on mental wellbeing, in both positive and negative ways, and may discourage help seeking when perceptions of other group members are negative.

[56]Tani and Vines (n 35).
[57]Eg Horwitz (n 5), and see, generally, n 8.
[58]Capece and Costa (n 12).
[59]Wakefield and others (n 19) 5.

Academic identity continually developed throughout participants' degrees and participants indicated this was linked with greater immersion and understanding of the subject and its applications, as well as adopting the norms expected of the subject groups' members (see *collaborative vs competitive participation*). A participant with a strong sense of identity was more likely to label themselves as a psychology or law student and, in turn, as part of the learning community. However, participants' academic identity and sense of community were not always linked in expected ways. While a strong social identity may lead to in-group favouritism, even when people do not know each other,[60] this does not automatically lead to a sense of community between in-group members if group norms are competitive and adversarial, despite members having a strong academic identity (see *collaborative vs competitive participation*). Law participants with a strong identity as a lawyer appeared to behave in line with competitive and adversarial norms, which may lead to decreased wellbeing as it may diminish peer support opportunities (see *collaborative vs competitive participation*). This is consistent with literature on the "social curse", which indicates that not all group memberships are healthy for us.[61] Literature on the mental health and wellbeing of law students supports this point.[62] Work by Bleasdale and Humphreys identified a comparable trend: music students worked collaboratively and medicine students provided each other with a "safety net", but law students were typically seen as competitive.[63] This is significant because a strong sense of community is an important contributor to positive mental wellbeing, as it can help to reduce stress by up to 30%.[64]

Among our participants, psychology students who reported good peer relationships and a strong sense of community reported greater help-seeking behaviours than law students, whose sense of community appeared orientated towards university staff (see *peer connections* and *staff connections*). As peer support is a significant influence on young people remaining in HE,[65] it would appear that group norms that are orientated towards competition are disadvantageous. When peers are supportive and participants felt able to turn to their peer community for help, it appeared to encourage help-seeking behaviours earlier in periods of difficulty rather than at the point a participant reached crisis. When negative views about other students exist, this may lead to reduced peer-to-peer support and students may instead rely on staff. Psychology participants could generally reach out via social media to a large number of peers when experiencing difficulties with an assessment (see *peer support*), but law participants turned to staff whose time is finite and typically accessible during office hours (see *staff support*).

While academic identity appeared to influence participants' mental wellbeing, their developing professional identity as either a "lawyer" or a "psychologist" was not reported as being significant. One reason participants gave for this is that their professional identity had not developed to a point where they identified as in-group members of the legal or psychological professions (see *professional membership*). Another reason

---

[60] See n 11.

[61] Blerina Kellezi and Stephen Reicher, "Social Cure or Social Curse? The Psychological Impact of Extreme Events during the Kosovo Conflict" in Jolanda Jetten, Catherine Haslam and S Alexander Haslam (eds), *The Social Cure: Identity, Health and Well-Being* (Psychology Press 2012).

[62] Howell and others (n 28).

[63] Lydia Bleasdale and Sarah Humphreys, *Undergraduate Resilience Research Project: Project Report* (Leeds Institute for Teaching Excellence, University of Leeds 2018).

[64] Duffy, Field and Shirley (n 9).

[65] Thomas (n 15).

may be that not all participants sought to become members of these professional communities and were instead pursuing other career paths, therefore a sense of professional identity as a lawyer or psychologist would be contingent on students following traditional career trajectories. University is a site of identity negotiation and transition for future professionals[66] and an academic setting creates opportunities to develop new cultural capitals.[67] Networking events are important spaces for students to "try on" professional identities,[68] assessing their compatibility and sense of belonging. However, it is students' own social and cultural capital that allows them to feel at ease within a professional environment.[69] As participants perceived a gap between "student" and "professional" identity (see *professional membership*), it is likely that participants did not yet possess sufficient capital to identify as in-group members of a profession. Thus, even if students aspire to join specific professions post degree, professional identity may not significantly influence wellbeing.

Conclusion

Consistent with social identity theory, students' academic identity and sense of community belonging may play an important role in their mental wellbeing. Strong identities, positive peer relationships and a sense of belonging to the learning community appeared to positively influence mental wellbeing and help-seeking behaviours. When peers were viewed as competitors or with suspicion, peer-to-peer support appeared less forthcoming, and this affected help-seeking behaviours. Trying to cope with challenges without support is likely to have a negative impact on mental wellbeing, whereas seeking and receiving support is likely to improve wellbeing.[70] If students are able to access support – and are encouraged to communicate and share their difficulties with each other and with staff – this may bolster their resilience and wellbeing. Belonging to a community of students and staff appeared to provide participants with access to a wide network of support during their degree.

Future research directions

We recruited participants from two academic schools in a research-intensive university in the Midlands. The region is traditionally associated with the coal and pottery industries; the student body will likely differ from rural or inner-city institutions. Student cohorts at Russell Group or post-92 institutions may also differ. A national study could be conducted across a range of institutions to better understand how students' identity and sense of community influence mental health. This study should also include a wider range of academic schools with both large and small cohorts, and subjects with links to professions (i.e. medicine, nursing, law) and those without. A future study should also explore how identity and sense of community develop

[66] Magali S Larson, *The Rise of Professionalism: A Sociological Analysis* (University of California Press 1977).

[67] Pierre Bourdieu, "The Forms of Capital" in John Richardson (ed), *Handbook of Theory and Research for the Sociology of Education* (Greenwood 1986) 241; Arthur Baxter and Carolyn Britton, "Risk, Identity and Change: Becoming a Mature Student" (2001) 11 International Studies in Sociology of Education 87.

[68] Desmond Manderson and Sarah Turner, "Coffee House: Habitus and Performance among Law Students" (2006) 31 Law & Social Inquiry 649, 665.

[69] ibid.

[70] Royal College of Psychiatrists, "Mental Health of Students in Higher Education: College Report CR166" (RCP 2011).

over time, as this study was only able to provide a snapshot in time during the autumn semester. For example, law students may develop a stronger professional identity towards the end of their third year of study as they approach vocational learning. Another future direction for research is to explore how we can create positive communities within academic schools of study that facilitate help-seeking behaviours and support mental health and wellbeing. This may involve challenging the culture in subjects based on competition and adversarialism by introducing a collaborative ethos and more group-based activities. To reduce competition and increase belonging, law schools could introduce greater opportunity for peer collaboration both in seminars and, more broadly, across the syllabus, such as joint research projects. These opportunities would need to be embedded into teaching from Year 1 and the value of collaboration would also need to be clearly and effectively communicated to students. Staff could act as collaborative role models by showcasing how collaboration adds value to their own research. Law schools might further aid such initiatives by implementing consistent membership of seminar groups across "core" modules to foster a sense of community and familiarity between students. To reduce the competitive elements of a law degree we must reflect on our own practices, how they may encourage or reduce competition, and be creative in how we deliver an effective and robust curriculum while developing a community to which students feel they belong, regardless of background or future aspirations.

Disclosure statement

No potential conflict of interest was reported by the authors.

Funding

This work was supported by the Society for Research in Higher Education [grant number 2017-044].

ORCID

Michael Fay http://orcid.org/0000-0001-7204-5038
Yvonne Skipper http://orcid.org/0000-0001-7011-3439

"Make glorious mistakes!" Fostering growth and wellbeing in HE transition

Stella Coyle and Hannah Gibbons-Jones

ABSTRACT

This paper uses Keele's Legal Essentials module as a case study to evaluate how curriculum design can promote wellbeing in first-year law students, by supporting their transition to higher education and fostering a sense of belonging to the Law School community. Module design is grounded in recognition that the orientation process for new law students should emphasise the importance of wellbeing[1] and that wellbeing initiatives are most effective when integrated into the curriculum.[2] Legal Essentials aims to give new law students an early experience of a community grounded in collaboration and authentic critical engagement, where risk-taking is fostered and supported. Module delivery incorporates co-teaching and panel-style discussions, including more senior students and members of the wider legal world. Academics, students, and professionals thereby share their own experiences of learning, practice, and wellbeing, modelling a community where vulnerability is not a weakness and collaboration is encouraged.

1. Introduction

This paper examines how curriculum design can promote wellbeing in first-year law students. It focuses on two vital, interrelated functions of legal education: how curriculum design can support students' transition to higher education (HE); and how it can help foster their sense of identity as members of the Law School community.[3] The paper uses Keele's new Legal Essentials module as a case study through which these questions can be analysed. It will describe how the module is designed to respond to the challenges facing student wellbeing, including recognition of some particular characteristics of law students revealed in the literature. It will examine the effect of traditional legal education on the wellbeing of both students and academics, with reference to the sense – or absence – of positive identity, community and belonging. The paper will then consider the issues raised

[1]Natalie Skead and Shane L Rogers, "Stress, Anxiety and Depression in Law Students: How Student Behaviours Affect Student Wellbeing" (2014) 40 Monash University Law Review 564.

[2]James Duffy, Rachael Field and Melinda Shirley, "Engaging Law Students to Promote Psychological Health" (2011) 36 Alt LJ 250.

[3]Sally Kift, Karen Nelson and John Clarke, "Transition Pedagogy: A Third-Generation Approach to FYE: A Case Study of Policy and Practice for the Higher Education Sector" (2010) 1(1) The International Journal of the First Year in Higher Education 1.

by transition to higher education, before going on to discuss Legal Essentials' curriculum design for wellbeing. It will conclude with an analysis of student feedback, team reflection, and suggestions for future module and curriculum development. Throughout the paper, the impact of Covid on student and staff wellbeing will be considered.

The data on student wellbeing is well documented,[4] and emerging research into the impact of Covid-19 on education reveals an additional risk of "reduced motivation toward studies, increased pressures to learn independently, abandonment of daily routines, and potentially higher rates of dropout" resulting in "an unprecedented mental health burden on students".[5] The literature also highlights long-standing concerns over law students in particular. Law students are highly vulnerable to comparing themselves negatively to others; they are concerned about not being as "smart" as other students, and they often feel "lost" because they believe that they do not understand as much as everyone else, especially in the first year.[6] Moreover, legal education, which tends to emphasise doctrinal content and linear thinking, has the effect of promoting "personality traits such as defensiveness, perfectionism and pessimism which can lead to unhappiness".[7] This is partly due to how law students are trained to approach legal issues; the LLB degree seeks to develop their logical, analytical and rational capabilities, as illustrated by concepts such as "thinking like a lawyer".[8] Law students find themselves early on in an adversarial environment, where legal issues are presented as problems, and where students are asked to advise one side. Legal Essentials was designed to respond to these problems and give new law students the experience of a community where vulnerability is not a weakness and collaboration is encouraged. It aims to develop students' sense of belonging through active engagement with the educational community.[9]

Why Legal Essentials?

Legal Essentials is a redesign and blending of Induction and the Legal Skills module, comprised of four concurrent and interrelated streams focused on "thinking", "making", "doing", and "being" law. *Thinking Law* encourages students to think critically and become confident in analysing and challenging legal concepts, arguments, and decisions. *Making Law* involves understanding and critically examining the English legal system, with an emphasis on access to justice. *Doing Law* focuses on scholarship and subject-related study skills. *Being Law* supports students to develop their personal and professional resources, helping to build affiliation with the school community and foster an authentic sense of identity that will benefit their wellbeing. Our motto is *"Make glorious mistakes!"*, borrowed from writer Neil Gaiman's 2011 New Year message

[4]See for example Craig Thorley, "Not by Degrees: Improving Student Mental Health in the UK's Universities" (Institute for Public Policy Research 2017); Emma Jones, *Emotions in the Law School: Transforming Legal Education through the Passions* (Routledge 2020) 126–29; Caroline Strevens and Clare Wilson, "Law Student Wellbeing in the UK: A Call for Curriculum Intervention" (2016) <http://law-school.open.ac.uk/sites/law-school.open.ac.uk/files/files/Law student wellbeing in the UK.pdf> accessed 29 October 2019.

[5]See for example Nicholas Grubic, Shaylea Badovinac and Amer M Johri, "Student Mental Health in the Midst of the COVID-19 Pandemic: A Call for Further Research and Immediate Solutions" (2020) 66 International Journal of Social Psychiatry 517.

[6]L Bleasdale and S Humphreys, *Undergraduate Resilience Research Project: Project Report* (Leeds Institute for Teaching Excellence, 2018) <http://teachingexcellence.leeds.ac.uk/wpcontent/uploads/2018/01/LITEbleasdalehumphreys_fullreport_online.pdf> accessed 7 January 2019.

[7]Duffy and others (n 2) 250.

[8]Emma Jones, "Transforming Legal Education through Emotions" (2018) 38 Legal Studies 450.

[9]Aidan Curzon-Hobson, "A Pedagogy of Trust in Higher Learning" (2002) 7 Teaching in Higher Education 265.

> I hope that in this year to come, you make mistakes. Because if you are making mistakes, then you are making new things, trying new things, learning, living, pushing yourself, changing yourself, changing your world. You're doing things you've never done before, and more importantly, you're Doing Something. So that's my wish for you ... Make New Mistakes. Make glorious, amazing mistakes. Make mistakes nobody's ever made before. Don't freeze, don't stop, don't worry that it isn't good enough, or it isn't perfect, whatever it is: art, or love, or work or family or life. Whatever it is you're scared of doing, do it. Make your mistakes, next year and forever.[10]

We include this message in our welcome and induction materials and refer to it throughout the module, to emphasise the importance of engagement and to encourage students to see their academic and personal development holistically, in a challenging but supportive and collaborative community.

Legal Essentials involves an intensive, high-contact, extended induction period in weeks 1–3, scaffolded by a further five weeks of skill- and self-development alongside the core law modules which begin in week 4. During the first three weeks, we deliver a range of knowledge, activity, skills, and wellbeing sessions through a mixture of seminars, workshops, lectures, and panel discussions, introducing the four Legal Essentials streams. Module assessment is a two-stage process: in week 5, an online multiple-choice quiz tests students' knowledge of the English legal system; and in week 9, students write a critical analysis of a short article on a current socio-legal issue, or an analysis of a topical case. Feedback on the written exercise is given before the main assessment period, so that students better understand how to approach their core module assessments.

Module delivery incorporates co-teaching, including "live performances" of critical discussion, to show that law and legal knowledge are up for debate – including team members' own research! We also use panel-style discussions, including more senior law students and members of the professional legal community. The teaching team models authenticity, vulnerability, and resilience (for example, by relating our own experiences of imposter syndrome and coping with setbacks and rejection – see further, section 4). Through teamwork, open discussion, and debate across the four streams, and the co-creation of some aspects of the module (see section 5), the aim is to give new law students an early experience of community grounded in collaboration and authentic critical engagement.

Of course, module delivery had to adapt to the move from in-situ to online learning during the Covid pandemic in 2020–21. One of the consequences of the online pivot was the loss of synchronous whole-cohort or large-group sessions – replaced by shorter, recorded lectures – with tutorials or seminars remaining "live", albeit online. This made sense for courses that were based on the traditional lecture and tutorial/seminar format, but the extended Induction part of Legal Essentials was not designed on this basis. We therefore had to lose our whole-cohort, co-taught, panel-style, live discussion and debate sessions, and we did not have the resources to deliver them across the small-group seminars in the same way. This meant we had to work harder to avoid lapsing back into the traditional educational approach.

---

[10] Neil Gaiman, "My New Year Wish" (*Journal*, 31 December 2011) <https://journal.neilgaiman.com/2011/12/my-new-year-wish.html> accessed 28 January 2021 and reproduced with kind permission of the author.

2. The effect of traditional legal education on wellbeing

Student wellbeing

Research suggests that law students experience a particular alienation from the personal dimension of their learning experience, whether online or in situ, which can negatively affect their mental health. Tani and Vines' comparative study[11] of law and medicine students highlighted some telling differences between the cohorts, including a prevalence of certain characteristics[12] amongst law students. For example, more law students are likely to be studying the degree for external reasons, such as parental influence; they are less likely to find their subject intrinsically interesting; are more likely to believe that employers look at grades rather than personal or social characteristics; tend to dislike group work; are less likely to say that they are at university to learn; and are more likely to view friendships through the prism of networking and career advancement opportunities. Such traits "may indeed have a significant impact on law students' likelihood of developing depression", particularly as "law students may have feelings of less autonomy and less social connectedness than may be optimal for mental health".[13] Moreover, the competitive nature of law students is a likely indication of reduced personal autonomy, as it suggests a dependence on external measures for self-evaluation and self-esteem.[14]

It is therefore important to foster a positive academic identity, and a sense of community belonging, to ameliorate these tendencies. Students' capacity to develop a strong academic identity is closely related to their social identity: to their concept of self, arising from their membership of – and sense of belonging to – a social group. People with stronger social identities are less likely to blame negative life events on internal causes such as personal shortcomings;[15] furthermore, social connectedness may enhance individual motivation.[16] Lack of social connectedness is the "strongest predictor of all adjustment outcomes" and a key risk factor in depression,[17] and such psychological issues can inhibit learning and promote disengagement.[18] Unfortunately, law students experience barriers to recognising and seeking support for their wellbeing, whether professionally or from their social networks.[19] Young people in general are less likely to feel they have someone to rely on or a sense of belonging in their neighbourhood,[20] yet good social networks and peer relationships clearly have

---

[11]Massimiliano Tani and Prue Vines, "Law Students' Attitudes to Legal Education: Pointers to Depression in the Legal Academy and the Profession?" (2009) 19(1) Legal Education Review, Article 2.

[12]Tani and Vines (n 11) 24–27.

[13]Tani and Vines (n 11) 25.

[14]Tani and Vines (n 11) 29.

[15]See for example Tegan Cruwys and others, "Depression and Social Identity: An Integrative Review" (2014) 18 Personality and Social Psychology Review 215; Jolanda Jetten, Catherine Haslam and S Alexander Haslam (eds), *The Social Cure: Identity, Health and Well-Being*(Psychology Press 2012).

[16]Katharine H Greenaway and others, "From 'We' to 'Me': Group Identification Enhances Perceived Personal Control with Consequences for Health and Wellbeing" (2015) 109 Journal of Personality and Social Psychology 53.

[17]Adele Bergin and Kenneth Pakenham, "Law Student Stress: Relationships between Academic Demands, Social Isolation, Career Pressure, Study/Life Imbalance and Adjustment Outcomes in Law Students" (2015) 22 Psychiatry, Psychology and Law 388, 400.

[18]Nikki Bromberger, "Enhancing Law Student Learning – The Nurturing Teacher" (2010) 20(1) Legal Education Review, Article 4.

[19]See for example Norm Kelk and others, *Courting the Blues: Attitudes towards Depression in Australian Law Students and Legal Practitioners*(Brain and Mind Research Institute, University of Sydney 2009).

[20]Office for National Statistics, "Measuring National Well-Being: Quality of Life in the UK, 2018" <www.ons.gov.uk/peoplepopulationandcommunity/wellbeing/articles/measuringnationalwellbeing/qualityoflifeintheuk2018> accessed 15 August 2018.

a protective influence against mental health difficulties.[21] It is important to recognise that mental health is not simply a problem for individuals,[22] but rather a problem for communities – including law schools.

The Law School during the Covid pandemic was, of course, a very different place. While we were keen to move away from some of the *content* of traditional legal education, we had not foreseen the move away from traditional *delivery* of legal education that happened in 2020–21. The online pivot meant that there was no "community" in the traditional, physical sense. Moreover, both students and staff were coping with a highly stressful set of circumstances. As Jones highlights, there is "evidence that high levels of stress and stress over a longer duration can result in memory impairment and inhibit neural plasticity. Students will 'worry more than learn' and begin to practice avoidance tactics".[23] This high level of stress on both sides, coupled with an unprecedented move away from in-person contact, was a clear challenge to the sense of community we were so keen to foster. There was a marked effect on staff wellbeing as a result.

Staff wellbeing

Peake and Mullings capture vividly the challenges facing the mental health of academic staff:

> Academics are possibly the worst "role models" for a different sort of academy, as the model that most of us embrace continues to be one of continuous achievement, and a capacity to take on work that is infinitely elastic. Indeed, we could be considered ideal neoliberal subjects because (supposedly) we respond well to the discourses of meritocracy and individual responsibility, achievement, advancement, persistence, competition, and the winner-takes-all ethos that currently structures and disciplines all in places of higher learning.[24]

Academic life is characterised by " ... isolated, individualized working practices; intense workloads and time pressures; long hours and the elision of barriers between work and home".[25] This situation was exacerbated during the pandemic. The first year of Legal Essentials – particularly the extended intensive induction period – was certainly stressful for the teaching team. We consciously tried to maintain our sense of team belonging; we met regularly in informal settings whenever we could and gave each other personal and practical support. During the pandemic, however, opportunities for informal support and stress relief had to be actively sought out rather than being readily available to us. It meant that it was much harder for us to be "leading by emotional example".[26]

Added to this is the emotional labour involved in teaching.[27] University lecturers report significantly higher levels of emotional labour than other occupations, including mental health nurses.[28] A key reason for this is the dissonance lecturers can experience

---

[21] Royal College of Psychiatrists, "Mental Health of Students in Higher Education: College Report CR166" (RCP 2011).

[22] Kelk and others (n 19).

[23] See Jones (n 8) 136.

[24] Linda J Peake and Beverley Mullings, "Critical Reflections on Mental and Emotional Distress in the Academy" (2016) 15 ACME: An International Journal for Critical Geographies 253, 273.

[25] John Horton and Faith Tucker, "Disabilities in Academic Workplaces: Experiences of Human and Physical Geographers" (2014) 39 Transactions of the Institute of British Geographers 76, 85.

[26] See Jones (n 8) 161.

[27] Mary Heath and others, "Learning to Feel Like a Lawyer: Law Teachers, Sessional Teaching and Emotional Labour in Legal Education" (2017) 26 Griffith Law Review 430.

[28] Karen Berry and Simon Cassidy, "Emotional Labour in University Lecturers: Considerations for Higher Education Institutions" (2013) 2(2) Journal of Curriculum and Teaching 22.

between their teaching personae and their true feelings.[29] But when emotional labour is conducted for the benefit of students, or for a teacher's own reward and satisfaction, rather than because of organisational demand display rules, job satisfaction can actually increase.[30] This is why authenticity in teaching and learning is so important. Unfortunately, it can be so difficult to achieve, especially in the present neoliberal university landscape, with its culture of individualism that fails to make adequate room for autonomy[31] or authenticity.[32]

In summary, while law students (and indeed law academics) may traditionally be trained and encouraged to think in a logical, rational manner, it is unrealistic to deny the centrality of emotion to law and legal education. Indeed, "the life of the law is, to a great extent, about the emotional life of a community; about its emotional relationships, its troubles and temptations, its conflicts and forms of resolving them".[33] So when law teachers "try to motivate students … they are appealing for an emotional response, a response which can become a launching pad for the emergence of the intellectual response".[34] Encouraging students to draw on their emotions to construct learning experiences can be a challenge, but it can also be a powerful tool. Legal Essentials' wellbeing focus is underpinned by these humanist and person-centred approaches[35] to design, delivery, and feedback and by bringing together a team of lecturers with diverse academic and personal histories to support students' transition to HE.

3. Law students at transition

Learning and teaching in higher education involve a transition from pedagogy towards andragogy. Andragogy constructs the learning experience as intrinsically motivated and self-directed.[36] Higher education institutions have traditionally assumed that students will arrive fully formed as self-motivating, organised, mature adults, but in fact we inherit new learners who are not necessarily equipped for active participation in, or recognition of, their learning. The challenge of moving from pedagogy to andragogy is due to two key gaps between further and higher education. First, there is an institutional gap, because further and higher education curricula are structured so differently. Secondly, there is an interpersonal gap, in how students relate to academics and their own peers, in the modified and student-led environment. The "active participant" in learning is an "individual and intricate interaction of values, goals, motivation, expectations and engagement … imbued with, and profoundly influenced by, emotions".[37] This suggests a significant emotional discrepancy occurring within the student at transition.

---

[29]Arlie Russell Hochschild, *The Managed Heart: Commercialization of Human Feeling* (University of California Press 1983).

[30]Sherianne Shuler and Beverly Davenport Sypher, "Seeking Emotional Labor: When Managing the Heart Enhances the Work Experience" (2000) 14 Management Communication Quarterly 50.

[31]Kennon M Sheldon and Lawrence S Krieger, "Understanding the Negative Effects of Legal Education on Law Students: A Longitudinal Test of Self-Determination Theory" (2007) 33 Personality and Social Psychology Bulletin 883.

[32]Lawrence S Krieger, "Institutional Denial about the Dark Side of Law School and Fresh Empirical Guidance for Constructively Breaking the Silence" (2002) 52(1–2) Journal of Legal Education 112, 119.

[33]Maksymilian Del Mar, "Legal Understanding and the Affective Imagination" in Paul Maharg and Caroline Maughan (eds), *Affect and Legal Education: Emotion in Learning and Teaching the Law*(Routledge 2011).

[34]Hugh Brayne, "Learning to Think Like a Lawyer – One Law Teacher's Exploration of the Relevance of Evolutionary Psychology" (2002) 9 International Journal of the Legal Profession 283, 297.

[35]Ian Reece and Stephen Walker, *Teaching, Training & Learning* (British Education Publishers Ltd 2004) 79–80.

[36]Andy Armitage and others, *Teaching and Training in Post-Compulsory Education* (OUP 2007).

[37]See Jones (n 8) 104.

Moreover, the process of transitioning to higher education also involves an expectation that students actively develop their own response to learning[38] (outside the institutional structure) and an ability to be able to think about their own thinking and learning (meta-cognition).[39] This may be a challenge for students who have not hitherto positively recognised themselves in the learning process. Legal Essentials incorporated tasks to support the development of meta-cognition, helping students recognise themselves and their actions within the transition process. The extended induction encourages students to reflect on their previous participation and activities in the learning process, providing opportunities for self-evaluation early in the module (see further, section 5). The aim is to move the student towards a positive self-image built on new experiences, and the confidence to accept change and challenge as part of the new learning process.[40] The significance of this opportunity for change mirrors the signposts towards a growth mindset.[41] A fixed mindset[42] at the transition stage creates a sense of low self-efficacy and hopelessness: "I don't understand" or "I can't do it" is seen, not as a temporary hurdle to overcome, but as a permanent obstruction. This, understandably, has a negative impact on both learning and wellbeing, and can lead to shame, anxiety, and disengagement. Module design was therefore underpinned by a focus on active participation, a move away from teacher-led learning[43] towards encouraging exploration, risk-taking, and the making of mistakes in the process. This shift in focus was also aimed at reducing the anxiety about changes to the teaching environment and study practices.[44] During the induction weeks, purposely positive dialogue was designed to build trust in the Law School community, allowing the student to trust that they would be supported and guided through the initial learning process[45] and their progression to other course modules. Recognising also that law students tend to take an instrumental, extrinsically motivated approach to their studies,[46] Legal Essentials has also drawn on self-determination theory to support and develop students' sense of autonomy, relatedness, and competence in the learning process (see further, section 5).[47]

4. Session design for wellbeing

Pilot: wellbeing awareness

Before Legal Essentials was implemented, we developed an hour-long pilot session on wellbeing awareness called "It's OK not to be OK",[48] to be delivered to the first-year cohort midway through the first semester. The session aimed to raise awareness that studying law can be psychologically and emotionally challenging; to remove stigma attached to mental health difficulties; and to encourage students to see the Law School

---

[38]Jones (n 8) 79.

[39]JH Favell, "Metacognitive Aspects of Problem Solving" in LB Resnick (ed), *The Nature of Intelligence* (Hillsdale 1972).

[40]Alan Rogers and Naomi Horrocks, *Teaching Adults* (OUP 2010) 275.

[41]Carol S Dweck, *Self-Theories: Their Role in Motivation, Personality, and Development* (Psychology Press 2000).

[42]Dweck (n 41).

[43]Robin Alexander, *Essays on Pedagogy* (Routledge 2008) 93.

[44]Rogers and Horrocks (n 40) 273.

[45]Alexander (n 43) 113.

[46]See Jones (n 8) 132.

[47]Richard M Ryan and Edward L Deci, "Self-Determination Theory and the Facilitation of Intrinsic Motivation, Social Development, and Well-Being" (2000) 55 American Psychologist 68.

[48]For a detailed analysis of this session, see Stella Coyle, "Using Mentimeter to Engage First Year Law Students in Wellbeing Awareness" (2021) 13 Journal of Academic Development and Education 49.

as a supportive community. During the session, we used Mentimeter to discover how students were feeling and how they were coping (or not). We used Mentimeter so that students could contribute anonymously – and we could respond – in real time. We also had a discussion panel made up of lecturers, our Learning Support specialist, and a PhD student who had also been a Keele undergraduate. The aim was to normalise the challenges facing students and to show that these challenges can be survived. We used the panel discussion as a means of modelling openness; panel members shared their own experiences and thereby gave students a real-life illustration of a supportive academic community.

Students' responses confirmed the research findings: 55% had already experienced a decline in their mental health by week 6, with "friends", "workload" and "stress" cited as the most common causes. As a result, students commonly felt "frustrated", "suicidal", and "low". In response to these worrying answers, the panel had to show we acknowledged their distress and were not going to shy away from difficult topics; the students had revealed their vulnerability and we had to give them a sense of safety and optimism. We shared our own experiences of similar feelings and talked about how we got through them. Importantly, we shared how we had experienced failure as academics, to show that setbacks were not a measure of their potential – they were, indeed, part of life. We emphasised how important it was to be kind to oneself and to seek support – and we gave them clear signposts to sources of this support.

Benefits. Students told us that they would take away messages such as "help", "talk to people", "coping strategies", "you're not alone", "it's OK not to be OK", and – our personal favourite – "everyone has shit"! The session was a good example of student-led teaching and co-creation of learning. We designed the session with a framework based on research into legal education, but most of the discussion was driven by students' answers to the poll. Some students actually asked questions during the session and shared their own feelings and difficulties. This showed that they felt safe in the environment we had created. Using Mentimeter to allow anonymity, and showing students that their peers – and their teachers – had similar feelings, seemed to give some of them the confidence to share their struggles out loud. The session was also a good example of modelling "community" by showing students what a collaborative and supportive learning community looks like. Following the session, our Learning Support specialist reported an increase in students being willing to disclose difficult feelings, as part of their academic skills discussions. We had similar feedback from personal tutors. This helped to inform our planning for the Legal Essentials module – treating first-year induction and skills training holistically, as a process involving the "whole student".

Limitations. Attendance at the session was less than 50%. The only slot available to us was a Friday morning, which may have been a disincentive, particularly as students knew it did not count towards assessment. In addition to this instrumental approach, it is likely that many students simply thought, "I'm already OK, thanks". During the session, there was a small reduction in the number of responses to our questions. Students may have found it difficult to articulate their feelings, or they may have felt inhibited in doing so. Some of the responses were immature, but the research on student response systems such as Mentimeter had warned us to expect this.[49] It is possible that such responses were driven by embarrassment or shame. We chose not to indulge these, and instead we focused on the meaningful responses.

It's OK not to be OK was delivered again as a standalone session in the first year of Legal Essentials (2019–20). Students' responses to the questions were broadly similar, confirming that the challenges to law student wellbeing at transition are ongoing. Delivery in the 2020–21 academic year was of course affected by the move to online teaching during the pandemic. As there was no synchronous large-group teaching, and the session design required a large group to provide the safety of anonymity, we tried instead to integrate wellbeing messages into other module sessions, as the following examples illustrate.

5. Integrating wellbeing into curriculum design

Skills development

Legal Essentials takes a holistic approach to legal skills and reminds students that they bring acquired academic skills with them on transition to HE. For example, in a week 1 seminar, we ask students to reflect on and share their existing characteristics and qualities – academic and personal – along with those they want to develop. We devised a skills template to aid thinking and discussion, and we shared our own experiences of personal and academic skills development – past and present – as examples. This enabled us to deliver the messages from the original themes of *It's OK not to be OK*: life and study – getting the balance right; coping when things go wrong; recognising when you are not OK; and support for wellbeing. We revisited this discussion in week 8 as our final seminar: we asked students to reflect on their development, celebrated any "wins" (academic or personal) and signposted them to sources of support where necessary.

Induction project: "It's not fair!"

This project was designed in response to the move to online learning in 2020–21 and took place during the first three weeks of the module. It aimed to acclimatise students to online learning and – through supported group work – to develop their sense of belonging to the Law School community. Students worked in small groups to devise and present arguments on a legal issue that made them feel "It's not fair!": a law that they would like to introduce, repeal, or amend. Popular topics included legalisation of drugs and prison abolition. Emphasis was placed on students working together to create interesting arguments. They were not required to undertake formal legal research, although research advice was available from our library colleague had they wished to do so. Mindful of programmes like "thinking like a lawyer" being criticised for having "pessimistic and depersonalizing"[50] effects and valorising the adversarial approach,[51] teams were *not* required to argue against each other; the ethos was cooperative rather than adversarial.

[49]See for example S Stuart, M Brown and S Draper, "Using an Electronic Voting System in Logic Lectures: One Practitioner's Application" (2004) 20 Journal of Computer Assisted Learning 95.

[50]Krieger (n 32) 117.

[51]Molly Townes O'Brien, Stephen Tang and Kath Hall, "No Time to Lose: Negative Impact on Law Student Wellbeing May Begin in Year One" (2011) 2(2) The International Journal of the First Year in Higher Education 49.

This was another good example of co-created teaching and learning, of building communities of practice through small-group activities. We wanted students to take risks and be creative in their ideas and arguments, and we did not want to place any barriers to their engagement, such as a requirement for specific skills or expertise.[52] However, students exceeded our expectations: they all undertook some research; all used visual aids in their presentations; and all team members took part in some way – even if it was simply managing the slideshow. Following each presentation, other members of the seminar group were invited to ask questions and/or make comments on the arguments presented, leading to some interesting discussions. And following the seminar, students completed a template giving constructive feedback on each other's presentations, for sharing within their seminar group. The project gave us an insight into the kinds of issues that students were interested in, and we were able to reflect their interests in the rest of the module and in the assessment. For example, in view of the popularity of the *Prison Abolition* topic, one of the subsequent critical analysis sessions was centred on an abolitionist article, and one of their critical writing assessment choices was an article on prison reform. This meant that we could relate the Induction project to their wider learning across the module.

What sort of lawyer am I?

Research suggests that the first year of the law degree should be used to encourage students to develop a "positive professional identity".[53] This positive identity can, in turn, increase intrinsic motivation and develop students' understanding of the broader role of legal education in society.[54] Students had evaluated positively a session given the previous year that included a panel of legal and law-related professionals, but for logistical reasons it was not possible to replicate this in the pivot to online delivery during 2020–21. Instead, one of the team liaised with a diverse group of legal professionals to record semi-structured videos for the students to watch asynchronously. We asked students to consider which professional(s) they most related to, and why, and what key messages they took from the videos. It was interesting – for us and the students – to note that all the professionals mentioned "authenticity" as being an important factor in their success and happiness. This was an important message for the students to hear, and it may have helped them see the link between work and wellbeing.

6. Research goals, methodology and results

Research goals

We collected data on the first year of delivery of Legal Essentials in 2019–20. Our aim was to understand students' experience of transition to HE, rather than simply to assess module delivery module resources. We did not want to simply duplicate the existing school survey which gathers data on the general student experience, teaching, and delivery of modules. Our survey questions aimed instead at focusing students on the

---

[52]Agnes Kukulska-Hulme and others, *Innovating Pedagogy 2021: Exploring New Forms of Teaching, Learning and Assessment, to Guide Educators and Policy Makers*(Open University 2021).

[53]Rachael Field, James Duffy and Anna Huggins, "Supporting Transition to Law School and Student Well-Being: The Role of Professional Legal Identity" (2013) 4(2) The International Journal of the First Year in Higher Education 15, 15.

[54]Tani and Vines (n 11).

utility or helpfulness of each teaching session.[55] We asked students to evaluate their own developing knowledge and skills; the extent to which they felt part of the Law School community; and how confident they felt in navigating sources of support.

Research method

We asked students to evaluate their own experience of the three-week extended induction by means of a brief[56] self-administered[57] online questionnaire,[58] before their core modules commenced in week 4. The questions comprised short statements with a numerical evaluation to indicate levels of agreement or disagreement. Our questionnaire was designed to capture both quantitative data in the form of numerical scores[59] and qualitative feedback through individual comments. We chose a questionnaire as the most efficient way of collecting data, although in future it would be useful to combine this method with a focus group to capture richer data.[60] The benefit of using the online survey included easier administration and distribution, as well as the data being automatically compiled.[61] The online aspect helped ensure the survey was anonymous, and meant students could choose whether or not they participated,[62] thereby limiting any effects that staff may have had on the survey process.[63] We reminded students that the survey was part of a teaching and learning design research project. We had explained the research as a team at the beginning of the induction process, and again at the point of questionnaire release, requesting consent to use the anonymous responses. The survey launch was supported by a question-and-answer session hosted by member of the teaching team. The whole level 4 cohort (193 students) was invited to complete the questionnaire; 43% (83 students) answered all or part of it.

Results

Respondents tended to favour the law-based sessions in the "Making Law" and "Thinking Law" streams, e.g. *Judicial Law-making, Legal Reasoning* and *Critical Analysis* – more than the explicitly "personal" sessions, e.g. *It's OK not to be OK, Team Building* and *Mindfulness in Study*. These findings seem to reflect the research on law students' instrumental approach to their studies, and their prioritisation of developing knowledge of law and legal study skills over the intra- and interpersonal realms. This suggests, in turn, that the cohort was more focused on the transition into the *subject* rather than the transition into higher education itself. Nevertheless, feedback does suggest that Legal Essentials has supported, at least to some extent, the wellbeing of students in their transition to HE. The efficacy of the "Being Law" stream is reflected in the data showing that, after three weeks, 95% of respondents had a clearer sense of the Law School community; 75% felt confident asking for help; and 80% felt supported by the school (Figure 1).

---

[55]Tehmina Basit, *Conducting Research in Educational Contexts* (Continuum 2010) 85.
[56]Alan Bryman, *Social Research Methods* (OUP 2016) 255.
[57]Bryman (n 56) 252.
[58]Bryman (n 56) 235.
[59]Basit (n 55) 17–18.
[60]Bryman (n 56) 223.
[61]Bryman (n 56) 231.
[62]Basit (n 55) 98.
[63]Bryman (n 56) 222.

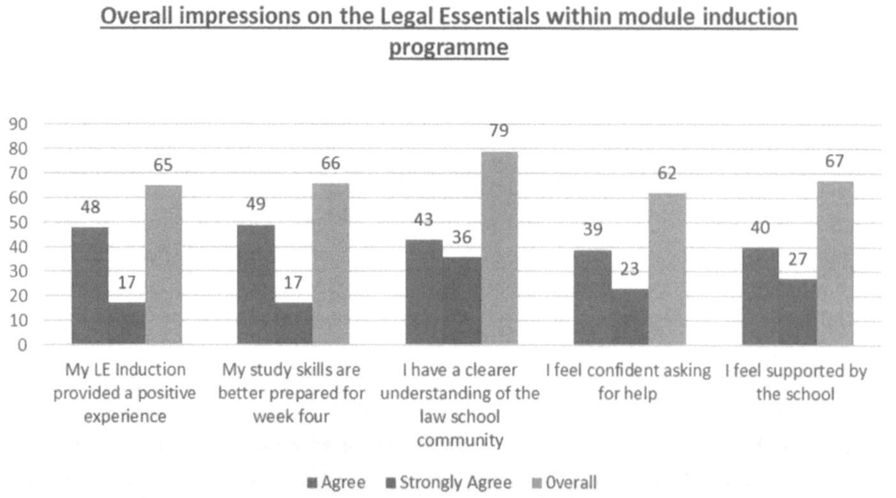

Figure 1. Overall impressions of the Legal Essentials within module induction programme. Note: Figure 1 shows the overall response to the Legal Essentials intensive induction, highlighting that most of the 83 respondents agreed or strongly agreed with the statements regarding their experience of transition to HE.

The responses emphasise the importance of integrating wellbeing more deeply, giving subliminal wellbeing messages throughout the course – in much the same way as a caregiver will smuggle vegetables into a pasta dish for a reluctant child! The danger of "smuggling" wellbeing messages into the module (and the curriculum more broadly) is that some students may not acknowledge the need to discuss their wellbeing openly. This can be ameliorated by making the messages a natural part of both teaching and general interactions with students. For example, we can begin sessions by encouraging students to "check in" with themselves (and we, as teachers, can also do this as a means of modelling self-awareness and self-care): how are they feeling today? Are they tired, confused, unprepared or bored? Are they excited by the topic but nervous about asking questions? Are they stressed about something outside their studies? And we can scaffold messages of support throughout the module by signposting to academic and emotional sources of help.

Finally, students were asked to identify the most important thing that they had learned during the three-week induction. Students found messages regarding *study, legal skills* and the *"make glorious mistakes"* ethos to be key learning points in their transition (Figure 2). These findings emphasise the need for induction to have a non-judgemental and practical underpinning, to support students in transition to the core modules and the degree as a whole. Aside from the development of practical skills, which enhance competence and confidence, a significant feature of the feedback was students' awareness that they were at the start of their undergraduate journey, with no expectation on them to be immediately accomplished in this new venture. Allowing the students to recognise that they can make mistakes is a powerful signpost towards the ongoing and voluntary nature of learning.[64] This initial examination of student voice gave us markers that would positively affect student wellbeing when integrated into the module and the degree.

[64]Rogers and Horrocks (n 40) 130–31.

Figure 2. The most important learning point in Legal Essentials. Note: Figure 2 captures the themes identified by 31 students who commented, as the most important thing that they had learnt from Legal Essentials during the three-week intensive induction.

7. Discussion and conclusions

What worked well, and why?

The team approach is integral to Legal Essentials. The collaborative approach to delivery enabled students to be introduced to staff they would be working with in core modules post-induction – again, aimed at enhancing the sense of community in the Law School. The collaborative approach to design also gave the teaching team a valuable sense of community, as evidenced in our team meetings. The team was also able to draw on support staff (librarians, career advisers and professional services) and student groups, including the Student Union and Law Society. Incorporating a range of voices and expertise (including the Head of School) encouraged the team to step out of traditional teaching mode and focus on the module goals in an authentic and innovative manner. Many of the team had previously been involved in pastoral care and student support roles, which helped us interrogate our goals and learning outcomes, and the routes to achieving them, in a safe and supportive environment. The experience has encouraged a new focus on teaching and learning theory as well as opening more avenues for personal reflective practice.

Furthermore, the design and delivery process enabled the team to consider their own learning experiences and individual teaching voice within a shared vision. This pedagogic "group consciousness" empowered the team to respond to in-session changes, technical issues, audience responsiveness, etc. in a mindful and cooperative manner. The allocation of teaching topics supported the specific skills and diverse teaching experience of the academics involved. The group approach to planning encouraged an examination and awareness of our different motivations, interests, skills, and limitations, which directly informed the development of the four streams (thinking, doing, being and making law). This thematic approach also encouraged the team to be persistently mindful of the individual student – their personal needs, educational needs, and inherited educational experiences – and how these could have an impact on their transition experience.

Sessions were delivered to a range of group sizes and incorporated a range of methods including peer learning, co-delivery, reflection, and panel discussions. There was an intentional balance between large- and small-group teaching, as the teaching team agreed that it was important for students to feel that they belonged to a whole cohort as well as their own seminar group. The module was underpinned by a strong ethos of community and social justice, which gave the project context and a foundation to build upon. The focus on connection was enhanced by the additional drop-in sessions, where students could meet with academics to ask questions about transition, timetabling, school administration, personal tutoring, and academic expectations.

The online pivot necessitated by Covid-19 did affect this aspect of delivery: our school did not offer synchronous whole-cohort or large-group sessions and so the sense of belonging to a whole year group was limited. We tried to ameliorate this through online drop-in sessions available to the whole cohort, where students were able to meet with students outside their own groups, and where common questions and concerns could be responded to. Some of these sessions were co-hosted, so that students could meet and converse with other members of the teaching team. In addition, the team made a conscious effort to communicate with the cohort through Microsoft Teams, sharing relevant news items and other information on a regular basis. We also used video recordings to welcome students, so that they had the experience of "meeting" the team and other colleagues such as learning support and library services.

The intensive, extended induction front-loaded the student experience. The team used the opportunity of the induction space to give the students time to think about their study of law before they began studying their core subjects. Induction to the university was run in parallel, enabling students to become integrated into both the school and the institution at an earlier point in the academic year. Delivery planning considered whether students had any fixed commitments to university activities or induction from other schools, which was especially important for students on combined degrees. The support from the Head of School, the senior management team, and professional services was also vital, due to the high level of staffing and intensive use of resources required to plan, design, and deliver the module – particularly the concentrated induction element.

What were (and are) the limitations?

Time is the biggest limitation! Time has several practical implications for planning and delivery. During the planning process, we have had to be aware of both staff workload allocation and staff turnover. Working within a large team means that such undertakings are incredibly resource intensive. It is therefore vital to get the whole Law School (and beyond) involved: the Head of School, Heads of Year, the wider pastoral team, careers team, library team, student union, student services, learning support, student representatives, and the Student Law Society. This supports the message of community in a practical manner and creates broader opportunities for direct contact with the students, supporting them to collaborate in an existing environment, rather than expecting them to go out and seek school links with little knowledge or affiliation. Having a large team inevitably means that some design goals will be diluted in response to practicalities, and so it is important to maintain an overall vision of what we want to achieve. Regular team meetings are important, not least to ensure that new members fully understand and commit to the module ethos. One way of responding to this need for consistency is to retain a core team to reflect and facilitate the development of the modules in response to student voice and assessment results.

There is a risk of staff and student burnout after the intensive three-week induction. The benefits of the extended induction must be balanced against the original impetus for Legal Essentials: our awareness of the challenges to law student engagement and wellbeing and our resulting desire for a more holistic approach to induction and legal skills. It is true to say that we, as a team, are still working on achieving this. The pivot to online and blended learning has inevitably disrupted module delivery for the 2020–21 and 2021–22 cohorts, making it increasingly important to address students' learning and personal challenges.

It may be true that most level 4 students come to HE with prior experience of a full timetable from further education (FE) (even if delivery has been largely online during the pandemic), and so we should not necessarily make assumptions about their capacity to cope with the intensive induction. Nevertheless, the impact of Covid-19 on the FE experience must still be considered, to mitigate any disrupted teaching that students have suffered. Students (and staff) were also more physically isolated for a protracted period, and some may have found the lack of in-person contact difficult to cope with. We should also recognise that the pandemic will have had a significant impact on students' motivation, energy levels and even their sense of structure, and this should be factored into post-Covid (more accurately, inter-Covid) module design. For the 2021–22 cohort, we have designed Legal Essentials as blended learning, with the express aim of facilitating students' adjustment back into a more structured educational environment. Daily teaching sessions will introduce students to, and maintain contact with, the Law School community from day one. We have designed weekly learning plans to help students navigate their timetables and the preparation and reflection work we are asking them to undertake. We release any asynchronous recordings on the Monday of each week, so that students have early access to the introductory materials that will be scaffolded in practice throughout the week.

The challenges for staff should not be underestimated. The pressure on the team, and the risk of early burnout, was brought into sharp relief during the pandemic. During the intensive three-week induction, team members are teaching over a full week programme as well as undertaking other teaching and administrative duties. At Keele, we have tried to mitigate the pressure by scheduling core level 4 modules to begin in week 4, after the intensive induction has ended. However, team members also teach at other undergraduate levels as well as on postgraduate programmes, and these all begin earlier. The support of the Head of School, senior management, and other module leaders is key in helping to manage staff workload so that those delivering the induction element are not overwhelmed. The awareness and commitment of the wider school team also are essential in supporting students to further translate and embed Legal Essentials messaging in subsequent modules. To support this, the team has found it useful to involve module leaders at a strategic and design level as well as in the delivery of teaching sessions. It is important that members of the wider Law School do not assume that students necessarily join core modules with the ability and confidence to navigate their new environment – they will not emerge from Legal Essentials magically transformed and ready to handle all aspects of their legal education! Early meetings with personal tutors, and the drop-in sessions, will help both students and staff to acknowledge where they stand in the learning process – and to recognise that transition itself is an individual process.

In terms of planning, the team is ultimately at the mercy of timetabling limitations: length of sessions, timing, staff availability and the availability of appropriate rooms for the sessions are all factors that must be considered. The timing of assessments also needs to be considered in conjunction with other teaching across the programme. For example, the MCQ assessment in week 5 of Legal Essentials risked a conflict in the focus of the learner, with students beginning their core modules a week previously. For 2021–22, there is no other delivery in Legal Essentials during the MCQ week, so that students can complete the assessment in the time that they would otherwise have spent in a teaching session. A broader solution is to ensure that students and staff use a year-based scheme of work to assist in planning commitments and to support awareness of activities outside the module.

What lessons can other law schools learn from Legal Essentials?

- We are not always afforded extensive planning time, and often due to the academic cycle this is not prioritised – but law schools should recognise that effective design is just as important as delivery.
- Colleagues expressed, during our meetings, that they considered the module design to have been enhanced by the team's diverse backgrounds; our team has had experience of legal practice, FE teaching, counselling, and even religious ministry!
- Law schools should look for natural opportunities to redevelop modules. Sometimes these occur due to organisational or curriculum modification, and each gap or change is an opportunity to try new things, not knowing whether they're going to work, but being open to the learning experience (as we would wish our students to be).
- Teaching creativity is fostered in the group setting, and that group includes both academic(s) and students. Being mindful of this collaboration encourages us to design teaching that places the student centre to the planning process – respecting both the individual as well as the learner.

Legal Essentials is still in the process of "becoming". Our initial design has been continually reflected on and moderated, through student and staff feedback and through the demands placed on HE during the pandemic. Nevertheless, we have retained our core principles and will continue to integrate wellbeing within legal skills teaching. We will also work towards better integration of wellbeing within the whole law degree – aiming to involve the whole school as well as the whole student. As Neil Gaiman says, "don't stop, don't worry that it isn't good enough, or it isn't perfect ... Whatever it is you're scared of doing, do it".[65]

---

[65] Gaiman (n 10).

Disclosure statement

No potential conflict of interest was reported by the authors.

ORCID

Stella Coyle http://orcid.org/0000-0001-9352-3350

OPEN ACCESS

Is using the term wellbeing with students a mistake? Evaluating a wellbeing intervention in a UK Law School – suggestions for repositioning strategies to address the impact of deficit-discourse

Denise Meyer and Caroline Strevens

ABSTRACT

This paper evaluates a curriculum-based and student co-created approach to improving student wellbeing and psychological resilience in a law school. The pilot employed an enhanced pedagogic framework informed by an evidence-based psychological literacy model compatible with self-determination theory (SDT). Level 4 students were introduced to a simple psychological model for recognising the role of emotion regulation in successful learning and the relevance to this of developing supportive connections and a sense of belonging within an inclusive learning community. Student "Wellbeing Champions" received further peer support and leadership training referencing this model and were then supported in developing the role primarily through community-building initiatives. Staff were also issued with a bespoke "Student Success" framework, encouraging them to support student motivation and success by incorporating activities for building relationships, creating a sense of community and belonging with safety to make mistakes, and scaffolding understanding of assessment and feedback. Recognising the limiting positions offered within a medicalised or deficit-focused narrative about wellbeing and mental health, the findings evaluate the effectiveness of the repositioning strategies represented within the pilot interventions, including a focus on learning success and leadership.

Introduction

Student wellbeing and mental health is now widely recognised as an important focus for the attention of university leaders and educators, with the launch in May 2021 of an award scheme for the University Mental Health Charter "created by thousands of staff and students to shape a future in which everyone in higher education can thrive".[1] The Charter clarifies detailed principles to action the landmark Universities UK #Stepchange

[1]Gareth Hughes and Leigh Spanner, "The University Mental Health Charter" (Student Minds, Leeds 2019). See for details of the Charter Programme and award scheme. <https://www.studentminds.org.uk/charter.html> accessed 9 February 2022.

framework, which advocated that universities "reconfigure themselves as health-promoting and supportive environments"[2] within a whole-institution approach to student mental health.

This paper outlines a collaborative innovation project compatible with these recommendations undertaken at a UK University Law School. Authors Professor Caroline Strevens, then Head of the Law School, and Dr Denise Meyer, Head of Wellbeing, at the University of Portsmouth, were awarded a Learning & Teaching Innovation grant building on their respective prior research and innovation work to run a pilot "whole-school" intervention in the Law School starting in September 2019. Employing an enhanced pedagogic framework informed by an evidence-based psychological literacy model[3] compatible with self-determination theory[4] the proposed project was intended to develop students' psychological literacy and skills for personal resilience with a focus on building a sense of belonging within an inclusive learning community. Level 4 students were introduced to a simple psychological model for recognising the role of emotion regulation in successful learning and the relevance to this of developing supportive connections and a sense of belonging within an inclusive learning community. Student "Wellbeing Champions" received further peer support and leadership training referencing this model and were then supported in developing the role primarily through community-building initiatives. Staff were also issued with a bespoke "Student Success" framework, encouraging them to support student motivation and success by incorporating activities for building relationships, creating a sense of community and belonging with safety to make mistakes, and scaffolding understanding of assessment and feedback.

This paper provides further detail of the intervention, sets out the theoretical context for the project in more detail, clarifies the research methodology, and reports on its findings. It considers the project as a piece of applied discourse analysis, using the framework of positioning theory aiming to "shift the direction of inquiry from reflecting or representing the social world, to actively transforming it".[5] It is based on analysis of qualitative data gathered via two focus group conversations with students and a survey conducted at the conclusion of the first year of the pilot intervention and considers the discourses shaping the positions taken up by students, staff and researchers as part of their reflections on strategies for improving student wellbeing and resilience.

Research method and intervention: pragmatic, co-created action

This pilot project was conducted during the 2019/20 academic year, as a piece of practical action research[6] planned and executed in collaboration with Law School staff and with student leaders from the student-led Law Society respectively.

[2]Originally launched in 2017, the #Stepchange framework was updated in 2020 to 'Stepchange: mentally healthy universities' - see <https://www.universitiesuk.ac.uk/what-we-do/policy-and-research/publications/stepchange-mentally-healthy-universities> accessed 9 February 2022.

[3]Paul Gilbert, *The Compassionate Mind* (1st edn, Hachette 2009).

[4]Edward L Deci and Richard M Ryan, "The General Causality Orientations Scale: Self-Determination in Personality" (1985) 19 Journal of Research in Personality 109.

[5]Kenneth J. Gergen, "A Constructionist Conversation with Positioning Theory" in Bo Allesoe Christensen (ed), *The Second Cognitive Revolution* (Springer 2019) 78.

[6]Hilary Bradbury (ed), *Handbook of Action Research* (3rd edn, Sage 2015) 1.

The intervention in the Law School had two parts. The first comprised a continuation and enlargement of a curriculum intervention within a core Level 4 module that introduced law students to the notion of personal values, motivation and wellbeing. This annual lecture and supporting seminar, designed by Strevens as part of her research interest into intentional curriculum design for wellbeing underpinned by self-determination theory (SDT), was supplemented with activities conducted within group personal tutorials introducing Meyer's simple psychological literacy model[7] for recognising the role of emotion regulation in successful learning and the relevance to this of identifying personal values and developing supportive connections and a sense of belonging within an inclusive learning community.

Concurrently, we worked with leaders from the student-led Law Society to develop a new volunteer peer support/leadership role, "Law Wellbeing Champion". A group of six student volunteers, mainly at Level 6, balanced in terms of gender and including students from minoritised ethnic backgrounds, were introduced to the psychological model within the context of peer support and leadership training, and then supported in developing the role mainly through devising and delivering extracurricular initiatives and events aimed at building an inclusive student community in the Law School.

In March 2020 the global pandemic brought about seismic changes with an inevitable impact on the project. Teaching staff no longer had capacity to continue developing the project interventions and it was no longer possible to collect a meaningful "after" measure of wellbeing to provide an indication of the impact of the project. However, we were able to gather data from two focus groups in July 2020, where we reflected with students as collaborators on practical actions taken within this outlined action research. The first focus group comprised students who had undertaken the leadership training tailored for law students (WBC focus group) whereas the second focus group comprised Level 4 and Level 5 law students who had experienced the first school-wide intervention (L4&5 focus group).

The eight students across the two focus groups had slightly more female than male participants, and included international students and/or students from minoritised ethnicities. Students were asked to evaluate their experience of the pilot intervention, their coping strategies in the current challenging circumstances, and their recommendations for improving student wellbeing, resilience and inclusion. The discussions were run using Zoom, with an anonymous Mentimeter poll running simultaneously to capture anonymous comments and reflections. In accordance with the ethical approval the recordings were transcribed for analysis without referring to the identity of these students.

In addition, 63 students from the School of Law, representing a range of demographic backgrounds and year groups, were among those who completed an all-student mixed method "Wellbeing in Difficult Times" (WiDT) survey as part of a separate piece of research into student wellbeing in the context of the pandemic. In addition to completing a battery of standardised measures relating to wellbeing, and belonging, survey participants could respond to open questions about their challenges and coping strategies during the pandemic; what they had learnt about themselves and their values; and their experience of the survey itself as an opportunity to reflect on their

[7]Denise Meyer, "Emotion Regulation for Learning: Skills for addressing the anxiety epidemic in the classroom." (Workshop at the Advance HE Learning and Teaching Conference, University of Northumbria, 3 July 2019). See also note 21.

wellbeing. The overall findings from the WiDT study are due to be reported elsewhere, but qualitative data from law student participants in the survey has been used to supplement the data from the focus groups as the basis for the analysis reported in this paper.

Research design and theoretical underpinning

Action research is a democratic and participative orientation to knowledge creation which "asks us to consider how we can act in intelligent and informed ways in a socially constructed world" – it is "about working towards practical outcomes, and also about creating new forms of understanding".[8] This paper serves as an extension of the reflection cycle within this piece of action research, drawing from a thematic analysis of the qualitative data collected and using the framework of positioning theory[9] to identify and consider the usefulness of the discourses shaping the positions taken up by students, staff and ourselves as action researchers when reflecting on strategies for improving student wellbeing and resilience in learning.

Positioning theory "recognises both the power of culturally available discourses to frame our experience and constrain our behaviour while allowing room for the person to actively engage with those discourses and employ them in social situations".[10] The theory suggests that we are both *positioned* by others – in direct interactions and/or by dominant cultural discursive practices – and also have a role in positioning ourselves, by claiming or resisting the positions offered. It thus offers a powerful framework, within social constructionist thought, for addressing issues of agency and change. Meyer has previously argued that:

> ... the dominant discourses around student distress or psychological difficulty – invoking diagnostic and medical categories as well as equality and disability measures – arguably offer relatively limited and limiting, overly binary positions from which to address these issues and challenges.[11]

We would add that the way in which this dominant deficit discourse feeds an "individualist presumption ... [means we] fail to explore the broader circumstances in which actions are enmeshed" – as Gergen rightly argues, "If my job is boring and my boss a tyrant, why should I be treated for my feelings of depression? Why not change the workplace?".[12] Similarly, Strevens has also argued, with others, for the ethical imperative to recognise the location of law student distress within "the context of the neoliberal university ... as a way of resisting the potential injustices and de-humanising tendencies of that paradigm"[13] quoting Parker in recognising the shaping power of discourse: "The ways that lawyers and academics talk and write about these issues are powerful – they create discourses that frame the way young lawyers see their situation, and the ways that the profession and public respond".[14]

[8] Peter Reason and Hilary Bradbury, "Inquiry and Participation in Search of a World Worthy of Human Aspiration" in Peter Reason and Hilary Bradbury (eds), *Handbook of Action Research* (Sage 2001) 2.

[9] B Davies and R Harré, "Positioning and Personhood" in Rom Harré and Luk Van Langenhove (eds), *Positioning Theory* (Blackwell 1999).

[10] Kenneth J. Gergen, "A Constructionist Conversation with Positioning Theory" in Bo Allesoe Christensen (ed), The Second Cognitive Revolution (Springer 2019) 78.

[11] Denise Meyer, "The Student Lifecycle: Pressure Points and Transitions" in Nicola Barden and Ruth Caleb (eds), *Student Mental Health & Wellbeing in Higher Education: A Practical Guide* (Sage 2019) 74.

[12] Kenneth J. Gergen, *An Invitation to Social Construction* (3rd edn, Sage 2015) 97.

[13] Nigel Duncan, Rachael Field and Caroline Strevens, "Ethical Imperatives for Legal Educators to Promote Law Student Wellbeing" (2020) 23 Legal Ethics 65, 72.

[14] ibid 77

Countering this dominant discourse, Meyer has argued for greater recognition of the "emotional discomfort, challenge and even distress ... [that is] an integral part of learning and the student experience"[15] and has introduced Gilbert's Compassionate Mind model for emotion regulation as shedding "new light" on the What Works? student retention findings,[16] "that the promotion of a sense of belonging is a crucial factor in successful student retention initiatives", with its recognition that the psychological security required to regulate this inevitable discomfort "is provided *in relationship* with others, through shared identity within an identifiable community and a sense of acceptance and belonging within that community".[17]

Strevens has long called for curriculum intervention to address law student wellbeing,[18] arguing (with others) for the ethical imperative to recognise and attend to law student stress and distress and proposing "ethical obligations for intentional curriculum design for the promotion of student wellbeing and the ongoing wellbeing of practitioners".[19] These publications have all investigated the application of Deci and Ryan's[20] self-determination theory within the context of legal education.

Self-determination theory (SDT) suggests that motivation for learning and growth is linked to three innate and universal psychological needs – competence, connection and autonomy.

This approach, aiming to facilitate autonomy, competence and relatedness, informed the Student Success policy which Strevens devised and disseminated to staff across the School of Law for the 2019/20 academic year, encouraging staff to support student motivation and success.

Highly compatible with self-determination theory, Meyer has developed an innovative application of Gilbert's three-system Compassionate Mind model for emotion regulation as a framework for psychological literacy in relation to teaching and learning[21] and as the basis for a distinctive whole-institution approach to mental health and wellbeing aiming to enhance psychological flexibility, resilience and learning mindsets with a focus on skills for building social connection, community and inclusion. The approach aligns with the key principles of self-determination theory with its emphasis on a sense of connection and belonging (i.e. relatedness) as a vital part of the soothing response helping to regulate the uncomfortable threat response emotions arising in response to learning and other challenges (i.e. challenges to a sense of competence), which in turn helps to successfully engage the drive response to pursue valued tasks and goals (i.e. establishing a sense of autonomy). Like self-determination theory, the model recognises the motivating role of personal values in helping to regulate emotions in the interests of persistence in the face of failure or other barriers in the pursuit of challenging goals.

---

[15]Denise Meyer, "The Student Lifecycle: Pressure Points and Transitions" in Nicola Barden and Ruth Caleb (eds), *Student Mental Health & Wellbeing in Higher Education: A Practical Guide* (Sage 2019) 74.

[16]Liz Thomas, "Building Student Engagement and Belonging in Higher Education at a Time of Change" (Final report from the What Works? Student Retention and Success Programme, Paul Hamlyn Foundation 2012).

[17]Note 15, page 76.

[18]Strevens, C., & Wilson, C. "Law student wellbeing in the UK: A call for curriculum intervention." (2016) Journal of Commonwealth Law and Legal Education, 11(1), 44-56.

[19]Note 13, page 65.

[20]Note 4.

[21]D Meyer, "Emotion Regulation for Learning: Skills for Addressing the Anxiety Epidemic in the Classroom" (Workshop at the Advance HE Learning & Teaching Conference, University of Northumbria, 3 July 2019).

The approach aims to undermine the overly dominant medicalising discourse by de-pathologising ordinary threat response emotions like anxiety or low mood, and offering a more constructive position presenting emotion regulation as a life skill which can be learnt and practised in the interests of learning success. In particular, the approach challenges the dominant deficit-focused narrative around the idea of "support" by depicting support as a basic human need, and mutually beneficial "supportive connections" as a central ingredient in learning success. This undermines the individualised responsibility for wellbeing implicit in the dominant discourse, and introduces the vital role of inclusion and belonging in promoting wellbeing and mental health for all. An introduction to the model has been captured within an engaging four-minute explanatory video animation entitled "Emotion Regulation for Learning and Life".[22]

The aim for the pilot project was to explore ways to introduce this psychological literacy model to students as an integral and deliberate part of the curriculum, complementary to the Student Success framework and offering "learning and tools for self-care and positive mental health" in a format consonant with the whole-institution approach recommended in the #Stepchange guidance. Likewise, the project enlisted students in developing the proactive "communities of learning and peer support"[23] recommended in the guidance.

Analysis: developing fruitful positions for wellbeing

The Covid-19 pandemic offered a ready-made opportunity to consider emotions and strategies in relation to the new challenges it posed. Under the rubric of "Wellbeing in Difficult Times" students participating in the survey and focus groups were asked about the move to online learning and other challenges they had faced personally, and what old and new coping strategies they used to help them face these challenges. All focus group students were also asked to reflect directly on their experience of the project interventions. The following analysis identifies discursive themes in how students are positioned or position themselves within these reflections about the two project interventions.

Part 1: student leadership

A key focus for the project was co-creation with students to foster and support student wellbeing in the Law School. Student leaders from the student-led Law Society, affiliated with the Students' Union (UPSU), had been keen to develop a peer support programme and agreed to work with us in the spirit of action research drawing on the learning from an existing institution-wide student leadership programme (led by Meyer) to develop a bespoke co-created scheme for the Law School.

The student leaders had initially envisaged setting up a traditional peer support scheme, seeing students as more likely to seek support from trained peers than from specialist services for anxiety, depression or other mental health difficulties. However,

[22]See https://myport.port.ac.uk/guidance-and-support/health-and-wellbeing/student-wellbeing-service/learning-well

[23]Phrases from the original 2017 #Stepchange framework - the refreshed Stepchange: Mentally Healthy Universities guidance can be found at https://www.universitiesuk.ac.uk/what-we-do/policy-and-research/publications/stepchange-mentally-healthy-universities accessed on 9 February 2022.

Meyer's experience in the initial stages of the institution-wide programme was that finding students eager to occupy supporter roles is easy, while meaningful engagement with their support is often disappointingly low.

The fatal flaw in traditional schemes is their inherent positioning along deficit lines, implicitly requiring users to identify themselves as "in need" of support – a vulnerable disempowered position avoided by most, particularly those sensitive to stereotype threat or imposter syndrome. By contrast, the "supporter" position is sought after as it delivers clear benefits, enhancing confidence and developing transferable skills to populate students' CVs. The training programme developed as part of the wider project explored the ethics of this with prospective supporters and used the Emotion Regulation for Learning model as a framework for rethinking the idea of "support", reframing peer support to focus on developing peer "leadership".

This approach positions student leaders as role models in upholding the values of the University's Student Charter, which emphasises a commitment to learning and self-development, respect, support and community building. Instead of focusing on one-to-one peer supporting skills, the training focuses on developing students' psychological literacy and self-respect as the basis for leadership skills such as empathic listening, facilitation of respectful and inclusive social interaction, bystander intervention and restorative conflict resolution. The leadership model positions students themselves as the agents of the supportive learning community which fosters learning success for all, encouraged to focus their leadership efforts on inclusion and community-building activities helping fellow students to make connections with their peers in order to develop a sense of belonging.

The six students who had been recruited for the Law School programme decided to call themselves "Law Wellbeing Champions" and the scheme they developed is described by one of them in a video recorded to share with other students:

> LWC video: We try to create a sense of community, a sense of belonging and an overall support network for Law Students. We help look after the wellbeing of students, we're a support system and we run different kind of events ... so we've run different workshops, like How to Deal With Rejection, How to Manage Your Time, so you're not too stressed, and we direct people to the help that they need and where they can find guidance.

Reviewing the benefits of their participation in their WBC focus group, the students recognised benefits similar to traditional peer support programmes through developing transferable skills, but also recognised the personal benefit:

> LWC2: that is definitely what brought me into it ... the fact that someone could train me and it's something to talk about at interviews and ... then I've had a community grow through that.

Others reflected on the personal benefit from learning the psychological literacy model – "I developed my emotional intelligence" and "[it] taught me to reach out for support", in addition to the wider skills such as developing their empathy and general people skills.

Overall as they reflected on how they would evaluate the success of their event programme, these students felt pleased with the events themselves and a perception that the students attending had found them beneficial, but disappointed that they had not attracted greater numbers. One student reflected:

> LWC1: One thing that keeps popping up with me is the stigma around the word "wellbeing". So, as soon as someone sees that it's a wellbeing event that's like a good 80% of people just gone, like that . . . I don't have a clue how to go and destigmatise the word "wellbeing" . . .

This participant's comment led to further explicit reflection in the focus group discussion about how people are positioned by the dominant discourses around mental health and wellbeing, with us respectively referencing our previous research and a reminder of how the co-creation discussion for the law wellbeing champion role had considered the effect of including the word "wellbeing" in the title. The general consensus was that it would be more effective not to badge a role or events with the word "wellbeing".

Students in the L4&5 focus group were also asked whether they had been aware of the student-led aspects of the project, or anything which had been effective at building a sense of community. Only one of the students was confident that they'd been fully aware of this part of the project, and felt that they had benefited personally, but wasn't sure how far it had reached

> I went to most of the Law Society events last year and I was aware of the Wellbeing Champions and everything. I have made new connections and some friends from attending events which is useful as it increased my sense of inclusion within the university.
>
> I'm not really sure if they were that well known, outside of the Society – I'm not really sure how far it got to students who didn't really integrate that much.

Several students commented on the benefit of a particular "Study with different years" event, agreeing that they had found it beneficial to extend their network to students from other years.

In the WBC focus group there was a more detailed discussion about the value of their supportive connections with others on their course for coping with the challenges of online learning:

> LWC2: I've actually felt quite lucky this year to have a good group of friends on my course and in the Law Society, 'cause I think in my first and second year I didn't have that. – my friends were all on different courses and I think I would have really struggled this year if there was no one else I could text or talk to, . . . who was going through the same thing.

This comment implies an element of randomness and "luck" relating to this sense of community with others on the course, and these students underlined their belief in the importance of their Wellbeing Champion role for a more proactive approach to inclusion.

The students' ideas for how to build on these findings are discussed in more detail below.

Part 2: curriculum intervention

The starting point for the project was the expectation that university-wide measures addressing student wellbeing would be most effective when embedded within academic departments and by academic members of staff, with reinforcement by student peers. From the perspective of positioning theory, embedding a focus on wellbeing within the curriculum in this way, along with peer endorsement, should go some way towards normalising conversations about wellbeing and at the very least providing a step forward in the battle against the stigma surrounding mental ill-health.

The main intervention in this context was through two tutorial sessions introducing the Emotion Regulation for Learning model. However, when the L4&5 focus group participants were asked to evaluate the curriculum interventions directly, only one of the five participants remembered having seen the Emotion Regulation for Learning video previously, and they suggested that introducing the model in a personal tutorial session might not have been the most effective method for dissemination

> Student 5: I'm afraid to admit it no, I haven't actually been to many tutor sessions because I've been working between uni . . . I just want to add though that that's no reflection on my tutor . . .

This was interesting as it echoed something the staff members had reflected upon during conversations to shape the intervention – staff were aware that attendance at tutorial sessions often tended to drop off quite significantly and had speculated that a "deficit" mentality might be affecting this, with students possibly seeing tutorials as something which were there mainly for those who "needed" more support or possibly for "remedial" skills development.

Staff were also aware that without credit-bearing status, tutorial sessions were likely to suffer from the strategic approach implied in Student 5's comments, with many students under financial pressure having to make difficult choices about how to allocate time to their studies and more likely to sacrifice sessions which did not have a direct bearing on credit-accrual.

Students in the L4&5 focus group also felt that tutorial sessions weren't as clearly signalled in the course timetable as other sessions, with comments like:

> Student 4: I did find that . . . some tutors weren't really making it aware that there was a session it would just be expected you just need to check your timetable . . . And then by the time [you] realised [you] had a tutor session, it was too late.

Other students agreed with this and suggested that email reminders from tutors would raise the profile of tutorial sessions more. The implication in this discussion was that this suggestion was not just about "nannying" students, but rather that tutors' actions (or inactions) were communicating something about their own valuing of the tutorial sessions and their content.

This exchange offers food for thought regarding choices about how and where wellbeing-related content is integrated into the curriculum, and what that communicates to students about staff members' perception of its importance and relevance. Lip-service level of attention to both wellbeing and inclusion is insufficient – psychological or wellbeing literacy may be a good starting point, but it is only through thorough embedding via changes in core, everyday practice that more fruitful possibilities and positions for action are properly opened up.

In the general L4&5 focus group, participants were shown the video animation to remind them of the model and were asked to reflect on what was helpful for themselves or other students from their understanding of the video's message. The students' comments made it clear that they could see the relevance of the key concepts communicated, one saying it was "interesting to learn about and useful to know . . . the different parts of why we feel different emotions". Another reflected the message that emotion regulation is a skill which can be acquired and practised:

> I think it's all very useful especially if students just keep these three things in the back of their head and strive for a compassionate mind throughout their university experience. Like the video said, it's about practising.

There was also clear recognition of the message regarding the relevance of wellbeing skills for dealing with common learning challenges:

> The part regarding the need to find a balance between the drive and the fear system. New students might tend to work too much since they fear failure so it is important to remind them to also take some time to look after their well-being.

This student's comment highlights the over-work and perfectionism that can arise in the pursuit of competence, and demonstrates how the model can provide reinforcement for the requirement in Strevens' Student Success policy for staff to structure in opportunities for students to make mistakes and experience fruitful failures.

One student's reflections on the helpfulness of the video very clearly identified the constructive benefit of the "de-pathologising" framing of anxiety in the model:

> "Running away is not helpful" as this is something that I struggled with when my anxiety developed during lockdown. I just wanted to forget about uni and socialising completely but [the video shows that] this is just my flight or fight instinct and it's fine.

The comment underlines the way in which the model aims to position students with the mindset to persist in the face of challenges, as one survey respondent also demonstrated: "I have been trying to stick with the task at hand, whereas previously I would give up. I have also been asking for help in more places".

When the L4&5 focus group students were asked what they did remember of the curriculum input about wellbeing it was the values session which stood out for them:

> . . . because it made me reflect on something I had never thought about before. During lockdown I was able to see how some of those values actually apply to me in reality.

Asked to reflect on learning from their pandemic experiences related to their values, survey respondents demonstrated development of greater psychological literacy in line with the model: "not to spend so much time stressing and completing work and learn to take a break", "some things not important and to just focus on what is important" and many of them found the survey itself a useful opportunity for self-evaluation: "It feels useful to reflect upon what specific things have helped me to keep motivated so I can use them further in my studies", "it is always good to pause and think to reflect on your own experiences and personality – this is so important in growth and adaptation to the next year of university".

These findings have helped to reinforce the intention to develop the curriculum intervention on the basis of a streamlined self-reflection tool which helps students to evaluate their psychological literacy and continue to monitor the associated skills as they progress.

The final comment on the helpful aspects of the model from the video animation focused on another fundamental aspect of its message, reinforcing aspects of the Student Success policy focusing on relatedness: "The part about protecting personal connections". Recognition of the importance of social support was a significant part of this focus group's reflections in relation to the challenges of the pandemic. They had initially focused on technical or practical barriers, like lack of access to computers and physical resources in the library, but as they reflected they recognised the wider wellbeing implications of losing a sense of being part of a learning community:

> I think it's not necessarily just the library ... but ... not being able to meet up and start to discuss it with people and to go to a social space and get yourself going for the day like, that kind of lack of routine, I think, is what throws a lot of people off when something like this happens.

Students also made an overt connection between wellbeing and a sense of inclusion: "you have to be somewhere that is inclusive and right for you". One student also recognised that her awareness of being "at a disadvantage because being a minority" meant that she felt she had to "isolate [herself to] work harder", thereby missing out on some of the fun of being a student and worrying about the impact of this: "I just don't want it to take a toll on my wellbeing".

A survey respondent who felt that having to do a lot of paid work had made it harder for her to enjoy a full student experience, affecting her sense of belonging and her mental health, said: "I hope the university uses this survey to help students ... who need the most because they come from disadvantaged backgrounds". Likewise, a focus group member from a minoritised background who had struggled to feel a sense of community on his course said: "I think it's the uni, and also the students that should be in it as well, to create a community so you feel close".

There is an interesting implicit point, when considering these students' comments, about how both material disadvantage and disadvantage through minoritised identity can affect students' access to the extracurricular or "optional extra" aspects of learning – and if wellbeing and belonging-focused activity are located here rather than in the core curriculum then this potentially compounds the learning advantage for those who already have the privilege of wider access. These students are clear about the university's responsibility to be more active in addressing disadvantages and lack of inclusion, in order to deliver a better student experience for all students.

Part 3: next steps

The latter part of the discussion in both focus groups moved from evaluation on to co-creation of next steps and further actions, which are summarised in this section.

The Wellbeing Champion group decided to drop the idea of a separate Wellbeing Champion role, but wanted to retain the value by ensuring that as many students as possible could benefit from the training and leadership experience for their CVs. They thought it would be better to build from the existing community-building function served by the student Law Society using the traditional "buddy" system used in student societies, where every new member is assigned an older member to welcome and induct them.

However, there was also an awareness of deficit positioning – that those who "need" something like this might be less likely to come forward, and miss out on the benefit. They were keen to see that such a system was made properly accessible and inclusive, by being automatically available for everybody. In order to achieve this they felt that the scheme should be embedded as part of the course, but they felt that it was difficult to know on what basis to match people, and that one-to-one pairings might also be a bit hit and miss, with a danger that "there's always going to be people who can't be bothered to do it as well":

> Student 4: ... and if you get put with someone who's just not interested, then that's also an issue because that's gonna make you feel a bit deflated.

They therefore preferred the idea of new students being assigned to peer groups with several trained senior students to facilitate – "that'll be quite cool to have a little support network".

The most obvious arena for taking forward some of these ideas was within the group tutorial system, as long as these were given a higher profile and prominence by staff. Students felt that there needed to be much more publicity, "more awareness at the start of the year on how to be involved, for people wanting to train and for people wanting to [participate]", as well as better communication generally, for example trying to "notify more students about their tutor sessions (by email) so they can get more involved".

In general, there was a feeling that involvement from tutors and other staff was essential – for structuring and promoting students' engagement with each other, and demonstrating the value of the activities – but with room for students to take the lead and set the agenda within this structure.

Discussion and findings

Positioning theory supports a "future forming sensitivity [which] shifts the direction of inquiry from reflecting or representing the social world, to actively transforming it" by "challenging existing traditions of understanding and offer[ing] new possibilities for action"[24] in the field of student wellbeing and mental health.

The action and reflection cycle described here has allowed for the development of a number of ways to position students and staff with fruitful possibilities for action circumventing some of the traps created by deficit discourses about wellbeing and mental health.

This analysis of reflections from the student focus groups gives some indication of the difficulty in promoting psychological literacy. Despite the amination being shown to groups of law students on several occasions, only one student could recall it and then in only general terms. This reinforces our view that measures need to be embedded into the curriculum and endorsed by academic staff.

We remain of the view that embedding university level mental wellbeing measures within the department and incorporating them, in addition, into the curriculum as opposed to into personal tutoring is likely to address some of the issues identified in this discourse analysis. Students highlighted problems with personal tutorial sessions that were not timetabled and not sufficiently promoted by academic staff and that resulted in low student participation.

Students recognised the limiting impact of the deficit model and the problem with using the term "wellbeing". They endorsed Meyer's approach to using leadership training and the practice of such leadership skills in building an inclusive community and increasing a sense of belonging as being both a personal benefit and of benefit to the wider student body. They reflected upon the benefit of creating peer learning communities where students were mixing with students from other levels. This could form a new model for either personal tutoring or a new group-based buddy system.

[24]Gergen (n 6) 78.

Students also valued input and commitment from their tutors and expressed the view that staff endorsement of student support measures would increase student engagement.

This pilot has reinforced our views about the power of co-creation with students and the importance of academic staff commitment. It has also reinforced our view of the need to increase students' engagement with personal tutoring and the possibility that the current lack of engagement may be as a result of students seeing this framed as addressing deficit.

We have been unable to comment upon any specific impact on students' academic motivation, resilience and confidence, given the confounding factors related to the global pandemic. However, useful practical resources and suggestions for structuring curriculum-based activity have been made, and the authors would welcome correspondence and discussion with colleagues in other contexts who would be interested in testing and further developing this approach in their own context.

Disclosure statement

No potential conflict of interest was reported by the authors.

ORCID

Caroline Strevens http://orcid.org/0000-0001-9016-839X

Influences on students' interest in a legal career, satisfaction with law school, & psychological distress: trends in New Zealand

Valerie Sotardi, Lynne Taylor, Erik Brogt, Ursula Cheer and Natalie Baird

ABSTRACT

This paper investigates cross-sectional and longitudinal trends in data collected from a self-selected cohort of law students enrolled at three New Zealand universities. From the beginning of their first year of study to the end of their third year, students were invited to complete questionnaires that documented a range of expectations, perceptions, and attitudes. Analysis was carried out to better understand students' interest in a legal career, satisfaction with law school, and psychological distress across their first three years at law school. Using descriptive and inferential statistics, we found that students' academic self-efficacy (i.e. perceived ability to be successful in law courses) and attitudes towards assessment emerged as noteworthy contributors to the law school experience. Students who persevered across three years of law school remained stable in their career interests and satisfaction with law school. However, two out of three students appeared at risk for mental health difficulties and we document an increase in psychological distress from the beginning of law school to the end of second year. Discussion focuses on how law schools might respond to these findings.

Introduction

The prevalence of mental health difficulties in university students is documented across jurisdictions. Approximately one in five students report symptoms of psychological disorders such as depression, anxiety, and substance use.[1] The early years of undergraduate study are a time of major academic and social transition for many,[2] and a peak period for the onset of mental health difficulties.[3]

[1] Randy Auerbach and others, "Mental Disorders among College Students in the World Health Organization World Mental Health Surveys" (2016) 46 Psychological Medicine 2955, 2970.

[2] Universities UK, *Student Mental Wellbeing in Higher Education: Good Practice Guide* (Universities UK 2015) 8.

[3] Ronald Kessler and others, "Age of Onset of Mental Disorders: A Review of Recent Literature" (2007) 20 Current Opinion in Psychiatry 359; G de Girolamo and others, "Age of Onset of Mental Disorders and Use of Mental Health Services: Needs, Opportunities and Obstacles" (2012) 21 Epidemiology and Psychiatric Sciences 47, 48; Randy Auerbach and others, "WHO World Mental Health Surveys International College Student Project: Prevalence and Distribution of Mental Disorders" (2018) 127 Journal of Abnormal Psychology 623, 625.

Studies across jurisdictions and time confirm that law students may be especially at risk for mental health difficulties.[4] Law students are reported as having rates of mental health difficulties higher than those reported in the general population.[5] In some instances, law students are reported as having higher rates of mental health difficulties than students enrolled in other disciplines.[6] Law students' reported levels of well-being have been shown to decline across their first year at law school,[7] and then to continue to decline across the remainder of their time at law school.[8] Law students are reported as reluctant to seek mental health support.[9] In the current context, the COVID-19 pandemic and the immediate switch to online teaching, learning and assessment has likely created additional stressors.[10] The potential effects of mental health difficulties are significant. The psychosocial functioning and physical health of affected students may be compromised, and so too may be their achievement motivation, academic performance and institutional retention.[11]

Less is known about the specific factors that give rise to the outcomes described above. Some evidence suggests that the social dimensions of law school may influence students' achievement motivation, satisfaction with their learning environment, academic engagement, and subjective well-being. For example, the well-being of law students in the United States appears sensitive to peer-related stress (such as bullying,

[4] See, for example, Natalie K Stead, Shane L Rogers and W Rupert Johnson, "The Role of Place, People and Perception in Law Student Well-Being" (2020) 73 International Journal of Law and Psychiatry, Article 101631; Natalie K Stead, Shane L Rogers and Jerome Doraisamy, "Looking Beyond the Mirror: Psychological Distress; Disordered Eating, Weight and Shape Concerns; and Maladaptive Eating Habits in Lawyers and Law Students" (2018) 61 International Journal of Law and Psychiatry 90.

[5] See, for example, Alan Reifman, Daniel N McIntosh and Phoebe C Ellsworth, "Depression and Affect among Law Students during Law School: A Longitudinal Study" (2001) 2(1) Journal of Emotional Abuse 93, 101; Norm Kelk and others, *Courting the Blues: Attitudes towards Depression in Australian Law Students and Lawyers* (Brain & Mind Research Institute 2009); Massimiliano Tani and Prue Vines, "Law Students' Attitudes to Education: Pointers to Depression in the Legal Academy and the Profession?" (2009) 19 Legal Education Review 3; Wendy Larcombe and others, "Does an Improved Experience of Law School Protect Students against Depression, Anxiety and Stress? An Empirical Study of Wellbeing and the Law School Experience of LLB and JD Students" (2013) 35 Sydney Law Review 407, 416; Jerome M Organ, David B Jaffe and Katherine M Bender, "Suffering in Silence: The Survey of Law Student Well-Being and the Reluctance of Law Students to Seek Help for Substance Use and Mental Health Concerns" (2016) 66 Journal of Legal Education 116, 137; Andrea Flynn, Yan Li and Bernadette Sánchez, "Law School Stress: Moving from Narratives to Measurement" (2017) 56 Washburn Law Journal 259, 273.

[6] Stephen B Shanfield and Andrew H Benjamin, "Psychiatric Distress in Law Students" (1985) 35 Journal of Legal Education 65, 69; Kelk and others (n 5) 12; Catherine Leahy and others, "Distress Levels and Self-Reported Treatment Rates for Medicine, Law, Psychology and Mechanical Engineering Tertiary Students: Cross-Sectional Study" (2010) 44 Australian and New Zealand Journal of Psychiatry 608, 611; Wendy Larcombe, Sue Finch and Rachel Sore, "Who's Distressed? Not Only Law Students: Psychological Distress Levels in University Students across Diverse Fields of Study" (2015) 37 Sydney Law Review 243, 260.

[7] Andrew Benjamin and others, "The Role of Legal Education in Producing Psychological Distress among Law Students and Lawyers" (1986) 11 Law & Social Inquiry 225, 246; Kennon M Sheldon and Lawrence S Krieger, "Does Legal Education Have Undermining Effects on Law Students? Evaluating Changes in Motivation, Values and Wellbeing" (2004) 22 Behavioral Sciences and the Law 261, 275; Molly Townes O'Brien, Stephen Tang and Kath Hall, "Changing Our Thinking: Empirical Research on Student Wellbeing, Thinking Styles and the Law Curriculum" (2011) 21 Legal Education Review 149, 159–60; Anthony Lester, Lloyd England and Natalia Antolak-Saper, "Health and Wellbeing in the First Year: The Law School Experience" (2011) 36 Alternative Law Journal 47, 48.

[8] Benjamin and others (n 7) 246; Sheldon and Kreiger (n 7) 280; Kennon M Sheldon and L Krieger, "Understanding the Negative Effects of Legal Education on Law Students: A Longitudinal Test and Extension of Self-Determination Theory" (2007) 33 Personality and Social Psychology Bulletin 883, 889.

[9] Kelk and others (n 5) 38; Organ, Jaffe and Bender (n 5) 141.

[10] Chris Ashford, "Law Teaching and the Coronavirus Pandemic" (2020) 54 The Law Teacher 167, 167.

[11] Auerbach (n 3) 625; Ronny Bruffaerts and others, "Mental Health Problems in College Freshmen: Prevalence and Academic Functioning" (2018) 225 Journal of Affective Disorders 97, 101.

cheating, and substance use), workload stress (such as time to complete coursework), and inadequate support and guidance.[12] Several other studies report how the law school learning environment may shape students' motivation, learning outcomes and well-being.[13] As such, it is reasonable to assert that adjustments to the learning environment can change –for better or for worse – law students' perceptions, attitudes, and actions.

In this paper, we investigate factors that shape students' subjective experiences at New Zealand law schools. Drawing on a social cognitive theoretical framework, we made an assumption that individuals appraise and evaluate their environment and that these subjective views have an impact on short- and long-term attitudes and behaviours. From this stance, we proposed that meaningful experiences in law school include students' career ambitions (e.g. "Do I want to pursue a career in the legal profession?"), their satisfaction with their respective academic programmes (e.g. "Does my law school meet my professional and personal needs?"), and personal well-being (e.g. "Do I feel physically and psychologically healthy in this environment?"). We sought to understand better students' interest in a legal career, satisfaction with law school, and levels of psychological distress across their first three years at law school.

The study of law in New Zealand

The study of law in New Zealand is a four-year undergraduate degree, the Bachelor of Laws. Six New Zealand universities[14] offer a Bachelor of Laws programme approved by the New Zealand Council of Legal Education (CLE). Completing an approved Bachelor of Laws programme is one prerequisite for admission as a Barrister and Solicitor of the High Court of New Zealand. The CLE's purposes include ensuring uniformity and the maintenance of common standards across New Zealand law degrees.[15] The CLE requires that students complete a series of compulsory courses for which it prescribes content, assessment modes, and moderation requirements. Law schools report pass rates and grade distributions in these courses annually to the CLE.

Students complete one of the CLE compulsory courses, "The Legal System", in their first year of study, with the balance of their enrolment made up of courses from other degrees (most commonly arts or commerce) and any other law-related courses required by the law school at which they are enrolled. Those who pass their first year courses and meet any additional limitation of entry requirement are eligible to enrol in second year programmes.[16] Students enrolled in full-time study[17] in their second and third years of

[12]Flynn, Yi and Sánchez (n 5).

[13]Wendy Larcombe and others, "Does an Improved Experience of Law School Protect Students against Depression, Anxiety and Stress? An Empirical Study of Wellbeing and the Law School Experience of LLB and JD Students" (2013) 35 Sydney Law Review 407, 432; Wendy Larcombe and Katherine Fethers, "Schooling the Blues? An Investigation of Factors Associated with Psychological Distress among Law Students" (2013) 36 University of New South Wales Law Review 390, 426; Paula J Manning, "Understanding the Impact of Inadequate Feedback: Means to Reduce Law Student Psychological Distress, Increase Motivation, and Improve Learning Outcomes" (2012) 43 Cumberland Law Review 225; Fiona McGaughey and others, "What Have We Here? The Relationship between Law Student Attendance and Wellbeing" (2019) 45 Monash University Law Review 695, 712.

[14]All six are Government funded, public universities.

[15]*Twenty Sixth Report of the New Zealand Council of Legal Education to the House of Representatives* (2016) 5.

[16]Both the University of Auckland and the University of Canterbury limit the numbers of passing first year students able to enrol in second year programmes.

[17]Approximately 80% of the students participating in this study were enrolled in full-time study.

study complete the following CLE prescribed courses:[18] the Law of Contract, the Law of Torts, Criminal Law, Public Law and Property Law (or both Land Law and Equity/Law of Succession).

The CLE does not mandate how compulsory courses are taught, but at all law schools this occurs through a combination of lectures (large classes) and tutorials (small classes) where hours of timetabled lectures far exceed those for tutorials.[19] This teaching model reflects both the large numbers of students that law schools must accommodate in compulsory courses[20] and the current university funding model. Nevertheless, the combination of external regulation and similarity in teaching models means that the students experience a comparable teaching and learning experience during their first three years at law school.[21] For their remaining years at law school, students complete a range of optional courses which vary in class size and teaching and assessment methods. The CLE does not regulate optional courses.

Social cognitive theory

Social cognitive theory is a psychological perspective in which a person's behaviour (e.g. motivation, learning and self-regulation) is examined according to varied influences emanating from the social environment.[22] Although there are multiple social cognitive perspectives, the most widely accepted framework is that proposed by Bandura.[23] Bandura assumes that individuals strive for a sense of agency over important events in their lives. To achieve agency, individuals draw on their subjective views of the environment and adjust their behaviour in ways that increase the likelihood of reaching their goals and aspirations. Bandura proposes that self-efficacy (e.g. an individual's perceived capabilities to perform actions successfully) is a key motivational process in social cognition. Indeed, feeling confident in one's environment serves as the glue between an individual's interpretation of the environment and their behavioural adjustments.

This paper uses social cognitive theory to frame students' reported experiences at law school. Our work extends the social cognitive research literature on perceptions of self-determination among law students[24] by drawing on multiple concepts and principles. Specifically, we posit that what law students want to achieve in the short term (their courses and university experience) and in the long term (their career and life), as well as their values, expectations, and personal well-being are a function of their individual perceptions of law school. A further assumption is that the teaching, standards, and support structures provided by law schools shape how students think about themselves. This, in turn, gives rise to agentic behaviours as each student follows their academic journey.

---

[18] *Professional Examinations in Law Regulations 2008* (NZ), reg 3(1).

[19] For example, at the University of Canterbury, students are timetabled for 72 hours of lectures and eight hours of lectures across the academic year.

[20] Enrolments at each of the courses exceed 200 students or more at each of the participating universities.

[21] Students' responses were analysed globally and by law school, but few differences of note were identified when the two sets of data were compared.

[22] DH Schunk and EL Usher, "Social Cognitive Theory and Motivation" in Richard M Ryan (ed), *The Oxford Handbook of Human Motivation* (2nd edn, OUP 2019) 11.

[23] Albert Bandura, *Social Foundations of Thought and Action: A Social Cognitive Theory* (Prentice Hall 1986); Albert Bandura, "Social Cognitive Theory: An Agentic Perspective" (2001) 52 Annual Review of Psychology 1.

[24] See, for example, see Larcombe and others (n 5); Leahy and others (n 6); Townes O'Brien, Tang and Hall (n 7).

A central tenet of Bandura's work is that triadic, reciprocal associations exist between a person, their behaviour, and environment.[25] For example, the amount of effort a student puts into an assessment task (behaviour) might be explained by their self-efficacy in being able to perform the assessment successfully (person) and the amount of quality academic support they have received (environment). These dynamics are reciprocal in that it is assumed that, for example, greater effort corresponds to greater self-efficacy over time and with experience. A social cognitive view assists in appreciating the complex, subjective processes that are a part of a student's law school experiences. Figure 1 below illustrates the framework and corresponding variables used in this study.

For the purposes of this paper, we explore the law student experience according to three personal characteristics: (a) students' interest in a legal career, (b) satisfaction with law school, and (c) difficulties with well-being (i.e. likely psychological distress). These particular characteristics are important in that they represent an understanding of students' drive and career ambitions, their global perception of their law school, and factors relating to mental health. We work on an assumption that a student who is uninterested, dissatisfied, and who struggles with mental health is at risk for poorer academic performance and early departure from law school. From a social cognitive perspective, we agree with the view that law schools have a responsibility to create a learning environment where students can be academically successful, but also have an ethical duty to promote student well-being and prevent a decline in their mental health.[26]

We investigate students' personal characteristics with respect to interest in a legal career at the beginning of their law studies alongside other dimensions of achievement motivation. Specifically, we posit that an interest in a legal career relates to (a) academic self-efficacy (i.e. students' perceived ability to be successful with their law courses), (b) effort expectancies (i.e. amount of time students expected devote to self-study outside lectures and tutorials), and (c) subjective task value (i.e. perceived importance of passing law courses). We use students' reported views of the support provided by academic law staff, grades coherence (i.e. perceived distance between students' anticipated and awarded grades), and assessment workload and timing to build on the "environment" element. We use students' reported academic engagement (i.e. rates of lecture attendance, working with others, and hours spent on self-study) to integrate the "behaviour" element. Lastly, we consider whether key variables within this model change over time.

Our research questions are:

(1) At the beginning of students' time at law school, are there meaningful associations between their current interest in a legal career and other dimensions of achievement motivation (i.e. academic self-efficacy, subjective task value, and effort expectancies)? To what extent do these factors differ as a function of demographic characteristics?

---

[25] DH Schunk and MK DiBenedetto, "Motivation and Social Cognitive Theory" (2020) 60 Contemporary Educational Psychology, Article 101832.

[26] Nigel Duncan, Rachel Field and Caroline Strevens, "Ethical Imperatives for Legal Educators to Promote Law Student Wellbeing" (2020) 23(1–2) Legal Ethics 65.

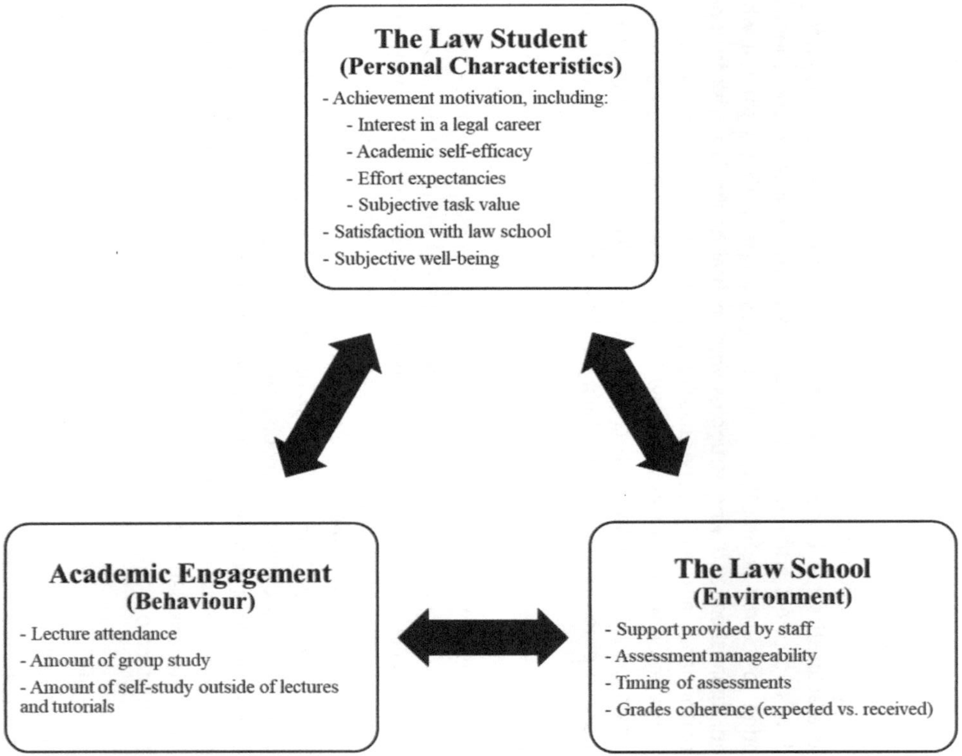

Figure 1. Triadic reciprocal causation model[a] representing theorised links between perceptions of the law student, their self-reported academic engagement, and their views of the law school environment. [a]Albert Bandura, *Social Foundations of Thought and Action* (Englewood Cliffs 1986) 23–28.

(2) At the end of students' first, second, and third years at law school, to what extent can personal characteristics, academic engagement, and the law school environment predict students' interest in a legal career, satisfaction with law school, and likely psychological distress, respectively?
(3) To what extent do students report change over time in relation to their subjective task value, effort expectancies, interest in a legal career, and satisfaction with law school? Do these trends differ as a function of student demographics and likely psychological distress?

Method

Participants

The initial study sample was a self-selected cohort of 785 first-year university students enrolled at three of the six New Zealand law schools.[27] Participants self-identified as female (61.9%), male (35.0%), or gender diverse (< 1%).[28] Participants' ages ranged from 16–17 years (13.1%), 18–20 years (70.2%), 21–25 years (6.5%), 26 and older (10.2%). Participants' reported ethnicity[29] was New Zealand European/Pākehā (42.9%), East Asian (14.8%), Pasifika (10.6%), other ethnicity (9.8%), New Zealand Māori (6.2%), Indian (6.0%), European (4.7%), and Australian (1.4%). Most participants began their studies on a full-time basis (81.8%).[30] Approximately one-third of participants reported having a family member with a connection to the legal profession (FMCL) (34.0%).

Procedures and design

The collection of data from students took place in accordance with protocols approved by the University of Canterbury Educational Research Human Ethics Committee.

Self-report data were collected from participants during their first three years of study via four anonymous online surveys. Students were contacted by email by an independent consultant and invited to take part in the first survey. Those who did were assigned a digital identifier, which was only used by the independent consultant to contact them for further surveys.

The overarching aim of the project was to collect data on students' law school experiences. Although some key questions were repeated in each survey, other questions were added or removed based on the findings of previous surveys. The first survey was administered at the beginning of students' first year of law school, and focused on their initial interest in a legal career, academic self-beliefs and attitudes, and expectations of their first year of law school. The second survey was administered at the end of students' first year of law school and focused on their satisfaction with law school, academic self-beliefs, performance-related attitudes, satisfaction with support provided by academic staff, academic engagement (class attendance, group study, and time spent on self-study), and

[27]The participating law schools were the University of Auckland, the University of Canterbury and Waikato University.
[28]Twenty participants (2.5%) did not report their gender.
[29]New Zealand Māori are the *tangata whenua* (indigenous people of the land) of New Zealand. The term Pākehā is a Māori-language term for New Zealanders primarily of European descent. The term Pasifika represents people living in New Zealand who have migrated from the Pacific Islands or self-identify with the Pacific Islands due to ancestry or heritage. Twenty-two participants (2.8%) did not report their ethnicity.
[30]We refer to this construct as "Rate of Study".

student debt levels. The third and fourth surveys were administered at the end of students' second and third years of law school and focused on interest in a legal career, satisfaction with law school, likely psychological distress, academic self-beliefs, attitudes towards grades and assessments, academic engagement, and student debt levels.

The number of participants reduced over time, as is typical in longitudinal studies. For ease of interpretation, sub-sample sizes, attrition rates, and demographic variables are described alongside findings in subsequent sections. Rather than use imputation procedures to manage missing cases, we present results as participants reported them. This is because it was not possible to determine whether incomplete responses were missing not at random (MNAR), missing at random (MAR), or missing completely at random (MCAR). It was not possible to identify students dropping out of university as opposed to those dropping out of the study, meaning that replacing missing cases would introduce substantial biases into the estimation of results.

Instruments

The majority of variables are estimated through single-item, Likert-style responses. The variables and the times in which they appeared in the student surveys are summarised in Table 1 below.

Psychological distress

Although there are extensive measures that focus on the presence of well-being, we focused on the presence of psychological distress. This was based on an assumption that we could more accurately estimate the extent to which students' perceptions and experiences in law school were predictive of difficulties with well-being. At the end of students' second and third years of law school, students completed the Kessler-6 scale, a set of questions used internationally to screen for likely non-specific psychological distress in large populations.[31] Participants were asked how often in the previous four weeks they had felt: "so sad nothing could cheer him or her up", "nervous", "restless or fidgety", "hopeless", "that everything was an effort", and "worthless". Participants answered using a five-point, Likert-style scale ranging from (1) "None of the time" to (5) "Almost all of the time". The sum of participant scores was calculated, and the total score categorised as follows: (1) those who score 6–11 are described as "likely to be mentally well", (2) those who score 12–19 are described as "likely to have a mild/moderate mental disorder", and (3) those who score 20–30 are described as "likely to have a severe mental disorder".[32] Reliability estimates for the current study were acceptable, with $\alpha = .86$ (end of Year 2) and $\alpha = .87$ (end of Year 3).

---

[31] Ronald Kessler and others, "Short Screening Scales to Monitor Population Prevalences and Trends in Non-Specific Psychological Distress" (2002) 32 Psychological Medicine 959; Ariana Krynen and others, "Measuring Psychological Distress in New Zealand: Item Response Properties and Demographic Differences in the Kessler-6 Screening Measure" (2013) 42 New Zealand Journal of Psychology 95, 95. "Psychological distress" includes a range of symptoms including anxiety, depression or rage: Ministry of Health, *The Health of New Zealand Adults 2011/12: Key Findings of the New Zealand Health Survey* (Ministry of Health 2012) 61.

[32] Although the Kessler-6 describes its categories in terms of "mental disorder", our sample comprises a non-clinical, student population and, therefore, we chose to appropriately adjust the terminology to the following categories: (1) "likely to be well", (2) "likely to have mild/moderate distress", and (3) "likely to have severe distress".

Table 1. Summary of variables, items, data collection and scaling used.

Variable name	Item or instrument	Data collection (wave)	Scaling used
Interest in a legal career	How interested are you at the moment in pursuing a legal career?	1, 2, 3, 4	1 (No interest) to 5 (Extremely interested)
Satisfaction with law school	How satisfied are you with your experience at law school?	2, 3, 4	1 (Very dissatisfied) to 5 (Very satisfied)
Psychological distress	Kessler-6 instrument (further details are described in this section)	3, 4	1 (None of the time) to 5 (All the time)
Academic self-efficacy	How confident are you in passing all of this year's law courses?	1, 3, 4	1 (Not confident at all) to 5 (Very confident)
Subjective task value	How important is passing your law courses this year to you?	1, 2	1 (Not important) to 5 (Very important)
Effort expectancies	Excluding your tutorials and lectures, how many hours of outside study do you expect to spend on your law courses?	2, 3, 4	1 = one or two hours 2 = three to five hours 3 = six to eight hours 4 = nine to ten hours 5 = more than 10 hours
Actual self-study	How many hours of study per week on average outside lectures and tutorials have you spent on your law courses?	2, 3, 4	1 = one or two hours 2 = three to five hours 3 = six to eight hours 4 = nine to ten hours 5 = more than 10 hours
Attendance	Please select the option that best describes your attendance at law lectures	4	1 = 81% – 100% 2 = 61% – 80% 3 = 41% – 60% 4 = 21% – 40% 5 = 0–20%
Amount of study with others	How often do you study with other law students?	2	5 = once a week or more 4 = every two weeks or so 3 = once a month 2 = less than once a month, 1 = only for tests/exams
Grades coherence	To what extent, on average, have the assessment results you have received in your law courses reflected your expectations?	2, 3, 4	1 (Much lower than expected) to 5 (Much higher than expected)
Assessment workload	My assessment load has been:	4	1 = Too low 2 = Low 3 = Acceptable 4 = High 5 = Too high
Assessment timing	The timing of my assessments has been manageable.	4	1 (Strongly disagree) to 5 (Strongly agree)

Analysis plan

We conducted our analyses in three steps. First, we examined descriptive statistics and bivariate correlations among the variables of interest for each time point of collected data. Second, we performed hierarchical multiple regression in SPSS version 25 to determine the extent to which dependent variables (for example, interest in a legal career, satisfaction with law school, and psychological distress) could be predicted based on a variety of relevant constructs. Each multiple regression included two steps. In the first step we added demographics: gender,[33] age, rate of study (full/part time), and whether students reported having a family member with a connection to the legal profession (FMCL). In the second step we added students' perceptions and experiences with law school, including their reported student debt. Preliminary analyses were conducted to confirm that the statistical approaches would be suitable based on the dataset. Last, we performed a series of one-way repeated-measures analyses of variance (ANOVA) to determine whether students' perceptions and experiences in law school had fluctuated over time while controlling for demographic differences in gender, age, rate of study, and family connection to a member of the legal profession.

Findings

At the beginning of Year 1 in law school

Our first research question asked: At the beginning of students' time at law school, are there meaningful associations between their current interest in a legal career and other dimensions of achievement motivation (i.e. academic self-efficacy, subjective task value, and effort expectancies)? To what extent do these factors differ as a function of demographic characteristics?

Means and standard deviations were: (1) interest in a legal career (M= 4.03, SD = .97); (2) academic self-efficacy (M = 3.72, SD = .74); (3) subjective task value (M = 4.77, SD = .57); and (4) effort expectancies (M = 4.05, SD = 1.10). The estimate for effort expectancies is equivalent to roughly 9–10 hours of study each week.

Results, illustrated in Table 2 below, show that students with more interest in a legal career reported higher academic self-efficacy, higher subjective task value, and greater effort expectancies. With respect to group differences, older students reported more

Table 2. Bivariate correlations for law students' perceptions and expectations at the beginning of law school (n = 785).

	Interest in a legal career	Academic self-efficacy	Subjective task value	Effort expectancies
Interest in a legal career	1	-	-	-
Academic self-efficacy	.10**	1	-	-
Subjective task value	.40**	.21**	1	-
Effort expectancies	.15**	.05	.15**	1

**p < .01.

[33]We tested for gender differences based only on participants who self-identified as male or female. This decision was made based on statistical power, as our sample included a very small, disproportional sub-sample of gender-diverse participants (< 1% of the sample).

interest in a legal career ($r = .12$, $p = .001$), higher academic self-efficacy ($r = .12$, $p = .001$), higher subjective task value ($r = .10$, $p = .004$), and greater effort expectancies ($r = .17$, $p < .001$). Independent-samples *t*-tests confirmed that, compared to male students, female students reported greater interest in a legal career;[34] t (680) = −2.06, $p = .04$. Female students, however, had lower academic self-efficacy; t (510.38) = 4.37, $p < .001$, and greater effort expectancies than their male counterparts; t (653) = −3.34, $p = .001$.

At the end of the first year in law school

Our second research question asked: At the end of students' first, second, and third years at law school, to what extent can personal characteristics, academic engagement, and the law school environment predict students' interest in a legal career, satisfaction with law school, and psychological distress, respectively?

At the end of their first year in law school, students were invited to complete a survey including a range of items designed to estimate their satisfaction with law school and the relationship between this, achievement motivation and academic engagement. Attrition resulted in a sub-sample of 597 participants. We performed chi-square tests for independence to determine whether attrition resulted in a different demographic composition. Results indicated no compositional differences on the basis of gender, age, rate of study, and family connection to the legal profession (FMCL). However, we detected a difference on the basis of student ethnicity; $\chi2$ (18) = 42.35, $p = .001$, specifically indicating that Pasifika, Korean, and multi-ethnic participants were less likely to have completed the end of Year 1 survey.[35]

Table 3. Bivariate correlations for law students' self-reported experiences at the end of Year 1 (n = 597).

	Satisfaction with law school	Satisfaction with lecturer support	Subjective task value	Grades coherence	Actual amount of self-study	Amount of study with classmates	Student debt
Satisfaction with law school	1	-	-	-	-	-	-
Satisfaction with lecturer support	.21**	1	-	-	-	-	-
Subjective task value	−.10*	.15**	1	-	-	-	-
Grades coherence	.24**	−0.03	−0.02	1	-	-	-
Actual amount of self-study	.15**	.10*	−.15**	0.02	1	-	-
Amount of study with classmates	0.05	0.03	−0.07	0.03	.13**	1	-
Student debt	−0.05	−0.04	−.12**	0.02	0.04	0.03	1

*$p < .05$. **$p < .01$.

[34]Note that the sample sizes differ due to incomplete demographic information.

[35]This does not mean that students from these ethnic backgrounds were more likely to depart from law school, but that the End of Year 1 sub-sample differed in terms of ethnicity from the Beginning of Year 1 sample.

We inspected descriptive statistics in terms of means and standard deviations. Results were as follows: (1) satisfaction with law school (*M*= 3.66, *SD* = .75), (2) satisfaction with lecturer support (*M* = 3.52, *SD* = .80), (3) subjective task value (*M*= 4.02, *SD* = 1.30), (4) grades coherence (*M*= 2.85, *SD* = .75), (5) amount of study with classmates (*M*= 3.30, *SD* = 1.20), (6) student debt (*M*= 2.70, *SD* = .94), and (7) actual amount of self-study (*M*= 2.46, *SD* = 1.10). The estimate for participants' actual amount of self-study is equivalent to roughly five to six hours of outside study each week.

Bivariate correlations ($n = 597$) are presented in Table 3 below. Students were more satisfied with law school when they were satisfied with the support provided by their lecturers, felt as though their grades reflected their expectations, and spent greater time on self-study. Notably, there was an inverse correlation between students' law school satisfaction and subjective task value. Although further investigation is needed, one possibility is that students who felt greater pressure to succeed academically also possessed higher standards and so were more critical of their law school experiences.

We sought to examine the extent to which these factors could predict students' satisfaction with law school (dependent variable). To achieve this, we performed a hierarchical multiple regression in SPSS version 25. In the first step, we included the following demographics: gender, age, rate of study, and FMCL. In the second step, we included the six predictor variables. Results revealed that greater reported hours of self-study ($\beta = .12, p = .002$), satisfaction with lecturer support ($\beta = .21, p < .001$), and grades coherence ($\beta = .26, p < .001$) contributed to greater overall satisfaction with law school; $F(9, 561) = 9.72, p < .001; R^2 = .14$. As the study progressed over time, we sought to gain a deeper understanding of these dynamics and their potential connections to psychological distress.

At the end of the second year in law school

Towards the end of their second year of law school, students ($n = 349$) completed a survey focusing on personal, environmental, and behavioural factors that might correspond to students' interest in a legal career, satisfaction with law school, levels of psychological distress. We identified no compositional differences due to attrition.

Descriptive statistics and bivariate correlations are presented in Table 4 below. The average student in our sub-sample reported a score of $M = 14.60$ ($SD = 4.06$) which on the Kessler-6 instrument reflects a likelihood of having mild-to-moderate psychological distress. Our results show that 68% of students at the end of their second year of law studies were likely to experience mild-to-moderate distress (49%) or severe distress (19%). Other key findings reveal that at the end of their second year of studies, students with more interest in a legal career and greater satisfaction with law school had higher academic self-efficacy and better academic engagement. Meanwhile, students with greater levels of psychological distress had less interest in a legal career and less satisfaction with law school. Not surprisingly, individuals with higher psychological distress also reported lower academic self-efficacy and grades coherence, poorer academic engagement, and higher levels of student debt.

We performed a hierarchical multiple regression to predict students' interest in a legal career while controlling for group differences as a function of demographics. Specifically, our full regression model showed that higher academic self-efficacy ($\beta = .27, p < .001$), greater hours of self-study ($\beta = .17, p < .001$), higher levels of student debt ($\beta = .14, p = .006$), and greater satisfaction with law school ($\beta = .24, p < .001$)

Table 4. Bivariate correlations for law students' self-reported experiences at the end of Year 2 (n = 249).

	Interest in a legal career	Satisfaction with law school	Academic self-efficacy	Grades coherence	Attendance	Student debt	Actual amount of self-study	Psychological Distress
Interest in a legal career	1	-	-	-	-	-	-	-
Satisfaction with law school	.35**	1	-	-	-	-	-	-
Academic self-efficacy	.35**	.47**	1	-	-	-	-	-
Grades coherence	0.05	.26**	.25**	1	-	-	-	-
Attendance	.15**	.17**	.20**	0.02	1	-	-	-
Student debt	0.02	−0.03	−.12*	0.07	−0.06	1	-	-
Actual amount of self-study	.23**	.18**	0.05	0.03	.14**	−0.01	1	-
Psychological distress	−.20**	−.28**	−.43**	−.11*	−.14**	.24**	0.04	1

$*p < .05$. $**p < .01$.

contributed to greater interest in a legal career; F (10, 328) = 12.26, $p < .001$; $R^2 = .27$. Female students ($\beta = .13$, $p = .009$) and older students ($\beta = .13$, $p = .02$) continued to show greater interest in a legal career. Although it is likely that moderation and attrition effects are at play, our results offer initial evidence that by the time students are at the end of their second year of law school, those who invest more time in their studies, feel competent in their abilities to perform academic tasks well, and hold a positive view of their law school tend to report greater interest in a legal career.

Next, we performed a hierarchical multiple regression to predict students' psychological distress while controlling for demographic characteristics. Specifically, our full regression model showed that students with more psychological distress reported lower academic self-efficacy ($\beta = -.31$, $p < .001$), had spent more time on self-study ($\beta = .12$, $p < .001$), had accrued more student debt ($\beta = .18$, $p < .001$), and were less satisfied with law school ($\beta = -14$, $p = .01$); F (10, 328) = 12.40, $p < .001$; $R^2 = .27$.

At the end of the third year in law school

Towards the end of students' third year of law school, students ($n = 173$) completed a further and expanded survey. We identified no compositional differences due to attrition in relation to the second dataset.

Descriptive statistics and bivariate correlations are presented in Table 5 below. As shown, students' interest in a legal career and their satisfaction with law school were positively associated with academic self-efficacy and attendance. Students' manageability of their assessments and their views on the adequacy of the timing of these assessments were positively associated with their satisfaction with law school (but not with interest in a legal career). Meanwhile, likely psychological distress was most strongly associated with lower academic self-efficacy and a view that the assessment workload was too high.

We performed a series of hierarchical multiple regressions. Students' interest in a legal career was influenced by their satisfaction with law school ($\beta = .32$, $p < .001$) and academic self-efficacy ($\beta = .18$, $p < .001$); F (12, 157) = 4.42, $p < .001$; $R^2 = .25$. Students' satisfaction with law school was influenced by their academic self-efficacy ($\beta = .35$, $p < .001$) and a perception that the timing of assessments was manageable ($\beta = .27$, $p < .001$); F (12, 158) = 4.92, $p < .001$; $R^2 = .26$. Lastly, psychological distress was influenced by having lower academic self-efficacy ($\beta = -.24$, $p = .003$), difficulties in managing their assessment workload ($\beta = .19$, $p = .02$), and poor satisfaction with law school ($\beta = -.18$, $p = .02$); F (12, 155) = 5.99, $p < .001$, $R^2 = .32$. Our results suggest that by the time students were at the end of their third year of law school, those who held a positive view of law school tended to report greater interest in a legal career, higher satisfaction with law school, and lower levels of psychological distress.

Law student perceptions: trends over time

Our third research question asked: To what extent do students report change over time in relation to their subjective task value, effort expectancies, interest in a legal career, and satisfaction with law school? Do these trends differ as a function of student demographics and likely levels of psychological distress?

Table 5. Bivariate correlations for law students' self-reported experiences at the end of Year 3 (n = 173).

	Interest in a legal career	Satisfaction with law school	Psychological distress	Academic self-efficacy	Grades coherence	Attendance	Student debt	Actual amount of self-study	Difficulties with assessment workload	Difficulties with assessment timing
Interest in a legal career	1	-	-	-	-	-	-	-	-	-
Satisfaction with law school	.38**	1	-	-	-	-	-	-	-	-
Psychological distress	−0.12	−.30**	1	-	-	-	-	-	-	-
Academic self-efficacy	.23**	.36**	−.44**	1	-	-	-	-	-	-
Grades coherence	−0.05	0.15	−0.13	.22**	1	-	-	-	-	-
Attendance	.156*	.17*	−0.14	0.13	−0.02	1	-	-	-	-
Student debt	−0.01	−0.03	.167*	−.27**	0.05	−0.04	1	-	-	-
Actual amount of self-study	0.14	−0.02	0.04	0.03	0.10	.16*	−0.05	1	-	-
Difficulties with assessment workload	−0.08	−0.14	.34**	−.32**	−0.11	−0.05	.19*	.18*	1	-
Difficulties with assessment timing	0.11	.30**	−.20*	.20**	0.08	0.03	−0.11	−0.07	−.39**	1

$^{*}p < .05$. $^{**}p < .01$.

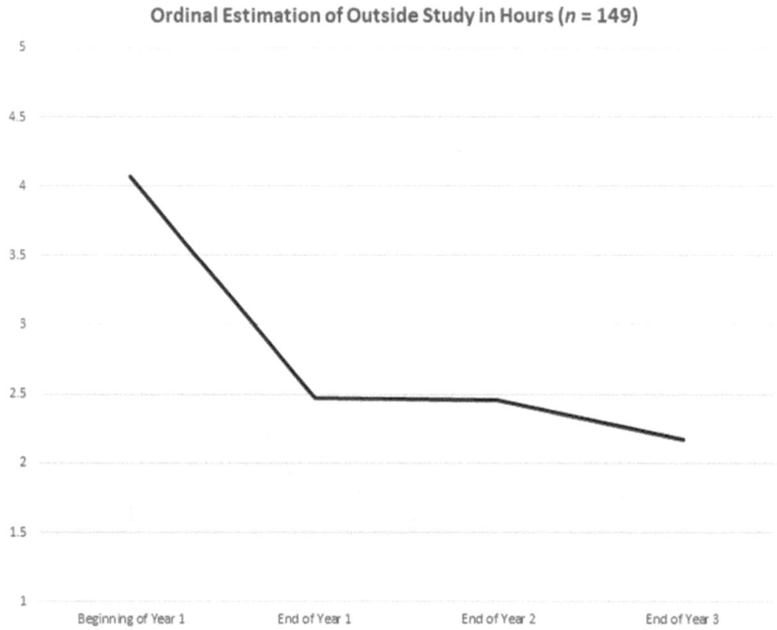

Figure 2. Trends in outside study in hours (per week) as reported by law students across three years of law school (n = 149).

Since the estimations of variables were different across waves of data collection, we report repeated-measures outcomes that compare responses across one, two, or three years. Our sample sizes differ slightly because of the attrition issues referred to above.

We began by analysing students' perceived importance of passing their law courses from the beginning of their university studies to the end of their first year. Using a repeated-measures ANOVA of gender, age, rate of study, and family connection to the legal profession (FMCL), our results confirm a small reduction in students' subjective task value; F (1, 569) = 4.14, p = .04; Wilks' λ = .99; partial η^2 = .01. We observed no group differences in this reduction according to student demographics.

Second, we considered changes in students' expected amount of time spent on self-study (in hours) at the beginning of law school (effort expectancies) and their actual amount of time for self-study across their first, second, and third years. As Figure 2 below shows, we identified a significant difference between the amount of hours that students anticipated they would spend on self-study at the beginning of their first year and the number of hours they actually spent on self-study over the next two years; F (3, 143) = 4.56, p = .004; Wilks' λ = .91; partial η^2 = .09. Means and standard deviations revealed that students anticipated studying roughly 9–10 hours per week on self-study, but actually reported 3–5 hours per week for self-study across their first, second, and third years of law school.

Third, we considered students' interest in a legal career and satisfaction with law school. We analysed students' interest in a legal career at the beginning of their first year, and the end of their second and third years of law school (n = 143). For the repeated-measures ANOVA, we included not only student demographics but also students' psychological distress as reported at the end of their second year of studies. Overall

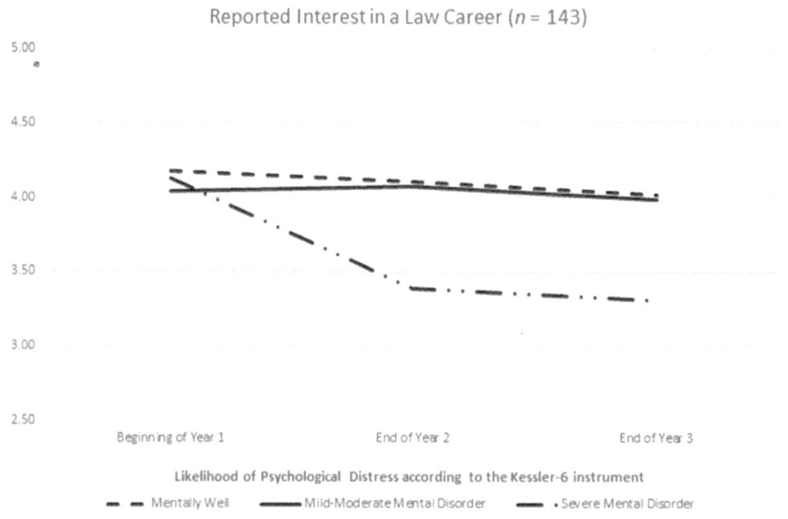

Figure 3. Trends in law students' interest in a legal career across three years of law school in relation to their levels of psychological distress (n = 143).

results show that students' interest in a legal career did not change across three years of study; F (2, 27) = 1.59, p = .22. Although we observed no group differences with respect to student demographics, changes in students' interest in a legal career were attributable to individual differences in psychological distress; F (124, 54) = 1.58, p= .03; Wilks' λ = .05; partial η^2 = .77. Keeping in mind the categories consistent with the Kessler-6 instrument (i.e. likely to be mentally well, likely to have a mild/moderate mental disorder, and likely to have a severe mental disorder), we report differences in students' interest in a legal career over time as a function of psychological distress in Figure 3 below. Although students' initial interest in a legal career did not differ, individual changes across the second year of law school were attributable to psychological distress. This reduction in interest remained unchanged at the end of students' third year at law school.

Using the same model, we analysed students' satisfaction with law school at the end of their first, second, and third years at law school. Similar to the trends observed with students' interest in a legal career, satisfaction with law school did not change as a function of time; F (2, 127) = 0.03, p= .98. However we observed important group differences. Changes in students' law school satisfaction differed according to gender; F (2, 127) = 3.02, p= .05; Wilks' λ = .96; partial η^2 = .05. As shown in Figure 4 below, female students' reported satisfaction with law school remained relatively consistent over time, but male students reported a slight decline over time. It was also clear that changes in students' law school satisfaction were attributed to individual differences in psychological distress; F (2, 127) = 6.78, p= .002; Wilks' λ = .90; partial η^2 = .10.

Figure 5 below shows differences in students' law school satisfaction over time as a function of second-year psychological distress. Students' satisfaction with law school at the end of the first year did not differ. Changes in law school satisfaction across students' second year were attributable to individual differences in psychological distress. These trends in law school satisfaction appeared to remain unchanged across students' third year at law school.

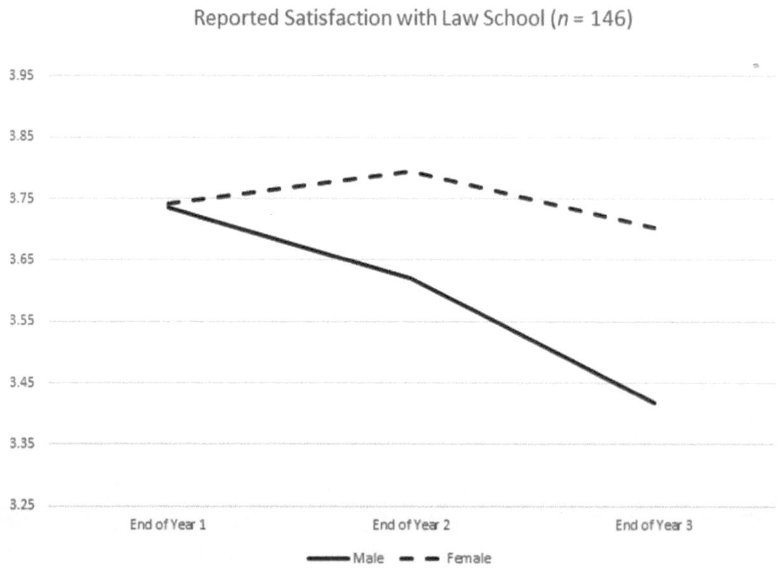

Figure 4. Trends in male and female law students' satisfaction with law school across three years (n = 146).

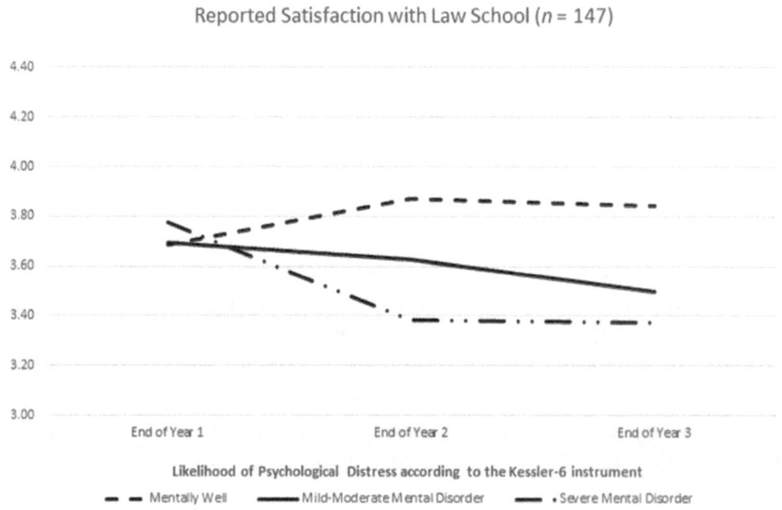

Figure 5. Trends in law students' satisfaction with law school across three years in relation to their levels of psychological distress (n = 147).

Discussion

Overall, our results offer evidence that positive and negative law school experiences have the potential to influence law students' interest in a legal career, satisfaction with law school, and levels of psychological distress. Consistent with a social cognitive view, our findings suggest that the law school environment may influence students' career ambitions, satisfaction with their respective academic programmes, and subjective well-being. Moreover, we report considerable shifts in students' expectations, perceptions, and experiences during their first two years at law school, which appear to stabilise in their third year. We note that stabilisation can be problematic when it includes chronic, unchanging levels of distress.

Incoming law students' interest in a legal career was linked to their initial levels of academic confidence and expectations of law school, a finding consistent with existing literature reporting that academic interest tends to be positively associated with self-efficacy.[36] Across multiple time points, greater interest in a legal career was linked to stronger confidence in ability to perform well in law school. This suggests that students tend to report less interest in a legal career when they also lack confidence in their ability to perform well in law school, a finding that aligns with well-established interest development frameworks in which levels of self-efficacy for learning and performance are by-products of individual interests.[37]

Our results show that the relation between interest in a legal career and self-efficacy beliefs is sensitive to students' early expectations of law school. For example, female law students reported less academic confidence and expected to spend more hours on self-study than male students at the start of their law studies. To accommodate and respond to this finding, we recommend that law schools ensure that the academic environment and non-academic opportunities are based on evidence-based, inclusive practices. Such inclusive practices might include ensuring diversity across teaching contexts (e.g. academic staffing and leadership opportunities) and non-academic contexts (e.g. extra-curricular activities and law student representatives). Beyond structural change, it may also be useful for institutions to create more explicit, proactive messages to students that academia and the legal profession benefit from diversity. After all, the legal profession should represent and reflect the communities it serves.

Second, our results confirm that, at different points in their law studies, students' interest in a legal career and satisfaction with law school appear to be influenced by contextual and situational perceptions. Two factors emerged as particularly relevant: lecturer support and attitudes towards assessment. For example, law school was judged by students as more satisfactory when lecturers provided what they perceived to be adequate levels of support. Although we did not differentiate between academic and pastoral forms of student support, it is likely that both contribute to this finding. This finding is consistent with the view expressed in legal education literature that a supportive learning environment is closely linked to student motivation and engagement.[38] Law students who feel as though they are being cared for, respected, and encouraged by law school academics in law school will likely see greater potential in themselves, and experience a sense of belonging and empowerment. Such attitudes may translate to not only greater law school satisfaction overall, but also short-term academic confidence and longer-term career interests.

Students' attitudes towards assessment were also meaningful contributors to their interest in a legal career and satisfaction with their law school experience. For example, satisfaction was influenced by the degree to which students felt as though the grades

---

[36] See Woogul Lee, Myung Lee and Mimi Bong, "Testing Interest and Self-Efficacy as Predictors of Academic Self-Regulation and Achievement" (2014) 39 Contemporary Educational Psychology 86.

[37] See Suzanne Hidi and K Ann Renninger, "The Four-Phase Model of Interest Development" (2006) 41 Educational Psychologist 111.

[38] Gerald Hess, "Heads and Hearts: The Teaching and Learning Environment in Law School" (2002) 52 Journal of Legal Education 75.

they received were consistent with their performance expectations. It is worth noting that educational research involving the concept of "satisfaction" warrants some degree of caution, as a customer-oriented perspective of the student experience may have little to do with effective learning, academic success, and reality (e.g. a student may be "satisfied" with their law school if the institution awards high marks for all assessments). Keeping this caution in mind, our findings do provide some evidence that students were less satisfied with law school when there was a greater distance between their anticipated and actual results. One possible explanation might stem from inaccurate expectations of academic performance. For example, a student who enters law school with a self- and socially ascribed identity as a "high achiever" may strive to maintain this positive image through the deployment of learning strategies previously used with successful results. However, if the student's performance standards are not aligned with those of their law school, then feeling surprised by underperformance could lead to frustration, self-doubt, loss of agency, and psychological distress.[39] Early formative assessment opportunities for students would provide a way to align expectations. However, given the mandated assessment structure in the core papers in the New Zealand law degree, it may be challenging to provide these opportunities in ways that authentically prepare students for summative assessments.

We confirm that satisfaction with law school is partly influenced by the degree to which students view their assessment workload as manageable. This result is consistent with the existing literature[40] and suggests that students' workload, particularly in relation to assessment, gives rise to individual differences in law school satisfaction. It is likely that perceived support from the wider law school exerts effects similar to the impact that teacher support has on students' motivation and engagement. For example, students who feel that their law school offers an unreasonable amount of assessment may in turn feel as though their goals are blocked, opportunities for success are limited, and that their failures are caused by factors beyond their control.[41] From a social cognitive view, students who feel a lack of agency over events that are important to them in their lives may struggle to cope adaptively. Our results underscore the importance of students' attitudes towards assessment. Such a perspective may have much to do with students' perceptions of a learning environment that helps them succeed and this has important implications for teaching and learning. When students perceive a lack of clarity with respect to assessment marking rubrics and/or insufficient attention to assessment design and timing, they may attribute failure to external causes and may not reflect on their study behaviours and strategies. Small changes at a programme level, in particular around student (assessment) workload management, could improve students' views of law school support and satisfaction, and motivate them to persist because of a perception that success is more clearly within their reach.[42] This may also have implications for students' reported distress levels.

---

[39] Albert Bandura, "Human Agency in Social Cognitive Theory" (1989) 44 American Psychologist 1175.

[40] Stephen Halpern, "On the Politics and Pathology of Legal Education" (1982) 32 Journal of Legal Education 383, 388; Hess (n 39) 78, 97.

[41] Bernard Weiner, *An Attributional Theory of Motivation and Emotion* (Springer-Verlag 1986).

[42] It is important to keep in mind that these results were measured during students' early experiences in law school. It is possible that such trends (for example, in relation to teacher support and assessment attitudes) change with greater experience, as the gap between actual and anticipated grades and coping with assessment workload could improve over students' time at law school.

Although most students in this study reported moderate interest in a legal career and satisfaction with law school, they also reported mild-to-moderate levels of psychological distress. Our results suggest that by the second year of law school, students' poor self-beliefs and negative attitudes towards law school contributed in part to greater levels of psychological distress. Clear patterns emerged during students' second and third years of law school. Students' psychological distress can be explained in part by factors relating to their confidence, amount of student debt, satisfaction with law school, assessment workload, and study practices.

Findings of student psychological distress are disconcerting for legal educators. However, these findings must be interpreted with some caution given the many factors at play. Findings with respect to students' self-beliefs, attitudes towards law school and psychological distress do not reflect causal trends. Students' encounters with law school may lead to reports of heightened distress, but it is also possible that law students with existing mental health problems may view their capabilities and law school environment in a less than positive light. Second, it is important to keep in mind that psychological distress is prevalent across university students worldwide. Our estimate that 19.1% of New Zealand law students fit the criteria for likely severe psychological distress is on a par with estimates using the Kessler-10 instrument in Australia (19.2%; $n = 6479$).[43] Moreover, the psychological distress reported in this sample does not necessarily mean that law school differs in this respect from other academic disciplines. Third, we note in the New Zealand context that law students do not have a full-time emphasis on the study of law until their second year at law school. Students go through an initial transition in their first year at university and then a second transition into the full-time study of law. It is not surprising that major acculturative shifts – along with their accompanying distress – are identified in this study.

Lastly, we report longitudinal trends involving a sub-sample of students who had the means and resources to persevere across three years of university study. Our findings may present a "best-case scenario". Students who discontinued their law studies may have had worse, or more extreme, experiences. However, even in the cohort of persisting students, our results confirm a reduction in the amount of hours of self-study that (persevering) students spent on their law studies as they progressed in law school. One possibility is that students who were comparatively "better" than those unable to persevere may have had very high expectations for academic success and then progressively realised that performing well was less important to them. Alternatively, they may have realised that it took less effort than expected for them to be successful. Although at first glance persevering students' interest in a legal career did not appear to change, one in five students signalled having serious psychological distress towards the end of their second year at law school, and for these students, interest in a legal career decreased substantially between their first and second years of study. Similarly, we found that second-year students reporting psychological distress had a considerable decrease in their satisfaction with law school. We add that psychological distress has the potential to explain individual differences in students' interests in a legal career and satisfaction with law school.

[43] Helen M Stallman, "Psychological Distress in University Students: A Comparison with General Population Data" 45 (2010) Australian Psychologist 249, 252.

Based on the existing literature and current findings, we recommend that law schools consider several steps. First, we propose that institutions conduct high-quality, educational research to gain a better understanding of their law students. Ideally, this research would consider the personal characteristics of each student in terms of motivation, satisfaction, and well-being, and would also be monitored across time to identify group trends. Second, we encourage institutions to perform a comprehensive needs assessment. Such an assessment could integrate information on academic success and mental health (from the previous step) in order to identify discrepancies between (a) what resources students need, (b) what resources students want, (c) what resources are assumed by the institution as available to students, and (d) what resources are actually provided to (and received by) students. Rooted in a social cognitive view, examining the subjective student perspective alongside what an institution thinks and does may be enlightening. Third, we recommend that law schools collaborate with teaching and learning experts in their respective institutions to develop strategies that can be realistically implemented to have a positive impact on the unique circumstances understood from steps one and two. Such strategies can be designed and targeted at different levels of scope, ranging from student cohorts (e.g. individuals from traditionally marginalised groups), lecturers and courses, programmes, or the larger institution. Last, a thorough analysis of these (anticipated) changes is necessary to determine whether the strategies are working (or not) and what needs to take place to optimise students' law school experiences.

Limitations

We examined cross-sectional and longitudinal data to understand the expectations, perceptions, and subjective well-being of New Zealand law students. Several limitations should be kept in mind. First, we relied on singular, self-report measures to serve as a snapshot of the variables of interest at different time points. We cast a wide net to identify key factors that influence law students' learning, motivation, and well-being. However, we acknowledge that single-item variables may affect reliability and validity. Not all measures were collected at every point of data collection, which limits our ability to draw conclusions around change over time. Second, although longitudinal data help to explain processes over time, participant attrition can pose difficulties with missing cases and interpretation of data. We chose to report only the data that were collected rather than use imputation methods. To improve data interpretability, we reported our findings in cross-sectional and longitudinal sections, with the latter representing only participants who had completed all questionnaires. Third, sample selection bias may be at play. It is possible that the New Zealand law students who participated in the study represent those who experienced especially negative or positive experiences in law school. Last, the Kessler-6 is a validated instrument that is used as a screening measure for anxiety and mood disorders. It is not equivalent to a clinical diagnosis.

Conclusion

This paper analysed cross-sectional and longitudinal trends in a cohort of law students enrolled at three New Zealand universities to better understand their interest in a legal career, satisfaction with law school, and psychological distress during their first three years at law school. Students' reported interest in a legal career when they started at law school was linked to their initial levels of academic confidence and expectations of law school. Across their time at law school, students' reported interest in a legal career and satisfaction with law school were influenced by their perceptions of law school support and attitudes towards assessment. Most students reported moderate interest in a legal career and mild-to-moderate levels of psychological distress. Factors identified as contributing to greater levels of psychological distress during students' second and third years of study were poor self-beliefs, student debt, satisfaction with law school, assessment workload and study practices. Whilst some factors, such as student debt, are outside the control of law schools, other factors are linked to law school policies and practices. This is evidence that law schools may utilise to enhance and/or improve the experience of their student body and of particular groups within it. This cyclical process includes conducting self-report research to learn about students' experiences in law school, performing a needs assessment to identify gaps within the system, and collaborating with experts to develop (and evaluate) realistic strategies that could better support the academic success and well-being of law students.

Acknowledgments

The author team are all members of the academic staff at the University of Canterbury, Christchurch, New Zealand. Valerie Sotardi is a Senior Lecturer in the School of Educational Studies and Leadership, Lynne Taylor is Professor of Law and Deputy Head of School, Erik Brogt is an Associate Professor in the Academic Quality Unit, Ursula Cheer is Dean and Professor of Law, and Natalie Baird is an Associate Professor of Law. We acknowledge with thanks the work of our research assistant, Maansa Bajaj Prakash.

Disclosure statement

No potential conflict of interest was reported by the author(s).

Funding

We acknowledge the funding received from Ako Aotearoa National Centre for Tertiary Teaching Excellence for the longitudinal study of law students which generated the data for this paper.

ORCID

Valerie Sotardi http://orcid.org/0000-0002-2720-6362
Lynne Taylor http://orcid.org/0000-0002-4197-8799
Erik Brogt http://orcid.org/0000-0003-2113-131X

"Hell is other people": rethinking the Socratic method for quiet law students

Rachel Spencer

ABSTRACT

This article is a reflective analysis of my own teaching methodology arising from my experience with teaching quiet law students, and reconciling this experience with a statement in Martin Seligman's *Flourish*, his best-selling work about positive psychology. Seligman asserts that Jean Paul Sartre's famous line "Hell is other people" in his play *No Exit* seems "wrongheaded" and "almost meaningless" today. This article will argue that Seligman's comments about Sartre's existentialist angst are the views of an extrovert. This article argues that much of the teaching in legal education today relies on the assumption that law students are extroverts, when the opposite is in fact often the case. It argues that catering only to extroverts is inappropriate. It explores the idea that pushing an aggressive agenda through the Socratic method of teaching diminishes the development of less aggressive legal techniques to resolve problems and ignores the learning needs of students with personalities that tend towards introversion. It argues that the Socratic method of teaching perpetuates a culture that has no place in modern legal practice. It also suggests that progressive approaches to law and dispute resolution require more contemplation, more active listening and less aggressive advocacy, and draws on the work of Susan Cain to demonstrate that recognising the needs and strengths of introverts is important in this process.

Introduction

The pedagogical rationale and methodologies of teaching students how to reflect and how to write reflectively have been the subjects of previous articles by me[1] that describe a scaffolded pedagogy of reflection and reflective writing. I have advocated that this pedagogical approach is useful within a clinical legal education

[1]Rachel Spencer, "Holding Up the Mirror: A Theoretical and Practical Analysis of the Role of Reflection in Clinical Legal Education" (2012) 18 International Journal of Clinical Legal Education 181; Rachel Spencer, "First They Tell Us to Ignore Our Emotions, Then They Tell Us to Reflect: The Development of a Reflective Writing Pedagogy in Clinical Legal Education through an Analysis of Student Perceptions of Reflective Writing" (2014) 21 International Journal of Clinical Legal Education 139; Rachel Spencer, "Private Lives: Confronting the Inherent Difficulties of Reflective Writing in Clinical Legal Education" (2014) 21 International Journal of Clinical Legal Education 177.

programme. This article provides a further reflective analysis of my own experiences as an educator within the Clinic context and reveals how I have broadened my views about reflective practice to accommodate the different learning styles of introverts and extroverts.

Part 1 of this article tells the story of my own "disorienting moment"[2] when I recognised deficiencies in my teaching practices that had hitherto failed to accommodate the needs of introverted students. This coincided with rereading a passage in Martin Seligman's *Flourish*[3] in which Seligman asserts that Jean Paul Sartre's famous line in the play *Huis Clos* – "Hell is other people" – "seems wrong-headed ... (because) today it is accepted without dissent that connections to other people and relationships are what give meaning and purpose to life".[4] Part 2 of this article describes my disagreement with Seligman's statement in the context of legal education and discusses my interpretation of Sartre's famous play. I explain that I take issue with Seligman because his contention about Sartre's "Hell is other people" line is skewed from the perspective of an extrovert. Part 2 examines some of the differences in the ways the extroverts and introverts learn, drawing on the work of Susan Cain[5] to explain this.

Part 3 then reflects on the Socratic method of teaching, not only as being an inappropriate vehicle for teaching introverted law students, but considering that the very fact that it requires, encourages and rewards extroverted behaviour may be producing lawyers who are not equipped with the emotional intelligence required for modern legal practice. Part 4 acknowledges the role of emotional intelligence in the modern lawyer's toolkit, and argues that if we expect our students to be emotionally intelligent and to be able to recognise emotions in others, law teachers must also develop emotional intelligence to recognise whether their students are experiencing frustration, anxiety, nervousness, overwhelm and the need for quiet and solitude. In turn, I argue that recognising a student's personality type, including whether they are introverted or extroverted, is an important aspect of student wellbeing. I conclude that adopting a teaching methodology that embraces both introverts and extroverts provides a superior learning environment for law students that will contribute to the development of more thoughtful, reflective lawyers.

I presented an earlier version of this article at the Australasian Law Teachers Association Conference in 2015. After my presentation, a number of audience members approached me, keen to discuss my ideas. Several of the audience members told me that they agreed with my views and suggested that this was an idea worth pursuing. I continued to develop my ideas about the introvert/extrovert dichotomy, noting that a number of scholars around the globe were similarly interested. This article is the culmination of my reflections on this topic over the past five years or so. It is a personal reflection that actively demonstrates the type of reflective writing that I encourage in my own students.

[2]Fran Quigley, "Seizing the Disorienting Moment: Adult Learning Theory and the Teaching of Social Justice in Law School Clinics" (1995) 2 Clinical Law Review 37.

[3]Martin Seligman, *Flourish* (Random House Australia 2011).

[4]Martin Seligman, *Authentic Happiness: Using the New Positive Psychology to Realize Your Potential for Lasting Fulfillment* (Free Press 2002) 17.

[5]Susan Cain, *Quiet* (Penguin Books 2012).

Part 1: my disorienting moment

Reflection and reflective writing are critical components of clinical legal education and, arguably, legal education generally. Susan Douglas recognises that "[r]eflective written exercises enable students to record their experiences, gain insight from them and use that insight to guide future action".[6] There is a vast literature on this topic which I have analysed in earlier articles.[7]

A critical component of my reflective writing pedagogy is the establishment of an appropriate environment where a relationship of trust (between student peers and between students and teacher) builds gradually and students are encouraged to disclose and analyse their reactions to events and experiences that have occurred within a clinic where they interview and provide advice (under supervision) to real clients. Classroom time is structured so that this relationship of trust builds gradually. Divulging personal reactions to work experiences involves an element of risk. In my experience, students are prepared to take that risk if they feel supported and know that the risk will produce a positive result in the form of a validation of their feelings and encouragement for the future.

Encouraging students to take such a risk is a scaffolded process involving a series of exercises. The first exercise involves students introducing themselves and articulating why they have chosen to enrol in the course. Subsequent written exercises involve personal goals, self-awareness, personality types, identification of strengths and recognition of opportunities for improvement. These exercises are private, and students are not required to divulge their thoughts. The next task involves discussing "an unexpected situation which I handled well" in pairs. Then they select a different partner with whom to discuss "an unexpected situation which I handled badly". After this, the pairs share each other's experiences with the class, leading to a discussion about strategies for dealing with unexpected situations that might occur on the placement or in a work environment. These early class exercises lay the foundation for later discussions about what they are learning in their clinical placement environments. As the term progresses, students are encouraged to relate experiences from which they have learned something.

The next step is to generate reflective writing from the material that is mined from class discussions. The translation of an informal discussion into an assessable piece of reflective writing is a complex progression involving "depth of reflection"[8] and an analysis of alternative perspectives. The reflective component of clinical legal education is strongly grounded in the development of competencies such as empathy, organisational awareness, relationship management, self-awareness and self-control which are now recognised as critical competencies for lawyers.[9]

---

[6]Susan Douglas, "Incorporating Emotional Intelligence in Legal Education: A Theoretical Perspective" (2015) 9(2) e-Journal of Business Education and Scholarship of Teaching 56, 65.

[7]See n 1.

[8]Claire Sparrow, "Reflective Student Practitioner – An Example Integrating Clinical Experience into the Curriculum" (2009) 14 International Journal of Clinical Legal Education 70, 73.

[9]See for example: Colin James, "Seeing Things as We Are – Emotional Intelligence and Clinical Legal Education" (2005) 8 International Journal of Clinical Legal Education 123; Claire Donohue, "Client, Self, Systems: A Framework for Integrated Skills – Justice Education" (2016) 29 Georgetown Journal of Legal Ethics 439, 457; Rachel Spencer and Susan L Brooks, "Reflecting on Reflection: A Dialogue across the Hemispheres on Teaching and Assessing Reflective Practice in Clinical Legal Education" (2019) 53 The Law Teacher 458; Susan L Brooks, "Listening and Relational Lawyering" in Debra L Worthington and Graham D Bodie (eds), *The Handbook of Listening* (John Wiley and Sons 2020) 361–71. See also Claire Donohue, "Client, Self, Systems: A Framework for Integrated Skills – Justice Education" (2016) 29 Georgetown Journal of Legal Ethics 439, 457.

About five years ago, at the Australasian Law Teachers Association Conference,[10] I presented a paper that was the forerunner to this article. A short time before that conference I had taught two separate cohorts of students within the clinical legal education programme that I had been teaching for many years. These two groups were particularly reticent when it came to orally reflecting and expressing their ideas in a classroom setting.

They were not lazy students. They attended classes, they were punctual, they were polite, and they produced excellent written work. They worked hard within the clinical programme and demonstrated deep empathy for their clients. Their written reflections about access to justice and the role of lawyers were intelligent and insightful. But they clearly were very uncomfortable talking in an informal, spontaneous situation. They were all reluctant to speak out in a classroom setting, unless they were standing at the front of the room for an assessable presentation, when they were well prepared, confident and articulate.

All of the students in this particular class were quiet, private, and reluctant to draw attention to themselves as individuals. But they were fully and deeply engaged. Their written work was evidence of this. I realised, after reading their work, that they were engaged quietly, thoughtfully, and intellectually, rather than in any demonstrative way. They chose not to draw attention to their engagement.

To begin with, I was worried about this group. My scaffolded approach that had been successful for many years, and my usual strategies for developing trust and developing momentum in the context of class discussions, were not working. So I rearranged the desks. I tried different prompts for initiating discussion. But the students did not want to answer my questions aloud. One day, in desperation, I asked them to write down their thoughts and hand them to me. The responses were astounding. They demonstrated deep engagement, thoughtful analysis and careful reflection.

Soon after that day, I went to a staff training seminar, where everyone was expected to be gregarious and interactive, a state of being that I find difficult, stressful and unproductive. And then the penny really dropped. In that moment I realised that my students were just like me.

My clinical teaching is grounded in Fran Quigley's concept of the "disorienting moment".[11] I encourage students to recognise their moments of disorientation as moments of learning. In that moment at the staff seminar, I recognised why my students were not responding to my usual approach. I empathised with them. In that disorienting moment, I recognised with a jolt that I had for years been disregarding the introverts. And that I was now dealing with a whole class of students whose personalities were at various levels of introversion.

The next time I met with that particular group of students in the classroom, I relaxed. I stopped trying to turn them all into extroverts. I stopped wanting them all to call out immediate answers to my questions. Instead, I used a variety of techniques with which readers of this journal will be familiar, including asking them to discuss issues in pairs or small groups (a strategy that was successful). By the end of that teaching term, I had developed a level of trust within the classroom that was comparable to the environment that I had been able to cultivate with previous classes. I had just reached that point in a different way.

[10]"Legal Education and Access to Justice" (ALTA Conference 2015, La Trobe University Law School, Melbourne, 16–18 July 2015).

[11]Quigley (n 2).

Part 2: Sartre and Seligman

This brings me to Martin Seligman who published *Flourish* in 2011.[12] The book is described on its cover as "a visionary new understanding of happiness and well-being". The overwhelming success of the book is testament to its value. Seligman's text is widely cited and used by clinical legal educators (including myself) in the context of self-awareness and the development of emotional intelligence.

Seligman's *Flourish* advocates "a tectonic upheaval in psychology":[13] a path to well-being through positive education, optimism, gratitude, love and growth, and the exploration of "what makes life worth living".[14] Seligman's work aligns with Aristotelian ethics which are based on the human desire to achieve happiness.[15] Seligman states that his "original view was closest to Aristotle's – that everything we do is done in order to make us happy" but then he proposes that "the monism of happiness" should be "dissolved into more workable terms".[16] *Flourish* explains Seligman's theory that extends beyond his earlier work *Authentic Happiness*.[17] According to Seligman, "the gold standard for measuring well-being is flourishing, and … the goal of positive psychology is to increase flourishing".[18] Seligman asserts that "human flourishing" comprises "happiness, flow, meaning, love, gratitude, accomplishment, growth, better relationships".[19]

Seligman explains that wellbeing theory has five elements: positive emotion, engagement, meaning, positive relationships and accomplishment. In further elaborating on the concept of "meaning" Seligman claims that meaning "is not solely a subjective state". He gives the example of Abraham Lincoln who (according to Seligman) judged his own life to be meaningless but that "we judge it pregnant with meaning".[20] Seligman goes on to say:

> Jean Paul Sartre's existentialist play *No Exit* might have been judged meaningful by him and his post-World War II devotees, but it now seems wrong-headed ("Hell is other people") and almost meaningless, since today it is accepted without dissent that connections to other people and relationships are what give meaning and purpose to life.[21]

Sartre's 1944 play, *Huis Clos* (*No Exit*)[22] is about three people, who have all died. Joseph Garcin, Inès Serrano and Estelle Rigault are brought to the same room in Hell and locked inside by a mysterious valet. They are each being punished for various transgressions in their lives[23] and locked into a room together for eternity. The famous line of the play is towards the end where Joseph concludes that Hell is not comprised of torture devices or physical punishment. Hell, he concludes, is other people.

---

[12]Seligman (n 3).
[13]ibid 1.
[14]ibid 1–2.
[15]ibid 9.
[16]ibid.
[17]Seligman (n 4).
[18]Seligman (n 3) 13.
[19]ibid 2.
[20]ibid 17.
[21]ibid.
[22]Literally translated into English as "closed door" or "behind closed doors". It is the French legal term for the English "in camera".
[23]Joseph cheated on and mistreated his wife; Inès seduced her cousin's wife while living with them; and Estelle had an affair and then killed the resulting child, prompting the child's father to commit suicide.

I interpret Sartre's phrase in a different way from Seligman. I take issue with Seligman for two reasons. First, Seligman's interpretation of "Hell is other people" is misconstrued. I think Sartre's message is partly that Hell for some people is their dependence upon the judgement of others. In *No Exit*, the characters judge each other and they are in Hell without the forgiveness of the others, but also because they cannot get away from each other. They are forced to be in the same room together for eternity. Jonathan Webber argues that Sartre's point was that the character Garcin's relationships with others "are poisoned in such a way as to make him overly reliant on those other people. Sartre clearly sees this as compatible with the idea that we are necessarily reliant on other people for our understanding of ourselves".[24]

The second way that I read Sartre differently from Seligman is because I believe Seligman's contention about relationships is focused through a prism of extraversion. For the introvert, Sartre's line "Hell is other people" is, to quote Seligman himself, "pregnant with meaning". The introvert experiences the lack of solitude as a form of Hell. Hell is a crowded room. Hell is other people sucking up the energy. Hell is noise and movement and distraction.

Susan Cain, a graduate of Harvard Law School and former transactional lawyer, explains that extroverts derive energy from other people. They are invigorated by engaging with others and prefer to "think out loud in the moment".[25] They are "generally more comfortable with conflict and less comfortable with solitude".[26] Extrovert students gladly share their thoughts and speak "off the cuff", happy to "bounce ideas around" – that common phrase that has entered management-speak. "Bouncing ideas around" is an extrovert's comfort zone. Introverts however, prefer to listen to others and then think things through. "Introverts tend to talk less and listen more, and think before participating in a conversation; they often feel they can better express themselves through writing than through conversation".[27] They also tend to do their best work alone.[28] This explains why my class of quiet students provided better written answers than they felt confident to provide orally.

Cain explains that the extrovert derives energy from the presence of others. The extrovert is inspired by external stimulation, like noise and social interaction. The introvert derives energy from "solitude" and periods of contemplation. Cain argues that society rewards the assertive, the charismatic and the vocal. Our work spaces and classrooms are geared towards the idea that creativity is only possible through group work.[29] But Susan Cain argues that solitude is a crucial ingredient in the creative process and we are undervaluing it to the point of calling introversion a personality flaw.

In 1965, two decades after the play was first published, an audio-recording was made of the play *Huis Clos* and Sartre recorded a preface at the beginning of the record. Sartre explained that the genesis of the play was his desire to write a play with three characters. He had three friends to take these roles. He wanted them all to be on stage at the same time, all the time, so that their parts were truly equal. He decided to

---

[24]Jonathan Webber, "There Is Something about Inez" (2011) 10(27) Think 45.
[25]Cain (n 5) 85.
[26]ibid.
[27]ibid 84.
[28]ibid 85.
[29]For a comprehensive analysis of group work and collaborative learning for law students with insights into the extrovert/introvert dimensions, see A Rachel Camp, "Creating Space for Silence in Law School Collaborations" (2016) 65 Journal of Legal Education 897-937.

put them in Hell and to make each one the executioner of the other two. Sartre explained that the phrase "Hell is other people" had been poorly understood ever since the play was first performed and that people thought he wanted to say that our relationships with others are always hellish.

"But what I really mean [said Sartre] is that when relationships with others are twisted or vitiated, then the 'other' can only be *l'enfer* (Hell) because the others are what is the most important in ourselves for our proper knowing of ourselves".[30] In the clinical legal education classroom setting, I interpret this to mean that if introverted students are not given the opportunity to think quietly, and reflect alone, their relationships with each other and with the teacher will become twisted and vitiated. The classroom can be Hell for the introvert.

Seligman's comment that "connections to other people and relationships are what give meaning and purpose to life"[31] is paradoxically exactly what Sartre was trying to say, in my view. For the introvert, connections to people are processed differently. It's not that introverts don't want to connect with people. It's more that we want to connect with others after we have had time to prepare ourselves for the connection. In interpreting Sartre through the concept of introversion, for some, Hell *is* other people. This does not mean that the introvert dislikes other people and does not want to communicate. But it means that the introvert needs time to prepare to connect and prepare to engage. When the teacher asks the class a question, the introvert prefers to think, to reflect, and then prepare an answer. Indeed, as Susan Cain explains so well,[32] the introvert feels most empowered and most energised when alone and quiet. Seligman's concept of "flourishing" needs to embrace recognising the introvert.

Part 3: the introvert and the Socratic method

Seligman's theory of authentic happiness relies on three components: positive emotion, engagement and meaning.[33] The quiet law student is often perceived as lacking engagement. This may be because the introverted student finds the Socratic method of teaching to be an ineffective means of engagement.

The Socratic method has been widely used in legal education "at the expense of virtually all other pedagogical tools".[34] The Socratic method of teaching is attributed to the ancient Athenian philosopher Socrates, whose student Plato described and recorded this teaching style in *The Republic*. The method involves the teacher asking a student to state a position and then the teacher asks a series of further questions to help the student think more deeply about the subject and also to expose weaknesses in the student's argument.[35]

The traditional Socratic method of teaching relies on vocal classroom interaction between the law teacher and individual class members. It is still used as the predominant method of teaching first-year law students in the USA and also used to varying

[30] *No Exit* in Michel Contat and Michel Rybalka (eds), *Sartre on Theater* (Quartet Books 1976) 199. This is a transcript of a spoken preface Sartre gave to a recording of the play published by the Deutsche Grammophon Gesellschaft. See also Kirk Woodward, "The Most Famous Thing Jean-Paul Sartre Never Said" (9 July 2010) <http://rickontheater.blogspot.com/2010/07/most-famous-thing-jean-paul-sartre.html> and Jonathan Webber, "There Is Something about Inez" (2011) 10(27) Think 45.

[31] Seligman (n 3).

[32] Cain (n 5).

[33] Seligman (n 3).

[34] Matt Hlinak, "The Socratic Method 2.0" (2014) 31 Journal of Legal Studies Education 1, 4.

[35] ibid 3.

levels of "dilution" in the United Kingdom, Australia and New Zealand.[36] It is alienating to many law students and has been criticised for disadvantaging female students in particular.[37] Paul Cain asserts that "[t]he Socratic method is designed to guide students (at least in theory) to 'think like lawyers'. It is not designed to enhance students' emotional acumen."[38] Perhaps the time is ripe for a study to ascertain whether it also disadvantages introverted students.

At this point, I know that the experienced (jaded) legal practitioner laments, "If they want to be lawyers, they need to get used to it! They need to think on their feet! If they can't express themselves and say what they think, then they should get out now! There's no room in the law for timidity!"

And indeed, that is exactly what I used to say when, many years ago, I first moved from legal practice to academia. They'd better get used to it, I'd say. They need to toughen up because it's tough out there. They'll get eaten alive. It's a jungle out there. They'll get thrown into the deep end. Any number of tired old clichés get hurled around when you start talking about preparation for the legal profession. Grant Morris and Kimberley Lewis (in examining modern legal education in New Zealand) note that law students have to learn to deal with an environment that is not empathetic and nurturing. They also conclude that "the processes by which students learn, and the teachers from whom they learn, can fail to create an empathetic and nurturing learning environment".[39] There is a strong push to equip students to deal with the savagery of legal practice. But this is changing too. In my own experience as a lawyer, I have noticed a marked rise in interest in wellbeing within the legal profession and a recognition that bullying and harassment are not acceptable. Twenty years ago, to suggest a continuing professional development seminar for lawyers about wellbeing would have been regarded with scepticism at best, and more likely condescension. Today, seminars and webinars on wellbeing abound and wellbeing has been officially accepted as a key component of the Standards for Australian Law Schools adopted by The Council of Australian Law Deans (CALD) which refer to a "commitment to sound educational methods and outcomes ... and the adoption of practical measures to promote student well-being".[40]

Aspasia Tsaoussi acknowledges that it is the "duty of the university teacher to impart to students the value of confidently and publicly stating their opinion".[41] I agree that developing such confidence is critical for a successful lawyer. But I also agree with Tsaoussi that the means by which students can develop such confidence can be done through methods other than dialogue-based pedagogy. There are other ways to engage students and to develop critical thinking. Tsaoussi argues that a compassionate teacher should "imagine what it must be like for timid, soft-spoken young women to become confident, vociferous law students". I suggest that this compassion should extend to all students, male, female, transgender and especially those whose natural disposition is not

---

[36] Lani Guinier and others, "Becoming Gentlemen: Women's Experiences at One Ivy League Law School" (1994) 143 University of Pennsylvania Law Review 41.

[37] Aspasia Tsaoussi, "Using Soft Skills Courses to Inspire Law Teachers: A New Methodology for a More Humanistic Legal Education" (2020) 54 The Law Teacher 1, 9.

[38] Cain (n 5) 4.

[39] Grant Morris and Kimberley Lewis, "Imaginings of Legal Education in New Zealand Fiction" (2010) 20 Legal Education Review 193, 195.

[40] Council of Australian Law Deans, Australian Law Schools Standards (2020) Clause 2.9 <https://cald.asn.au/wp-content/uploads/2020/07/Australian-Law-School-Standards-v1.3-30-Jul-2020.pdf>

[41] Tsaoussi (n 37) 11.

to be vociferous. A good lawyer does not have to be loud. In fact, as a legal practitioner, Susan Cain came to realise that lawyers who were "more measured and deliberate ... inspired the trust of both clients and adversaries".[42]

The concepts of introversion and extraversion are founded in Jungian psychology. Carl Jung's early twentieth-century theory of analytical psychology was later developed into the Myers-Briggs Type Indicator. This is a test that assesses a person's personality type. The scope of this article does not extend to a broad analysis of Jung's division of personalities into "introversion" and "extraversion" but I agree with Rachel Camp's view that "[u]nderstanding the specific behaviours associated with these terms, how those behaviours manifest themselves, and how our culture values or devalues those behaviours is critical to understanding how different individuals approach group work".[43]

According to Susan Cain, a third to a half of the population are introverts – that's one out of every two or three people. Leslie Gordon notes that more than half of lawyers are introverts.[44] Susan Greene notes a "disproportionate representation of introverts in the field of law".[45] This means we have a lot of students whose natural inclination is introversion. But teachers tend to gravitate towards the extroverts. We love it when someone asks a question, or even better, *answers* a question because it generates energy and interest, whether that is in a real classroom with everyone present or via an online platform where everyone is separate but connected on the screen. Against the background buzzwords of "student engagement" and "flipped learning" law teachers are encouraged, even forced, to design our teaching around catering to the extroverts. Those who like to sit and listen are labelled "passive", a term laced with negativity. Contemporary flipped learning strategies tend to focus on classroom discussion and interaction, the success of which is often measured by the level of noise in the room.

Seligman acknowledges that the introvert/extrovert dichotomy is relevant in the acknowledgement of "happiness". Seligman notes that "[i]ntroverts are much less cheery than extraverts, but if public policy is based ... on maximizing happiness in the mood sense, extroverts get a much greater vote than introverts. The decision to build a circus rather than a library based on how much additional happiness will be produced counts those less capable of cheerful mood more heavily than those less capable."[46] In a similar way, a teacher who relies on the shouters in the class to measure the level of engagement is ignoring the engagement of those who choose not to shout about it.

In 2020, a global pandemic changed everything and the classroom became a screen. Covid-19 not only changed the way we teach and interact with students but it also highlighted the different needs and strengths of introverted students. When all my clinic teaching was done in lockdown, remotely, through a screen, I spent time one on one with each of my students to discuss how they were individually coping with the lockdown circumstances. Particular challenges arose for the extroverts in my classes who missed the social interaction from which they would normally derive considerable energy. But many introverts thrived in the solitude of working at home. Interacting with

---

[42] Leslie A Gordon, "Introverts in an Extroverts' World" (2016) 102(1) American Bar Association Journal 36.

[43] A Rachel Camp, "Creating Space for Silence in Law School Collaborations" (2016) 65 Journal of Legal Education 897, 911.

[44] Gordon (n 42). Gordon cites a study completed by Eva Wisnik, president of the legal training and placement firm Wisnik Career Enterprises.

[45] Susan Greene, "Mindful Practices for Law Practices" (2020) 46 Ohio Northern University Law Review 53.

[46] Seligman (n 3) 14.

others on a daily basis through a screen presented other challenges. The scope of this paper does not extend to a broader discussion of the differences in remote learning for introverts and extroverts but it is important to note that any bias that teachers might have towards extroverts exists in the online environment as much as it does in a real classroom or lecture theatre.

The Socratic method of teaching is acknowledged as a means of developing a law student's ability to think critically and respond quickly to a difficult question.[47] It is also hailed as an excellent training ground for confident public speaking and problem-solving skills.[48] However, legal professionalism extends far beyond the skill of public speaking. Legal expertise requires careful reasoning and specialised advocacy. Success as a lawyer comes from clarity of thought, precision in language and logical argument. It requires tenacity and staying power. It requires the ability to think and concentrate for long periods of time. It requires deep understanding of complex theories and concepts. And it requires an empathic understanding of clients and their motivations for decision-making. Are we encouraging the wrong personality type in encouraging the extroverts?

If law students are consistently berated for not being loud enough, not being heard enough, there is perhaps a risk that they are being groomed to be loud, to be aggressive, to have the last word. This is the language of competition rather than the discourse of conciliation. We constantly reward those who are comfortable calling out the first thing that comes into their head by giving marks for class participation or by developing an unconscious bias in favour of the loudest in the class. In doing so, we may be developing a type of lawyer who lacks insight, lacks the ability to think carefully and expects to be successful by virtue of a domineering presence.

Law schools have been advocating the value of alternative dispute resolution (ADR) for many years. But the shadow of the adversarial system is long and far-reaching and it lurks behind and over all aspects of legal education. Its legacy remains in the competitive way that we train law students. The modern lawyer needs to be far more relationship-focused. The legal profession and the justice system are less focused on litigation and more attentive to mediation, collaborative lawyering, conciliation, settlement, compromise, negotiation, and relational lawyering. The courts are moving towards therapeutic jurisprudence and court diversion programmes. All of these progressive approaches to law and dispute resolution involve an approach that requires more contemplation, and more active listening than aggressive advocacy. The students who really learn how to listen may well be better prepared for the legal profession of the future than those whose expertise is only to talk.

My experience with my class of quiet students leads me to believe that perhaps as law teachers we are misreading the quiet students. Instead of labelling unresponsive students as lazy, disengaged and uninterested, I now recognise their quietness as a legitimate manifestation of engagement. As Wisnik explains "[i]t's tempting to confuse introversion with a lack of assertion, shyness or arrogance. But they're not the same thing ... it's about whether someone does most of their processing internally or prefers to talk it out."[49] I have relaxed into an expectation and acceptance of those students whose preferred state is to be contemplative.

[47]Hlinak (n 34).

[48]Tsaoussi (n 37) 2. See also Joseph A Dickinson, "Understanding the Socratic Method in Law School Teaching after the Carnegie Foundation's *Educating Lawyers*" (2009) 31 Western New England Law Review 97.

[49]Gordon (n 42) 3, 40

Part 4: emotional intelligence

Research is revealing that emotional intelligence is extremely important in a cognitively dominant profession such as law and that a good lawyer requires emotional competencies as well as technical skill.[50] Paul Cain states that helping law students deal with the emotional side of practising law is "at least as demanding, and perhaps more demanding"[51] than helping the students prepare their cases. Cain suggests that this may be due to the school curriculum focusing on the fundamental legal principles. After providing an emotional intelligence class in an internship programme, Paul Cain concludes that law schools "must train students to effectively and intelligently interact with people on an emotional basis if we are to train students to be effective, good lawyers".[52] And if law teachers expect students to be emotionally intelligent and to be able to recognise emotions in others, law teachers themselves must also develop emotional intelligence to recognise the emotions of their students. This includes emotions like frustration, anxiety, nervousness, overwhelm and the need for quiet and solitude.

An acceptance of quietness does not mean that students remain passive absorbers of information. In clinical legal education, teachers have the opportunity to spend much more "one on one" time with students than in black letter law courses. They have the opportunity to learn about their students' personality types and how they best learn. Clinical class sizes are generally smaller than in black letter law subjects. I agree with Rachel Camp that "legal educators must push students beyond their comfort zone and ask them to take risks, stretch themselves, and develop skills necessary for working with others".[53] I also agree with Camp that "in doing so, they must be careful to not ask all students to learn in ways that are best for one particular learning style".[54] I have developed new techniques for encouraging engagement at a more personal level. Where previously I encouraged (and indeed rewarded) extrovert behaviour that manifested itself in the form of comments, questions, discussion and interaction, now I allow that to happen through a more gradual process involving time for students to write and articulate their thoughts which they then submit to me or discuss with me personally. I select certain comments and ideas from their written submissions and then ask the students to discuss these particular issues in pairs or groups of three. Because they have had time to think about the overall ideas (such as client-centred practice, power differential between lawyer and client, access to justice, self-represented litigants, the role of the lawyer, ethical issues) I have found that students are more prepared to share their thoughts with others, even if that might be only one other person to start with. Gradually the discussion in pairs can extend to the larger group through my facilitation. This produces thoughtful and invigorating stimulation of ideas. I also ask my students to complete a Myers-Briggs test to determine their personality type, and we spend classroom time discussing how this affects the way that students interact with each other and also with their clients. Recognising one's own personality type is a key element of self-awareness which in turn is a significant component of empathy and emotional intelligence.

[50]See Marjorie Silver, "Emotional Intelligence and Legal Education" (1999) 5 Psychology, Public Policy & Law 1173 and Jean R Sternlight and Jennifer K Robbennolt, "Psychology and Effective Lawyering: Insights for Legal Educators" (2015) 64 Journal of Legal Education 365.

[51]Paul Cain, "A First Step Toward Introducing Emotional Intelligence into the Law School Curriculum: The 'Emotional Intelligence and the Clinic Student' Class" (2003–2004) 14 Legal Education Review 1, 4.

[52]ibid 1.

[53]Camp (n 43) 899.

[54]ibid.

Emotional intelligence has been defined as "the ability to sense, understand, and effectively apply the power and acumen of emotions as a source of human energy, information, connection, and influence".[55] Emotional intelligence also includes "self-control, zeal and persistence, and the ability to motivate oneself"[56] and "being able ... to rein in emotional impulse; to read another's innermost feelings; to handle relationships smoothly".[57] Paul Cain acknowledges that the works of the early pioneers of emotional intelligence in the 1930s and 1940s was essentially ignored until 1983, when Howard Gardner published his work describing intrapersonal and interpersonal intelligence. In 1990, emotional intelligence was further developed into five domains: knowing one's emotions, managing emotions, motivating oneself, recognising emotions in others and handling relationships.[58]

I agree with Susan Douglas that in order to develop emotional intelligence, a student needs to "think about their personal experience and communication of emotion, a client's experience and expression of emotion and the relevance of those experiences to issues of practice".[59] These topics are not easily broached and necessitate deep thought and analysis. It is understandable that many students may wish to contemplate these issues privately before articulating their thoughts publicly.

Since I first started to think about considering the personality types of law students, a number of scholars have written about the need for a more humanistic education. Aspasia Tsaoussi argues that "[l]egal pedagogy today focuses disproportionately on the model of the 'thinking lawyer', when it should equally empower students to develop the skills of a 'feeling lawyer'".[60] Tsaoussi argues that there should be a better balance between so-called "soft skills" (a term I don't like, but let's go with it for now) and "hard skills" within law curricula. Tassaousi's goal "is to gradually bring about a cultural paradigm shift".[61] This cultural paradigm shift can be extended to the way that we expect law students to be extroverts, by adapting our teaching to suit multiple personality types.

Tsaoussi proposes "a set of pedagogical principles revolving around four axes: compassionate, attentive, reason-based and empathetic teaching (CARE)".[62] Tsaoussi advocates compassionate teaching of law by "a mature, calm and reserved master of legal knowledge who is primarily responsible for creating a friendly learning environment".[63] I suggest that a consideration of the needs of introverted students in the classroom forms part of this CARE approach and would facilitate "a greater number of law professors [to] inspire their students to develop a quiet passion for the law".[64]

Compassionate teaching includes recognising a student's personality type, including whether they are introverted or extroverted. This is an important aspect of student wellbeing, a position that supports Seligman's argument about flourishing. I have elsewhere argued that law teachers have a duty to teach for the wellbeing of

[55]Robert K Cooper and Ayman Sawaf, *Executive EQ: Emotional Intelligence in Leadership and Organizations* (The Berkley Publishing Group 1998) xiii.
[56]Daniel Goleman, *Emotional Intelligence* (Bantam Books 1997) xii.
[57]ibid xiii.
[58]ibid 42.
[59]Douglas (n 6) 65.
[60]Tsaoussi (n 37) 2.
[61]ibid 3.
[62]ibid 8.
[63]ibid 9.
[64]ibid 8.

students.[65] An extensive literature is developing about the prevalence of mental illness within the legal profession and the links between emotional intelligence and wellbeing. Some research has concluded that law students suffer from anxiety and depression more than other university students and that lawyers suffer from depression more than other professionals.[66] Douglas provides a helpful overview of the literature relating to the wellbeing of law students and the legal profession and concludes that "[w]ithout further empirical research it is not possible to conclusively assert that lawyers and law students suffer higher rates and degrees of psychological distress than other professionals and student cohorts".[67] However she notes that the "existing research has been sufficient to raise real concern within the profession and the academy".[68]

The acceptance of different personality types within a cohort of students accords with the commitment to adopt practical measures to promote student wellbeing. This can be done in the same spirit in which we adapt our teaching practices for students with disabilities and health issues, including mental health issues. We also practise cultural awareness to ensure inclusivity for all students. I am advocating an awareness of different personality types as a form of modelling emotional intelligence in our teaching. I have found Camp's work useful here. Camp is of the view that "the best teachers would not ask a student who processes information in writing to instead prefer to process it orally".[69] Camp cautions against "asking a student who needs time to reflect and consider a problem before engaging, to assume a preference for discussing ideas before reflecting, and vice versa".[70]

Importantly, Camp also points out that "lawyers tend towards introversion more than the general population"[71] and that "for many lawyers, solitude is critical to creativity".[72] I crave silence and solitude when I need to write or to think through a complex or difficult problem. I also prefer to think through complex issues by myself before discussing them with others. It is only after I have struggled with a problem by myself, thinking through the pros and cons and grappling with my own attitudes, values and goals, that I am ready to share my ideas with others. There are undoubtedly many law students whose thoughts are harnessed in the same way. Recognising the strengths of introverts includes valuing those strengths and harnessing them in creative ways. This ensures deep learning for those students and facilitates more productive conversations when they are ready to share their thoughts. It also contributes to the wellbeing of everyone on the class. Importantly, Eva Wisnik observes that "introverts make good lawyers, especially for clients who want a thoughtful answer".[73]

---

[65] Claire Carroll and Rachel Spencer, "Chapter 10: On Being a Legal Educator: Responsible Teaching for Law, Justice and Wellness" in Judith Marychurch and Adiva Sifris (eds), *Wellness for Law: Making Wellness Core Business* (Lexis Nexis Butterworths 2020).

[66] Norm Kelk and others, *Courting the Blues: Attitudes towards Depression in Australian Law Students and Lawyers* (Brain and Mind Research Institute University of Sydney 2009).

[67] Douglas (n 6) 60.

[68] ibid.

[69] Camp (n 43) 899–900.

[70] ibid.

[71] ibid 900.

[72] ibid 900–01.

[73] Gordon (n 42) 1, 38

Lauren Carasik argues that "[t]his is a time of unprecedented opportunity to undertake a comprehensive and unflinching evaluation of the deeply entrenched and inflexible system of legal education"[74] in the USA. Carasik notes that "Socratic teaching, law school's 'signature pedagogy', has been widely deconstructed. Some argue that it is by its very nature damaging".[75] Carasik describes the Socratic method of teaching law as "unrelenting pressure" and "humiliating".[76] Jason Dolin declares that "the Socratic-Casebook method through which law students are taught is not only pedagogically ineffective, but is downright damaging to their mental and emotional health".[77] I have grave concerns that the Socratic method normalises the process of humiliation and that law students learn that this is how to "teach". Then they carry this normalised bullying behaviour into their professional lives and perpetuate it by the way they subsequently treat new graduates. And so the culture festers. Surely there is a kinder way. Does training lawyers have to be so mean spirited?

With a new focus on wellbeing in the legal profession, our law schools need to lead the way. The way we teach law students to interact needs to start with the way we interact with them. If we want to develop a compassionate, collegiate profession where mutual respect and empathy are the cornerstones of our practice, we should be focusing our energies on being good listeners and careful thinkers instead of competing to be the loudest and the quickest responders. Benjamin Barton is of the view that "inside the classroom, the Socratic method and semester exams encourage students to answer every question as quickly and thoroughly as possible, frequently regardless of whether they truly know the answers".[78]

The scope of this article does not extend to a thorough analysis of the Socratic method of teaching, but the Socratic method is mentioned as an example of a teaching methodology that is intimidating and alienating for law students who may be introverts. What I want to suggest here is not necessarily that the Socratic method be abandoned completely but that it be adapted to accommodate all students, including those who learn by speaking up, as well as those who learn more effectively by listening and thinking.

Conclusion

I wrote the abstract for this article pre-Covid. Since the pandemic, so much has changed, but it has reinforced the ideas that I have expressed in this article. This article has argued that much of the teaching in legal education today relies on the assumption that law students are extroverts, when the opposite is in fact often the case and that this should be considered in the context of law student wellbeing. It has explored the idea that although Seligman's argument that "connections to other people and relationships are what give meaning and purpose to life" may be true, his comments about Sartre's existentialist angst are the views of an extrovert. It has expressed agreement with Camp's views that "recognizing the importance of silence, space, and opportunity for

[74]Lauren Carasik, "Renaissance or Retrenchment: Legal Education at a Crossroads" (2011) 44 Indiana Law Review 735, 736.
[75]ibid 748.
[76]ibid 750.
[77]Jason M Dolin, "Opportunity Lost: How Law School Disappoints Law Students, the Public, and the Legal Profession" (2007) 44 California Western Law Review 219, 224.
[78]Benjamin H Barton, "A Tale of Two Case Methods" (2008) 75 Tennessee Law Review 233, 240.

reflection, legal educators [should] create an environment that implicitly and explicitly values not only contributions and approaches of the loudest and most assertive, but those of the more contemplative and deliberate".[79] It has also supported the views of Susan Cain that introverts require solitude and quietness in order to feel empowered and energised and that law teachers should be aware of this. It has explored the idea that pushing the assertive agenda is a symptom of the adversarial system that diminishes the development of less aggressive legal techniques to resolve problems like alternative dispute resolution, mediation and mindfulness. It has also suggested that progressive approaches to law and dispute resolution involve an approach that requires more contemplation, more active listening and less aggressive advocacy. I suggest that adopting a teaching methodology that embraces both introverts and extroverts not only "enrich[es] the learning environment"[80] of law students but will contribute to a kinder, more thoughtful, more reflective profession.

Acknowledgments

I am grateful to Jessica Coles-Black who provided valuable research assistance for this article.

Disclosure statement

No potential conflict of interest was reported by the author.

ORCID

Rachel Spencer http://orcid.org/0000-0002-2193-7180

[79]Camp (n 43) 934.
[80]ibid 935.

Feeling feedback: screencasting assessment feedback for tutor and student well-being

Alison Turnbull

ABSTRACT

Assessment feedback in higher education has the potential to have an impact on the well-being of both tutors and students: tutors feel their feedback workloads, while students often engage emotionally as well as cognitively with their feedback. Relatively little is written about the effects of feedback practice on tutor and student well-being. This study examined law tutors' feedback values and practices within the shifting contexts of higher education, and findings suggest that tutors experience professional tensions between their feedback values and practice. In response to this, the study also examined both tutors' and students' perceptions of the use of audio-visual feedback. The findings indicate that tutors may save time in providing their feedback in this way, and that students welcomed the relational dimensions of the medium, as well as asserting positive impacts on their feedback engagement. The findings are significant in that they offer a response to growing feedback demands which can threaten tutor well-being, as well as offering socio-affective feedback affordances for students.

Introduction

The importance of assessment feedback

Feedback should help students learn but has been described as: "less like a 'gift of learning' and more like a colonoscopy".[1] Shute[2] likens assessment feedback to a good murder where the learner needs her "MMO": her motive (a desire for feedback); her means (the ability to use it effectively); and her opportunity (future occasions to use what she has learned). Good learning design should therefore incorporate frequent, clearly signposted feedback opportunities, since these represent: "the mechanism through which students discover whether ... they are on track to meet expectations".[3] Feedback can be the single most powerful influence on student

[1] Douglas Stone and Sheila Heen, *Thanks for the Feedback: The Science and Art of Receiving Feedback Well* (1st edn, Penguin Random House 2015) 7.

[2] Valerie Shute, "Focus on Formative Feedback" (2008) 78 American Educational Research Association Review of Educational Research 153.

[3] David Boud and Elizabeth Molloy, *Feedback in Higher and Professional Education: Understanding It and Doing It Well* (1st edn, Routledge 2013) 1.

achievement, even out-stripping tutor–student in-class activity,[4] however: "higher education institutions are criticised more for inadequacies in feedback ... than for almost any other aspect of their courses".[5] The reasons for this are complex and the literature suggests that there is a dissonance between tutor and student perceptions of what constitutes good feedback.[6] However, for feedback to have any effect students clearly need to engage with it in some way and tutors need to help them achieve this. To that end, tutors are often exhorted in the feedback literature to adopt feedback practices based on social constructivism, the fundamental premise of which is that learning is experienced through language and interaction.[7] Within a feedback context, a social constructivist approach reminds us that feedback is, or should be, a two-way process involving not only tutor delivery, but also student receipt and response. This feedback partnership or "educational alliance"[8] emphasises the social process element of the feedback relationship, and Carless[9] notes a relatively recent shift in the literature on assessment feedback which aligns with this co-constructivist approach, recasting the learner as an active agent in the feedback process, while switching the tutor's role to that of feedback enabler. Malecka, Boud and Carless[10] describe these new learner-centred models as new paradigm feedback processes,[11] and Gravett[12] notes that these new models assume that students are equipped to respond to feedback, which raises questions around emotional as well as cognitive response, or as others have put it: requiring tutors to view feedback as something that students not only understand, but also feel.[13] Emotions may therefore be important not just for building rapport,[14] but also may influence future feedback engagement. Feedback which is 'done with' students rather than 'done to' them has the potential to foster both self-regulation and more sustainable feedback effects.[15]

These shifts in designing feedback practice towards more learner-focused models ask much of tutors in constructing their feedback strategies. Seeking to understand how feedback is constructed by tutors demands an understanding of the context within which the feedback is given, and how this context may interact with tutors' own feedback roles and values.

---

[4]John Hattie and Helen Timperley, "The Power of Feedback" (2007) 77 Review of Educational Research 81.

[5]Boud and Molloy (n 3) 698.

[6]Lucy Yeatman and Louise Hewitt, "Feedback: A Reflection on the Use of Nicol and Macfarlane-Dick's Feedback Principles to Engage Learners" (2021) 55 The Law Teacher 227.

[7]Erik Duval, Mike Sharples and Rosamund Sutherland (eds), *Technology Enhanced Learning: Research Themes*(1st edn, Springer International Publishing 2017).

[8]Summer Telio, Rola Ajjawi and Glenn Regehr, "The 'Educational Alliance' as a Framework for Reconceptualizing Feedback in Medical Education" (2015) 90 Academic Medicine 609.

[9]David Carless, "From Teacher Transmission of Information to Student Feedback Literacy: Activating the Learner Role in Feedback Processes" (2020) Active Learning in Higher Education (forthcoming).

[10]Bianka Malecka, David Boud and David Carless, "Eliciting, Processing and Enacting Feedback: Mechanisms for Embedding Student Feedback Literacy within the Curriculum" (2020) Teaching in Higher Education (forthcoming).

[11]Naomi Winstone and David Carless, *Designing Effective Feedback Processes in Higher Education: A Learning-Focused Approach* (Society for Research into Higher Education 2020).

[12]Karen Gravett, "Developing Students' Feedback Literacies" in Patrick Baughan (ed), *On Your Marks: Learner-Focused Feedback Practices and Feedback Literacy* (Advance HE 2020) 152.

[13]Naomi Winstone and others, "'It'd Be Useful, But I Wouldn't Use It': Barriers to University Students' Feedback Seeking and Recipience" (2017) 42 Studies in Higher Education 2026.

[14]Stephen Dixon, "The Pastoral Potential of Audio Feedback: A Review of the Literature" (2015) 33 Pastoral Care in Education: An International Journal of Personal, Social and Emotional Development 96.

[15]Sean Conley, "Dancing with Feedback: Inquiry-Based Feedback and Teacher Learning" (Doctorate in Education thesis, Columbia University 2020).

Contextual change and assessment feedback practice

The UK higher education sector continues to undergo profound change. The last 20 years have seen substantial rises in student numbers with falling levels of face-to-face teaching[16] and a diversification of the student body which some view as problematic due to the challenges which may accompany a widening participation in higher education.[17] Others assert that tuition fees and the growing industry around higher education audit in England and further afield[18] are producing not only performativity concerns for tutors,[19] but also a marketised view of higher education in general[20] and a commodification of assessment feedback in particular.[21] Political and institutional contextual shifts have the potential to influence, for good or ill, pedagogic practice around assessment feedback which finds itself situated in a fast-changing socio-political context. Some assert[22] that sound feedback practices are difficult to implement productively within the constraints of a mass higher education system, and that contextual shifts are leading to "impoverished dialogue"[23] in assessment feedback and to an issue of obstructed values for tutors.[24]

If such feedback strains do exist for tutors, what can they do in response? One part of the literature around feedback practice concerns itself with the use of audio-visual screencast technology and its potential affordances and limitations for learning, as well as tutor and student well-being. As part of a doctoral study, two research questions were framed to examine first, tutors' views around their feedback practice in the changing landscape of higher education and second, tutors' and students' perceptions of working with audio-visual feedback. An intervention was designed in which a team of tutors in a post-1992 university law school provided formative feedback on an undergraduate law degree module using audio-visual screencast technology.

Methodology and methods

The research questions demanded a conceptual framework based on an interpretive approach[25] and a flexible, qualitative research design using a case study methodology[26] was employed, sited in an LLB second year undergraduate core module. A purposive sample of four tutors teaching on the module completed contemporaneous reflective journals, took part in semi-structured interviews and attended a focus group to discuss their feedback practice and their experiences of using the screencast technology. A volunteer sample of 14 students also provided data via reflective journals and focus

---

[16]Dai Hounsell and others, "The Quality of Guidance and Feedback to Students" (2008) 27 Higher Education Research and Development 55.

[17]Stephen Dixon, "Hearing Voices: First Year Undergraduate Experience of Audio Feedback" (Doctorate in Education thesis, University of Wolverhampton 2017).

[18]Carol Evans, "Making Sense of Assessment Feedback in Higher Education" (2013) 83 Review of Educational Research 70.

[19]John Kenny, "Academic Work and Performativity" (2017) 74 Higher Education 897.

[20]Elizabeth Nixon, Richard Scullion and Robert Hearn, "Her Majesty the Student: Marketised Higher Education and the Narcissistic (Dis)satisfactions of the Student-Consumer" (2018) 43 Studies in Higher Education 927.

[21]ibid.

[22]Winstone and Carless (n 11).

[23]David Nicol, "From Monologue to Dialogue" (2010) 35 Assessment and Evaluation in Higher Education 501.

[24]J Clare Wilson and Caroline Strevens, "Perceptions of Psychological Well-Being in UK Law Academics" (2018) 52 The Law Teacher 335.

[25]Louis Cohen, Lawrence Manion and Keith Morrison, *Research Methods in Education* (7th edn, Routledge 2011).

[26]Robert K Yin, *Case Study Research: Design and Methods* (4th edn, SAGE 2009).

groups examining their experiences of working with the audio-visual feedback, their perceived relational and affective responses, and whether and how these responses might affect their subsequent feedback engagement. As so often with case study research (especially single site case studies), the number of participants was small, self-selecting and self-reporting. However, any claims for generalisability from the findings would be limited to the theoretical level using concepts of transferability or fittingness[27] rather than predictive approaches when seeking to enquire whether the data might reliably transfer to another site. The data from the study were analysed thematically using a constant comparative method,[28] and the main findings as they relate to tutor and student well-being are discussed below where participants' identities are protected via the use of pseudonyms.

Findings and discussion

A concern: tutors' feedback values, roles and well-being

The main findings relating to tutors' feedback values and their changing feedback practices were twofold: first, that professional tension existed arising from a conflict between tutors' feedback values and their feedback practice. This was experienced most acutely by tutors when delivering feedback to larger numbers of students, and tutors expressed growing concerns around viewing their feedback primarily through a work, rather than a teaching, lens. Second, the data suggested that tutors were also concerned about a growing de-professionalisation of their feedback practice resulting from what they saw as marketised approaches to learning and a commodification of feedback.

1. Tutor feedback roles and values

All tutors in the sample independently described professional, sometimes vocational, tensions between their espoused feedback values and their espoused feedback practice. These tensions were thought to flow predominantly from external shifts leading to greater student numbers, and they felt that the resultant workload intensification was the most significant negative contextual influence on their feedback practice:

> It's the numbers, because that stops you doing feedback how you really want to do [it] . . . I don't know students' names, and I can't remember when that changed. (Tutor Tess)

When asked about their feedback *values*, the tutors described feedback values centred around student support and development, often using pastoral language and an occasionally nostalgic narrative around changed feedback practice. By contrast, when asked to describe their feedback *practice*, they did so almost exclusively in terms of work, and felt that the role of feedback as work had become more dominant, describing a change towards a more process-oriented experience where performativity was becoming a professional issue for them:

> I'd like to be the teacher, but I'm somewhere between teacher and worker, because . . . I know what I'd like to do, but I can't do it that way. (Tutor Tess)

---

[27] Yvonna S Lincoln and Egon G Guba in Roger Gomm, Martyn Hammersley and Peter Foster, "Chapter 2" in *Case Study Method: Key Issues, Key Texts* (1st edn, SAGE 2002).

[28] Matthew B Miles and Michael Huberman, *Qualitative Data Analysis: An Expanded Sourcebook* (2nd edn, SAGE 1994).

There are fewer studies into tutors' than students' feedback experiences,[29] and fewer still into tutors' reflections around their feedback roles and practices.[30] Research into the changing nature of tutors' feedback roles and values also represents a limited area of discourse which has been developed, in part, by the work of Tuck.[31] Tuck examines feedback-giving as a social practice and asserts that tutors experience conflicting feedback roles: as *markers*, fulfilling institutional audit requirements; as *workers*, fulfilling contractual obligations; and as *teachers*, seeking to engage in feedback dialogue. Tuck's view that the different feedback roles produce tutor dissonance was strongly borne out by the data from the study. Tuck's description of tutors experiencing "disengagement and weariness"[32] when acting or attempting to act as "teachers" certainly found resonance, but this was thought by the tutors in the study to be caused mostly by increased student numbers, rather than the internal institutional quality assurance constraints identified by Tuck's participants, and was more reminiscent of Nicol when he states:

> most teachers feel overwhelmed by the workload associated with providing ... feedback when numbers are large.[33]

There was also strong data in the current study showing that the tutors were beginning to view their feedback more through a 'work' lens than a 'teaching' lens. As Tuck notes, analysis of feedback-giving as *work* has been "relatively absent from previous studies",[34] but the data here supports her view that feedback practice is in danger of becoming a work-dominated aspect of academic practice. The evidence of a professional, and in some cases vocational, tension where tutors feel that their feedback practice and values chafe, supports the view of Isomottonen[35] that tutors may find themselves: "'squeezed between' two stakeholders: students and administration",[36] and that the tensions felt are largely tacit. That these tensions were strongly associated with growing student numbers chimes with the work of Kenny[37] who asserts that sector changes have led not only to increased workloads, but also to increased stress for academic tutors, and Jones and others[38] describe this as a threat to tutors' well-being.

2. Marketisation and de-professionalisation

The tutors in the study expressed strong feelings around the impacts of a perceived marketisation of higher education which they felt made their feedback practice more high-risk. This manifested for them in two ways: first, they felt that tuition fees encouraged a growing consumerist student mentality resulting in grade fixation and a commodification of assessment feedback; and second, they felt that this had led to a challenge and complaint culture around feedback as well as assessment grades. Both

---

[29] Evans (n 18).
[30] Nicola Reimann and Ian Sadler, "Personal Understanding of Assessment and the Link to Assessment Practice: The Perspectives of Higher Education Staff" (2017) 42 Assessment and Evaluation in Higher Education 724.
[31] Jackie Tuck, "Feedback-Giving as Social Practice: Teachers' Perspectives on Feedback as Institutional Requirement, Work and Dialogue" (2012) 17 Teaching in Higher Education 209.
[32] ibid 217.
[33] Nicol (n 23) 511.
[34] Tuck (n 31) 215.
[35] Ville Isomottonen, "For the Oppressed Teacher: Stay Real!" (2018) 23 Teaching in Higher Education 869.
[36] ibid 870.
[37] Kenny (n 19).
[38] Emma Jones and others, "Student Well-Being and Assessment in Higher Education: A Balancing Act" (2021) 46 Assessment and Evaluation in Higher Education 438.

these shifts were described by them as having the potential to threaten their professional status. They felt that students were increasingly viewing themselves as consumers of a feedback product, rather than engaging in a feedback process:

> [but] we're not talking about a product, we're talking about people and people's education, which to me isn't a product, so they don't . . . sit very easily for me. (Tutor Cherie)

The discourse around the interface between higher education and the marketplace continues to grow apace, and since the introduction of tuition fees in 2004 there has been an understandable concern within the academy around standards and the possible effects of a consumer mentality on learning and teaching. The view of Collini that: "the paradox of real learning is that you don't get what you 'want' and you certainly can't buy it"[39] has at its heart a concern around student ends-focused expectations, and the dissonance which can occur when seeking to apply market ideology to the often unpredictable landscape of learning and personal development, where criticism and perseverance may be what is needed, but not wanted. Cheng[40] asserts that while an interest in the quality of education is both legitimate and desirable, the application of free market logic to the student–tutor relationship increases attention on grades, prioritises financial over educational outcomes, and can switch focus from student effort in learning to a more passive reception of educational merchandise. This, Cheng claims, ignores both the emancipatory power of higher education and what he terms: "the people-building purpose of higher education".[41] This refocusing to product rather than process becomes, in the context of assessment feedback, a potential issue of commodification.

Nixon and others[42] take the discussion around commodification a stage further and, while welcoming accountability structures which improve the quality of educational offering, suggest that a novel shift is occurring where the student in a marketised context can operate not just as a passive consumer of education, but as an active *customer*. This, they suggest, lies at the root of a new and disturbing pattern of unwarranted student complaint which finds echoes in the current study where tutors described changing academic behaviour to accommodate what they saw as a more litigious climate. This concern may be justified in light of reports from the Office of the Independent Adjudicator for Higher Education of an increase of over 70% in the number of student complaints between 2016 and 2020. In the context of legal education, the number of complaints in 2020 was ranked fifth highest by discipline.[43] Additional market mechanisms such as student charters, the institutionalisation of complaints procedures and the application of consumer law to the provision of higher education may all serve to heighten consumerist approaches on the part of students. The compelling evidence of concern among the tutor sample that students were engaging in consumerist approaches to learning in general, and to feedback in particular, appears to support the work of both Nixon and Cheng.

---

[39] Stefan Collini, "From Robbins to McKinsey" (2011) 33 London Review of Books 3.

[40] Ming Cheng, "Reclaiming Quality in Higher Education: A Human Factor Approach" (2017) 23 Quality in Higher Education 153.

[41] ibid 156.

[42] Nixon and others (n 20).

[43] Office of the Independent Adjudicator, Annual Report 2020 <https://www.oiahe.org.uk/media/2470/oia-annual-report-2019.pdf> accessed 12 May 2021.

A response: screencasting feedback for well-being

The tutors in the study gave screencast feedback to their students and the data from both tutors and students were analysed for practical, relational and affective potentials for tutor and student well-being.

1. Practical dimensions

While acknowledging the 'halo effect' of using a novel technology,the literature concludes that audio-visual feedback is, on the whole, welcomed by students,[44] who report generally higher levels of satisfaction with it compared to written feedback.[45] This was largely borne out by the students in the study. While tutors' views on audio-visual feedback are currently under-researched,[46] many studies also show that tutors generally support its use[47] and, again, the tutors in the study mainly echoed this, some even reporting a renewed enthusiasm for their feedback practice, echoing tutors in the study of Henderson and Phillips.[48]

There was agreement among the tutor sample that producing written feedback could be time-consuming and that providing feedback via audio-visual means had the potential to lighten feedback workloads. However, there was some difference of view around how they worked with the screencast technology and whether it had in fact saved them time. All the tutors felt that their reliance on detailed written notes to support their audio-visual performance reduced significantly as they progressed, though to differing degrees, and these variations in approach were similar to the practices of the tutors in the study of Vincelette and Bostic.[49] The tutors also felt that since they were not trained typists, there was the potential for them to save time by giving their feedback in the audio form. However, they expressed concern that they were not able to use generic or 'cut and paste' feedback when working with audio-visual technology as they might when giving written feedback, reporting that they accordingly spent time making the same points many times over to different students. Acknowledging technological challenges,[50] three of the four tutors concluded that they saved time overall compared to their written feedback practice, and while this issue remains hotly contested in the literature, the majority view of the tutors aligns with most of the previous research,[51] while challenging the work of others including Borup and others.[52] Significantly, all the tutors reported giving more feedback, more feedforward and more explanatory comment, and three out of four maintained that they did so while still saving time overall.

---

[44]Elizaveta Sopina and Rob McNeill, "Investigating the Relationship between Quality, Format and Delivery of Feedback for Written Assignments in Higher Education" (2015) 40 Assessment and Evaluation in Higher Education 666.

[45]Susanne Voelkel and Luciane Mello, "Audio Feedback – Better Feedback?" (2014) 22 Bioscience Education 16.

[46]Trevor Kettle, "Using Audio Podcasts to Provide Student Feedback: Exploring the Issues" (2007) Working Papers in Health Sciences 1.

[47]Paige Mahoney, Susie Macfarlane and Rola Ajjawi, "A Qualitative Synthesis of Video Feedback in Higher Education" (2019) 24 Teaching in Higher Education 157.

[48]Michael Henderson and Michael Phillips, "Video-Based Feedback on Student Assessment: Scarily Personal" (2015) 31 Australasian Journal of Educational Technology 51.

[49]Elizabeth Jackson Vincelette and Timothy Bostic, "Show and Tell: Student and Instructor Perceptions of Screencast Assessment" (2013) 18 Assessing Writing 257.

[50]Alan Cann, "Engaging Students with Audio Feedback" (2014) 22 Bioscience Education 31.

[51]John West and Will Turner, "Enhancing the Assessment Experience: Improving Student Perceptions, Engagement and Understanding Using Online Video Feedback" (2016) 53 Innovations in Education and Teaching International 400.

[52]Jered Borup, Richard E West and Rebecca Thomas, "The Impact of Text Versus Video Communication on Instructor Feedback in Blended Courses" (2015) 63 Educational Technology Research and Development 161.

All the tutors agreed that physical *workspace* had become a challenge in their feedback practice since they all worked in shared offices, some with over a dozen academic colleagues, and accordingly recording audio-visual feedback at work was, they felt, often impractical. They cited difficulties in achieving the seclusion they felt they needed for audio-visual feedback in the office, with some also experiencing difficulties recording their feedback at home. This is in line with other work where tutors report needing to: "set aside space and time"[53] to allow for the performance elements of the medium. These issues around workspace represented an emerging issue and continued to be reported while tutors worked at home during the lockdown periods of the pandemic.

The students in the study welcomed the flexibility of audio-visual feedback and some reported that using the technology to access their feedback found some synergy with their private lives, with student Megan reporting accessing her audio feedback on her mobile telephone while cooking her tea. Some have termed this the "Martini effect"[54] and these findings are in sharp contrast to the recent work of Kay and Bahula who describe negative accessibility potentials of the medium.[55] In terms of potential reverberation on student feedback use, audio-visual delivery seems to promise potential for students to engage more fully with their feedback by offering increased flexibility.[56]

Difficulties with navigating through audio-visual feedback and later returning to review it were, however, noted by both tutors and students as posing challenges to engagement with the medium. Many students preferred written feedback in this regard, which they felt was easier and quicker for them to navigate, and this aligns with the majority of the studies in the area.[57] There was some suggestion in the study that students were forced to engage differently with audio-visual feedback, and that the multi-modal nature of audio-visual feedback can encourage deeper feedback engagement due to the cognitive demands it places on students to work with it, and this issue of qualitatively different feedback engagement is a theme in the work of both Orlando[58] and Dixon.[59] The students in the study, however, did not welcome spending more time and cognitive effort engaging with their feedback, and intimated that the additional effort required in this regard could negatively affect their feedback engagement.

2. Relational dimensions: presence, connection and care

Mahoney and others (2019) assert that the potential of audio-visual feedback lies principally in its relational possibilities and may serve to strengthen tutor–student relationships. In terms of student well-being, the relational dimensions of receiving

---

[53]ibid 168.

[54]Sally Quinn and Julian Oldmeadow, "The Martini Effect and Social Networking Sites: Early Adolescents, Mobile Social Networking and Connectedness to Friends" (2013) 12 Mobile Media and Communication 237.

[55]Robin Kay and Timothy Bahula, "A Systematic Review of the Literature on Video Feedback Used in Higher Education" (12th International Conference on Education and New Learning Technologies, 2020, University of Ontario Institute of Technology, Canada, 6th and 7th July 2020, DOI 10.21125/edulearn.2020.0606).

[56]Michael Carmichael, Abigail-Kate Reid and Jeffrey D Karpicke, "Assessing the Impact of Educational Video on Student Engagement, Critical Thinking and Learning: The Current State of Play" (SAGE 2018).

[57]For example, Edd Pitt and Lin Norton, "'Now That's the Feedback I Want!' Students' Reactions to Feedback on Graded Work and What They Do with It" (2017) 42 Assessment and Evaluation in Higher Education 499.

[58]John Orlando, "A Comparison of Text, Voice and Screencasting Feedback to Online Students" (2016) 30 American Journal of Distance Education 156.

[59]Dixon (n 17).

audio-visual feedback loomed large in the study and two themes with the potential to have an impact on well-being arose for consideration: perceptions of presence and connection; and perceptions of care.

In terms of perceptions of presence, some students reported feeling that their audio-visual feedback was akin to 'meeting' with their tutor. This aligns with the works of Grigoryan[60] and Kay and Bahula[61] who assert that audio-visual feedback has the potential to produce perceptions of social presence via an illusion of transparency or non-mediation, supporting the earlier theoretical work of Lehman.[62] There was strong data from both tutors and students that these perceptions of presence led on, for some, to perceptions of connection between them. Students talked in terms of 'walls' or 'barriers' being removed by the audio-visual medium: "I feel that it removes the wall that tends to be built up through the words ... used in feedback when it is written" (Student Alia). Appreciation of these feelings of connection was noted with particular strength in the reflective journals of the six students in the sample who spoke English as a second language (hereinafter referred to as 'international' students), and also by student Jenny who disclosed a life-long mental health condition. The tutors giving the audio feedback also welcomed what they saw as the enhanced relational possibilities of audio delivery:

> I felt more connected with the student doing it that way ... because I'd call them by their name ... it gave me a bit more of a connection with them ... It's a human thing, isn't it? (Tutor Sarah)

These perceptions of presence and connection were taken further by some of the students who described enhanced feelings of *care* on the part of their tutors. For some, this took the form of caring more about their work and their academic progress supporting the work of Knauf,[63] while others felt that their tutors cared more about them and reported feeling more supported by their tutors, echoing Dixon's study.[64] Additional significance of these perceptions of connection and care may lie in their potential to positively affect feedback engagement, and this seemed again to be particularly the case for the international students in the study and for student Jenny, who asserted that her audio-visual feedback helped relieve the anxiety associated with her mental health condition.

Perceptions of presence, connection and care have led some to laud the audio-visual medium for its rapport-building or pastoral potentialities,[65] and this was borne out by tutor Cherie's data in particular when she reported an increased number of students to whom she had given audio-visual feedback later seeking her out for pastoral as well as further academic advice. She wondered whether this could be due to a reduction in social distance associated with the medium. If so, this would align with the views of

---

[60] Anna Grigoryan, "Audiovisual Commentary as a Way to Reduce Transactional Distance and Increasing Teaching Presence in Online Writing Instruction: Student Perceptions and Preferences" (2017) 3 Journal of Response to Writing 83.

[61] Kay and Bahula (n 56).

[62] Rosemary Lehman, "The Role of Emotion in Creating Instructor and Learner Presence in the Distance Learning Experience" (2006) 2 Journal of Cognitive and Affective Learning 12.

[63] Helen Knauf, "Reading, Listening and Feeling: Audio Feedback as a Component of an Inclusive Learning Culture at Universities" (2016) 41 Assessment and Evaluation in Higher Education 442.

[64] Stephen Dixon, "The Pastoral Potential of Audio Feedback: A Review of the Literature" (2015) 33 Pastoral Care in Education: An International Journal of Personal, Social and Emotional Development 96.

[65] ibid.

both Brearley and Cullen[66] and Mahoney, Macfarlane and Ajjawi[67] and may signal interesting shifts in the tutor/student feedback relationship. Knauf[68] asserts that the use of audio-visual feedback can contribute not only to feelings of connection and care, but also more generally to the development of an inclusive university. The data of the international students in the study suggests that the medium offers particularly significant potentialities for such students by encouraging their access to and use of feedback. Some of these students described feeling less anxious in relation to their audio-visual feedback, and this builds on the recent work of Olave-Encina and others,[69] who suggest that such students' relationship with assessment feedback is largely negative, and that building trust and connection is crucial. Student Jenny's feedback experience suggests that there might be similar affordances for students facing mental health challenges, and develops the recent work of Jones and others[70] who examine assessment and well-being and assert that feedback is becoming a pastoral as well as a pedagogic practice.

3. Affective dimensions

Molloy and others assert that: "feedback is an inherently emotional business [that] can have a lasting impact beyond its intent",[71] and many of the student participants talked with some passion about how they responded to feedback (both generally and in relation to the feedback in the study) at both cognitive and affective levels, asserting that their emotional response could eclipse their rational response at least in the short term, and this finds echoes in the literature.[72] The interaction between emotions and assessment feedback is a relatively under-researched area, despite the existence of an already established literature around emotions and learning more generally.[73] Emotional reactions to feedback can be significant since they can alter a student's perception and acceptance of her feedback, as well as changing her engagement with it. The students in the study acknowledged that their reactions to feedback could be variable, but, significantly, felt that the medium of feedback delivery could affect how they viewed their feedback, lending weight to the recent work of Winstone and Carless who advocate[74] that the medium of feedback delivery can strongly affect the extent to which students both accept and engage with their feedback.

The students were asked how they normally felt when receiving written feedback and while acknowledging that different students may have different affective responses to feedback, and deal with those responses in different ways, there was strong evidence from the students that they often experienced negative feelings on written feedback

---

[66] Francis Q Brearley and W Rod Cullen, "Providing Students with Formative Audio Feedback" (2012) 20 Bioscience Education 22.

[67] Mahoney, Macfarlane and Ajjawi (n 48).

[68] Knauf (n 64).

[69] Karen Olave-Encina, Karen Moni and Peter Renshaw, "Exploring the Emotions of International Students about Their Feedback Experiences" (2021) 40 Higher Education Research & Development 810.

[70] Jones and others (n 38).

[71] Elizabeth Molloy, Francesc Borrell-Carrion and Ron Epstein, "The Impact of Emotions in Feedback" in David Boud and Elizabeth Molloy (eds), *Feedback in Higher and Professional Education: Understanding It and Doing It Well* (Routledge 2013) 51.

[72] Tony Dowden and others, "Students' Perceptions of Written Feedback in Teacher Education: Ideally Feedback Is a Continuing Two-Way Communication that Encourages Progress" (2013) 38 Assessment and Evaluation in Higher Education 349.

[73] Anna D Rowe, Julie Fitness and Leigh N Wood, "The Role and Functionality of Emotions in Feedback at University: A Qualitative Study" (2014) 41 The Australian Association for Research in Education 283.

[74] Winstone and Carless (n 11).

receipt. This echoes the work of Pitt and Norton who assert that negative feelings are often associated with feedback and can produce what they term "emotional backwash".[75] The tutors, while acknowledging that feedback receipt was an affective as well as a cognitive experience, thought that students' negative responses to feedback could be attributable not only to the judgements involved in the feedback process, but also to the higher-risk landscape of higher education involving tuition fees and, for many law students, the prospect of entering a progressively competitive job market. They felt that this could produce feelings of vulnerability and affect the emotions students attached to their grades and feedback. In addition, some of the tutors felt that students could suffer from what they saw as a lack of emotional resilience and advocated the need for students to build what has been termed "academic buoyancy".[76] Shafi and others[77] argue that an active process of feedback dialogue which includes socio-emotional support could be key in developing this academic buoyancy and mediating emotional response.

The students in the study were also asked to describe the feelings which they had associated with their screencast feedback. They reported two principal responses: feeling 'encouraged' and feeling 'motivated'. They asserted that their audio-visual feedback was, in the main, less judgemental than they were used to and spoke more to the positives than the negatives of their work, which some of them found encouraging and which they associated with higher levels of support from their tutors. The significance of feeling encouraged for some students was that they felt this increased their motivation to engage with their feedback or with their studies more generally. The largely positive emotions associated with audio-visual feedback lend strength to the work of those such as Winstone and others[78] who assert that feedback is not only something which students understand and do, but is also something which they *feel*, and challenges the recent work of Kay and Bahula[79] who conclude that evocation of negative emotions is a danger of the audio-visual medium. The data from the students around the effect their emotions could have on their feedback engagement also aligns with the work of Shafi and others,[80] who argue that emotional response can be used to positively affect feedback engagement and can move students towards what Winstone terms "pro-active feedback recipience".[81]

Responses to feedback, whether positive or negative, may of course be highly nuanced, with affective responses mediated by a number of factors, including a student's disposition, her prior feedback experiences and, one might add, her state of digestion, resulting in a considerable variety of feedback response.[82] One area which attracted more discussion than any other in relation to feedback and feelings related to students' receipt of feedback criticism. The tutors were alive to the potential affective consequences of their feedback and some felt that audio-visual feedback could allow

---

[75] Pitt and Norton (n 58) 1.

[76] Adeela Ahmed Shafi and others, "The Role of Assessment Feedback in Developing Academic Buoyancy" (2018) 43 Assessment and Evaluation in Higher Education 415.

[77] ibid.

[78] Naomi Winstone and others, "'It'd Be Useful, But I Wouldn't Use It': Barriers to University Students' Feedback Seeking and Recipience" (2017) 42 Studies in Higher Education 2026.

[79] Kay and Bahula (n 56).

[80] Shafi and others (n 77).

[81] Winstone and others (n 79) 2041.

[82] Mantz Yorke, "Formative Assessment in Higher Education: Moves Towards Theory and the Enhancement of Pedagogic Practice" (2003) 45 Higher Education 477.

them to 'soften the blows' of criticism: "It made it easier to deliver feedback that might have seemed 'colder' in writing ... to tell somebody ... in a way that was more constructive" (Tutor Cherie). Once again, student Jenny found receiving feedback via audio to be particularly helpful to her, and she shared that she normally did not access her written feedback at all, since it triggered anxiety which was associated with her otherwise well-controlled mental health condition. She found the socio-affective affordances of the medium helped her to access and accept critique: "Receiving the feedback felt a lot more personal, making the improvements needed seem less like failing" (Student Jenny). Other students, however, felt that audio may not be well suited to the delivery of a lot of feedback criticism: "Imagine ... eight minutes of 'this is wrong, this is wrong', [laughter] probably wouldn't be very motivating" (Student Marea).

Conclusions

The findings from this study are drawn from a small-scale study from which one cannot generalise, save at a theoretical level. They also appear against a particular contextual backdrop involving an ongoing neoliberalisation of the higher education sector which continues to exert pressure in various forms upon universities and their employees. It has been noted that tutors' feedback practices and experiences represent an under-researched area. The data suggest that there is evidence of professional dissonance resulting from fractured feedback relationships and practices linked to higher education contextual change, and that professional feedback tensions exist, in part, due to obstructed feedback values and practices. This finds particular support in the work of Tuck,[83] most especially in relation to a shift to a work, rather than a teaching, feedback lens. The study also builds on Tuck's work where tutors expressed strong concerns around feedback commodification, student feedback complaint and personal reputational risk. The finding in relation to pressures around feedback workspace seems to represent an emerging issue.

Screencasting feedback might be a useful, partial response to these feedback practice strains. The findings around the intervention align in large part with existing literature to support the proposition that feedback generally can often produce negative emotional 'backwash', and that screencast technology offers particular affordances in relation to its socio-affective dimensions. Principally, the study advocates the advantages of flexibility, tutor time saving, and enhanced perceptions of social presence, connection and caring. The study also aligns with existing work in relation to the limitations of the medium in terms of navigation and reviewability. The findings challenge prior work which suggests that negative emotions are often associated with the receipt of audio-visual feedback; and that tutors in higher education are insufficiently aware of the emotional dimensions of their feedback practice. The findings are significant in that first, the relational affordances of the medium were of particular importance to the international students in the sample, as well as to a student facing mental health challenges, and positive impacts on these students' feedback engagement were reported by them. Second, audio-visual feedback may stimulate subsequent dialogue of a pastoral as well as pedagogic nature, which may be of significance in building inclusivity and student well-being.

[83] Tuck (n 31).

The existing research on audio-visual feedback suffers from a number of limitations, but most significantly Mahoney and others[84] assert that the current state of play of the research into audio-visual feedback discloses little evidence of any *impact* on students' subsequent academic performance, with few studies reporting on whether the relational or other affordances of the medium translate into student action or any measurable learning gains. They conclude that current findings on the impact of the medium are limited and that merely viewing a practice through a socio-constructivist lens does not avoid the fact that many studies have: "merely substituted one medium (written) for another (video)".[85] Their central concern remains that audio-visual feedback, while perhaps creating an illusion of dialogue, may still offer limited avenues for students to respond and to develop agency.

Feedback is, however, not just about its impacts, but also about the subjective experiences of those giving and receiving it. While it may be fair to assert that tutors should avoid unnecessarily wounding their students in providing feedback, it may equally be contended that students cannot and should not seek to escape the discomfort or emotional pain associated with challenge or failure, which is often a valuable part of the human learning experience.[86] Beard and others[87] argue, however, that we need richer conceptions of students as affective as well as cognitive beings, and a clearer theorisation of the role of emotion in educational encounters which can be achieved, they assert, without a collapse into therapeutic discourse.

As incentive to reflect further on our own feedback practice, one might consider whether it is true that: "individuals at any point on their path from novice to expert are able to recount a 'painful feedback anecdote'".[88] One challenge tutors face is that feedback is largely a sub-silencio practice[89] open to quick fixes or 'nostrums', often based neither on sound theory nor on evaluated practice.[90] Audio-visual feedback must therefore be seen as only one part of a more holistic, person-centred response to student learning and, as our feedback practice develops, it is a wise person who knows what to embrace and what to leave behind.[91] To reclaim feedback well-being for both tutors and students involves institutional commitment of time and resource, and there can be no clearer driver for this than the consistently low National Student Survey results for assessment and feedback, which for most universities persist year on year.[92] Audio-visual technologies may have something to offer in the rebuilding of emotionally aware pedagogic relationships fractured by contextual change, and its reported affordances, both pedagogic and socio-affective, suggest that it may be worth considering as part of our feedback practice. In the particular context of law

---

[84] Mahoney, Macfarlane and Ajjawi (n 48).

[85] ibid 170.

[86] AlexForsythe and Sophie Johnson, "Thanks, But No Thanks for the Feedback" (2017) 42 Assessment and Evaluation in Higher Education 850.

[87] Colin Beard, Sue Clegg and Karen Smith, "Acknowledging the Affective in Higher Education" (2007) 33 British Educational Research Journal 235.

[88] Molloy and others (n 72) 17.

[89] David Boud, "Reframing Assessment as if Learning Was Important" in David Boud and Nancy Falchikov (eds), *Rethinking Assessment in Higher Education: Learning for the Longer Term* (Routledge 2007).

[90] Boud and Molloy (n 3).

[91] Antonio Martinez-Arboleda, "Student Feedback through Desktop Capture: Creative Screencasting" (Seventh International Conference on E-Learning and E-Technologies in Education, Lodz, Poland, ICEEE, 17-19 September 2018).

[92] Alistair Blair and others, "What Feedback Do Students Want?" (2013) 33 Learning and Teaching in Politics and International Studies 66.

tutoring, Jones notes: "emotions have a fundamental role to play in student learning … in the emotional well-being of law students and in relation to both the work and well-being of legal academics".[93]

Acknowledgments

With thanks to the tutors and students who engaged in this research and to my colleagues who reviewed drafts of this work.

Disclosure statement

No potential conflict of interest was reported by the author.

[93]Emma Jones, "Transforming Legal Education through Emotions" (2018) 38 Legal Studies 450-465.

The role of employer/educator collaboration in improving the wellbeing of lawyers

Nigel Jones

ABSTRACT

Well before Covid struck, wellbeing was already being taken seriously by organisations involved in both the education and employment of lawyers. Both groups were looking for ways to help lawyers keep themselves well, build their personal resilience and help them thrive in the profession. The crisis has added further impetus to those endeavours, and made wellbeing an even higher priority. This paper considers whether the chances of achieving those objectives would be increased if the two stakeholder groups collaborated more effectively, and what that collaboration might look like. Its focus is on the UK profession. It is written from the employer perspective, in particular that of large law firms based in the City of London. And it is primarily based on the first-hand experience of the author. It also considers the approach of other employers and the broader stakeholder community (including in the third sector), based on personal communications and published literature. It explains why those employers are taking lawyer wellbeing more seriously, what steps they have taken and which they believe are having a positive impact, and how the training of their future employees might be changed in order to help maintain their health. Its objective is to promote debate between educators and employees about what better collaboration might look like.

> To be a good lawyer, one has to be a healthy lawyer. Sadly, our profession is falling short when it comes to well-being.

So said a 2017 report on the state of the US legal profession.[1] Many would say the comments apply equally to the UK profession. This paper advocates greater collaboration between employers[2] and educators to change things for the better.[3] Its aim is to stimulate both debate and action.

---

[1]See <www.americanbar.org/groups/lawyer_assistance/task_force_report/>, December 2019 providing an update on progress since the publication in August 2017 of a report entitled "National Task Force on Lawyer Well-Being: Creating a Movement to Improve Well-Being in the Legal Profession", page 1 (14 August 2017) (also accessible through this link). The report went on to say this: ". . . too many lawyers and law students experience chronic stress and high rates of depression and substance use. These findings are incompatible with a sustainable legal profession, and they raise troubling implications for many lawyers' basic competence. This research suggests that the current state of lawyers' health cannot support a profession dedicated to client service and dependent on the public trust", page 1.

[2]Throughout this paper, I use "employer" as shorthand for all such organisations, including those in which lawyers operate in other capacities (eg sole practitioners (whether solicitors or barristers), partners and consultants).

[3]It is based on a paper originally prepared as pre-reading for a November 2019 discussion at York Law School on whether increased employer/educator collaboration would help, and, if so, what it might look like. The consensus from that discussion was that it would. That is consistent with input the author has received from

Introduction

Wellbeing is now taken seriously by most UK organisations in which lawyers work. And many of those organisations are taking action to help lawyers look after themselves. The fact that so many City law firms are active members of the City Mental Health Alliance, and are implementing many of the lessons shared through that organisation, illustrates the increased commitment being made to this topic. The same goes for many other stakeholders in the legal and higher education communities – including the Law Society, the Bar Council, universities and law schools, charities and other bodies.

Widespread cynicism remains, however, about whether employers are really committed to change, or whether, as a 2019 *Law Society Gazette* article claimed, at least some – including City law firms – are "bribing people back into the [broken] culture" on the basis that "you always have enough people queueing up to train and to get some good money".[4] Many lawyers, particularly those who are relatively new to the profession, cite examples of people in senior management positions in employer organisations not "walking the talk" – and of employers which they believe pay lip service to their stress management or wellbeing policies in their day-to-day working arrangements. And even those whose commitment is clear recognise that this remains a significant issue and that more can and should be done.[5] There is no doubt that the Covid-19 crisis has caused everyone in the legal community (and of course elsewhere) to take wellbeing even more seriously. But that has still not translated into 100% compliance with what many would regard as good practice, and in some cases it has made matters worse.

Remote working has, for example, made it possible to schedule back-to-back calls (or virtual meetings) throughout the day and into the evening (and in many cases beyond). That prevents people taking critically important regular breaks, leaves people with no time to prepare healthy meals, take exercise or pause for reflection – and in many cases negatively affects sleep patterns. When prompted to consider whether any of those developments are good for business, senior people generally realise that the answer is a

a range of other stakeholders. So this amended version takes that as its premise. (The author would like to express his gratitude to York faculty members Peter Harrison and Dimitrios Tsarapatsanis for issuing the invitation to lead that discussion, and, in doing so, encouraging him to consider this issue in more detail; and to the many others who kindly commented on the discussion paper, and whose views the author has sought to reflect here.) It has been updated only to a limited extent since the Covid-19 crisis struck, as the key messages have not been changed by the crisis.

[4]"City Firms 'Bribing' NQs to Tolerate 'Broken Culture'" *Law Society Gazette* (30 September 2019) <www.lawgazette.co.uk/news/city-firms-bribing-nqs-to-tolerate-broken-culture/5101602.article>.

[5]The fact that lawyers (both in education and in the workforce) face higher risks of mental illness than other professions has been established by authors such as Martin Seligman, PhD (eg in his 2002 book *Authentic Happiness,* Free Press) and Kennon Sheldon and Lawrence Krieger (eg in "Understanding the Negative Effects of Legal Education on Law Students: A Longitudinal Test of Self-Determination Theory" (2007) 33 Personality and Social Psychology Bulletin 883). Reliable statistics directly relevant to lawyers in the UK are hard to come by, but the following examples demonstrate the scale of the broader issue, including for younger people: (a) about half of millennials and 75% of Gen Z'ers have left a job for mental health reasons (see Kelly Greenwood, Vivek Bapat and Mike Maughan, "Research: People Want Their Employers to Talk about Mental Health" Harvard Business Review (October 2019) <https://hbr.org/2019/10/research-people-want-their-employers-to-talk-about-mental-health>); (b) poor mental health costs the UK economy between £74 billion and £99 billion a year; and (c) analysis by Deloitte commissioned in the Farmer/Stevenson report shows that the cost to employers is between £33 billion and £42 billion of this number (see P Farmer and D Stevenson, "Thriving at Work: The Stevenson/Farmer Review on Mental Health and Employers" (2017) <https://assets.publishing.service.gov.uk/government/uploads/system/uploads/attachment_data/file/658145/thriving-at-work-stevenson-farmer-review.pdf>).

clear no: tired, demotivated people perform less well, make more mistakes, stay with employers for shorter periods, and describe the work environment to future potential employees very negatively. It is bad for business whichever way it is viewed. Yet it continues, and in the author's view will continue as remote working becomes part of the norm – unless leaders take positive steps to address it.

Remote working also makes many aspects of a positive work experience more difficult: the "water cooler" informal chats; getting to know (really know) your boss/work colleagues so that you can build trusting relationships; seeking and receiving authentic, valuable, constructive feedback (only really possible in face-to-face conversations); creativity; and effective learning and development (which for the author worked best through in-person interaction – including while sharing an office with his principal as an articled clerk in the 1980s, a process which, even pre-Covid, seemed to be gradually disappearing from many workplaces and which has been impossible while working from home).

Collaboration is already helping: with competing law firms working together on the topic, and engaging more constructively with clients and the Bar.

Clients can play an important role in catalysing change in this area, just as they have done in relation for example to diversity and inclusion and environmental issues. Many already are (for example in leading on the Mindful Business Charter (see below) and those who already include wellbeing as one of the criteria taken into account when selecting law firms). But many are not, and the demands of some clients are cited by many law firms as the reason they can't risk changing.

Similar considerations apply to the way solicitors interact with barristers, and within barristers' chambers themselves (e.g. the way clerks allocate work). The best working relationships the author had with members of the Bar were those in which everyone in the team knew what commitments others had outside the workplace (caring responsibilities, artistic or sporting interests/rehearsals, family/religious commitments, etc.), respected those commitments when planning the work schedule and avoided unhelpful/snide comments about "working from home" (now, of course, rightly respected as at least as effective, if not more so, than being in an office or chambers), "slacking" (when not available to take evening or weekend calls) or failing to pull their weight – and instead focused on how to use the skills and time of each team member most efficiently. Conversely, the worst such relationships tended to be those in which the team leader assumed that everyone would be available whenever he (generally, rather than she) might decide he would like their input, without any forward planning to consider what else team members might need or want to be spending their time doing.

Before suggesting what educator/employer collaboration might look like, this paper summarises what some employers are doing to help their people keep themselves well (focusing on City law firms but also touching on others), then considers from the employer perspective what law schools might do differently to help in that endeavour. Again, the Covid-19 crisis has not fundamentally changed employers' approaches, other than requiring them to make all interactions virtual.

Employers: attitudes and actions

Many employers have for many years provided employee benefits, and engaged in broader initiatives, directed at helping people to keep themselves physically healthy and ease access to treatment for physical sickness. Examples include private medical insurance, on-site GPs, staff restaurants offering healthy meals, and subsidised gym membership. And in that respect, many lawyers have for some time been getting a better deal than people in other workplaces. People working in small and medium size enterprises (including many law firms), for example, will seldom have those benefits, and their availability in many non-legal corporate, public or third sector employers will be (or certainly in the past has been) much more limited.

More recently, increasing numbers of employers have added measures to address what they refer to as "mental health" – though in reality many were instead simply providing safety nets to help deal with mental *ill* health.

It has however taken most organisations longer to recognise that the overall health of their people (with physical and mental being inextricably linked) is fundamental to their success.[6] That it should be a top business priority. That they should be focusing not only on how to help sick employees recover, but also (and to an even greater extent) on how to help them keep themselves well and able to thrive in the workplace.

Many organisations who have now come to this view have changed the way they work and seen the resulting benefits. Examples of these changes are set out below. The positive consequences these organisations have experienced include: improved recruitment and retention of the best people, particularly among the younger generation; greater credibility of their commitment to diversity and inclusion; and increased profitability.[7] And many have contributed to a shift in attitudes to mental illness; encouraging more open and honest discussion of factors that might contribute to ill health (physical and mental); and helping to reduce stigma and to improve the language used to talk about it ("mental health literacy" as some call it).

But many challenges remain, not least in determining what practical steps really have a positive impact. That in part results from difficulties in finding reliable evidence on the effectiveness of the extensive range of choices – including healthier eating initiatives, mindfulness, yoga, and resilience[8] training in its various forms. In turn that

[6]The World Health Organization definition of health includes "a state of complete physical and mental wellbeing and not only the absence of disease and infirmity", and as being both "a resource for living a full life" and "the ability to recover and bounce back from illness and other problems" https://www.who.int/data/gho/data/major-themes/health-and-well-being, page 1. And some refer to the latter point in defining resilience as the ability to bounce back/recover from set-backs, failures or mistakes.

[7]It is hard to obtain hard evidence to support the link between these benefits and the increased commitment to wellbeing. But the anecdotal support, at least from firms based in the City, is strong: strong, active and consistent, sustained support for the sorts of initiatives referred to elsewhere (including CMHA) – support which would have been unlikely unless firms saw benefits from them in all these areas, and almost certainly stopped if it had been perceived to have a negative impact on eg profitability; senior leaders speaking increasingly publicly about their experiences and how the reactions of their colleagues/organisations contributed to their recovery; and the ability of firms to continue to attract good people while increasing their focus on wellbeing relative to some of the other attractions previously emphasised.

[8]The use of the term "resilience" in this context evokes mixed reactions. Some prefer self-confidence or mental toughness, considering *resilience* inappropriate because to them it suggests that people need to learn to adapt or mould themselves to toxic work environments rather than seeking to change them – ie that you can't be both *resilient* and *resistant*. Some also consider it to be sexist – suggesting a trait of inherent strength more often associated with men than women. Those are not meanings with which the term is intended to be associated in this paper. Instead, it is intended to focus (as do most dictionary definitions) on a person's ability to *bounce back or recover* from misfortune. The ability to get up again when they fall (or fail), not that they have learnt never to fall (or fail) in the first place – an unrealistic and counterproductive belief which can severely damage self-confidence when faced with new challenges. And it's meant to be combined with, not to be an alternative to, the ability to strive to make the ground more even so that we reduce the risk of falling (or perceiving oneself to have failed) in the first place.

can lead to difficulties in persuading key stakeholders to make the necessary investment (both financial – answering the Chief Finance Officer's questions about return on investment; and in behaviour change – including dealing with leaders whose attitude is displayed by comments like: "I didn't get where I am today by encouraging malingering!"). And it presents major headaches for those responsible for determining which of the plethora of wellbeing providers to engage, particularly with their necessarily limited budget.

What works?

None of these questions is easy to answer. And there is no "one size fits all" solution. But the following approaches have been found by some organisations to be effective – when working both in the office and remotely (e.g. as during the Covid-19-induced lockdowns).

- **Demonstrate leadership from the very top** – if the words and actions of the most senior people in the organisation are consistent with and reinforce the messages from HR and others, your wellbeing initiative has a chance of succeeding. If they are inconsistent, it will probably fail, and prove to have been a counterproductive waste of time and money.
- **Combine top-down leadership with "bottom-up" initiatives** – empower junior, less-experienced and younger people to create their own initiatives. They are likely to be better suited to their needs than those imposed from the top.[9] And in doing so, recognise that different things will work for different people. Some will find mindfulness helpful, others will hate it. So too with yoga, gym sessions, retail therapy, singing, cooking, gardening. Offer a range of options so that people can work out what's best for them.
- **Encourage story-telling** – significant benefits have come from people sharing their experience of mental ill health, and how they came through it and went on to achieve success. Such story-telling helps break the stigma, it motivates and empowers, and it encourages greater openness. Sharing stories of how organisations have developed and implemented a wellbeing strategy, including things that have not worked, also helps.
- **Collaborate rather than compete** – collaboration between law firms and between them and their clients has been key to the success of many initiatives in this area, including the City Mental Health Alliance (CMHA) and the Mindful Business Charter;[10] and a much more productive approach than competing to be number one in a race without any reliable way of determining what "success" looks like.
- **Build the business case** – many consider this simply to be the right thing to do from a moral and ethical perspective. But that may not be enough to persuade the CFO to release the funds needed to make appropriate investments. Focus instead on the positive impact it will have on the bottom line/

[9] For example, the Junior Lawyers Division of the Law Society and the "Thriving from the Start" initiative of the City Mental Health Alliance (CMHA), run by and for those entering the City to help them address the challenges that transition involves and work out how to thrive in that environment <http://citymha.org.uk/supporting-graduate-mental-health/>.

[10] <https://mindfulbusinesscharter.com/#what-is-the-charter>.

profits. Healthy people are more productive, generate higher quality work more consistently, make fewer mistakes and generate fewer claims on your professional indemnity and private medical insurance. They are also likely to stay with the organisation longer, and become its ambassadors, rather than its enemies, when they move on.

- **Change the way you view/use technology** – on the one hand, manage potentially negative effects of technology, for example by agreeing email management rules with your internal team and with your clients, and ensure that everyone, including those at the senior end of the organisation, comply with them. And on the other hand, enhance its ability to generate positive effects, through using technology-enabled wellbeing products and services.[11] But don't overdo it. As one mental health tech CEO put it: "People like doing things with other people. There is no killer app."[12] This has become a particular challenge with so many forced by the Covid-19 crisis to work remotely, having to spend so much more time online and leading to the new, and very real, phenomenon of "Zoom fatigue".
- **Be human** – engage with staff as people not units of production. Listen more, particularly on non-work subjects. Build empathy. Identify people willing to act as mental health champions. Spot changes in people's behaviour which might be early signs of potential ill health, and make time to listen to people's concerns. The old adage "A problem shared is a problem halved" often proves accurate, and helps people move up rather than down the health curve. As one in-house occupational health practitioner once told me, the most important thing senior people can do to help is listen more – evidence of the value occupational health can provide when developing and implementing an effective wellbeing strategy.[13]
- **Provide resilience[14] and/or mental health first aid training** – the former comes in a range of forms, from external experts giving lectures to internally facilitated discussions. And there are several high-quality, reliable providers of the latter.[15] Work out what you want to achieve, consider which approach is most likely to fit with your culture and budget, give it a go, refine as appropriate.

These approaches are being used not only by City law firms but also by many others: law firms based elsewhere, the Bar[16] and in-house legal departments in the corporate, public (e.g. Government Legal Service) and third sectors. (They are

[11]Examples include BetterSpace, Unmind and CorLife (in all of which, in the interests of transparency, I own shares). And there are many others.

[12]For an interesting, informative, and practical discussion of how to build "e-resilience" see <https://thepsychologist.bps.org.uk/developing-e-resilience>.

[13]For more information, see the website of the Society of Occupational Medicine <www.som.org.uk>.

[14]See n 8.

[15]For example Mental Health First Aid England <https://mhfaengland.org/>. It is widely recognised that this can be helpful in raising awareness of mental health issues, including by law firms which have adopted it, but evidence of its effectiveness in the workplace is limited – see for example Public Health England's 2018 report <www.hse.gov.uk/research/rrhtm/rr1135.htm>.

[16]See summary at <www.wellbeingatthebar.org.uk/>.

also being applied by many other organisations, for example the Big Four accountants, banks and other corporates. But they are beyond the scope of this paper.)

Contributions of others

And there are many other organisations working in this area. Those primarily focusing on lawyers include our professional bodies and the charity LawCare.[17] For over 20 years, LawCare has been providing 24/7, 365 days a year support for lawyers on a broad range of challenges they face. But far too many in the profession are unaware that it even exists.

Others whose focus is on the broader mental health field include those to which I have already referred (CMHA and MHFA England) as well as Mind[18] and the Mental Health Foundation,[19] two of the UK's leading mental health charities. And those focusing on higher education more generally include Student Minds,[20] the Charlie Waller Memorial Trust,[21] the Matthew Elvidge Trust[22] and MindEd.[23] The websites of all of these organisations contain a great deal of valuable, practical guidance on how we can all look after ourselves and those around us for mutual benefit and the benefit of the organisations and communities in which we work and live.

Having established that much is already being done, including by organisations in which lawyers work, I turn to the role of those who educate them, in particular law schools, then offer a few suggestions on how the two stakeholder groups might emulate the collaboration which has proven effective elsewhere.

The role of law schools: perceived gaps

I left law school over 35 years ago, and my university days are an even more distant memory. So I clearly do not have first-hand, up-to-date knowledge of what life is like today for those entering those communities. Nor do I claim expertise in the new Solicitors Qualifying Examination (SQE), though I am aware that the changes involved have provoked significant controversy and concern, and that views vary on the extent to which its introduction will provide greater flexibility on what and how students are taught.

I am also aware that many legal academics consider their primary role to be to teach law, not to prepare students for a career in the legal profession – understandably given that only a minority of law graduates actually enter the legal profession (and, like the author, those in that profession never studied law as an academic subject). But even those academics (as well as those teaching other subjects), at least arguably, have a responsibility for the wellbeing of their students, and for helping them develop skills which will help them in whatever career they choose after leaving their academic

---

[17] Again, I declare my interest, as one of its champions.
[18] <www.mind.org.uk>.
[19] <www.mentalhealth.org.uk>.
[20] <www.studentminds.org.uk/charter.html>.
[21] <https://charliewaller.org>.
[22] <www.thematthewelvidgetrust.com/our-work/>.
[23] <www.minded.org.uk/>.

institute. And for those working in institutions whose primary role is to prepare for a career in the legal profession (as the Chancery Lane Law School was in the mid 1980s for the author), that responsibility is even more clear.

So while my legal academic experience is old, and may be regarded by some legal academics as only indirectly relevant, what is in my view relevant is my direct and recent experience of the attributes with which many law school graduates emerge into the world of work, and the extent to which those attributes help or hinder their prospects of thriving in the profession. I also know what younger generations are experiencing, including people who have recently completed their higher education and are entering or at an early stage of their legal careers.

On the basis of that experience, I see significant gaps between the needs of employers (and of those wanting to thrive as their employees and in due course leaders) and the skills of those entering the workforce. And I believe that some may be the result of law schools providing an education which may not always achieve the right balance between skills that employers value and those which are not as important to them as they may have been in the past.

There are many reasons for law schools operating the way they do,[24] and many other causes of these perceived gaps. Some are probably linked to much broader and complex issues relating to parenting philosophies, the impact of technology and social media, and the broader education system in the UK. Others may be the result of employers failing to explain clearly to educators what they do and do not value. So I am not suggesting that law schools are at fault. Instead, by identifying the gaps and encouraging a discussion about whether others also see them, I hope to catalyse a debate which will identify practical steps which will benefit everyone in the profession – and hopefully the wider community.

The gap which is most relevant for this paper is in junior lawyers' knowledge and understanding of how to look after themselves in new and/or challenging environments, and how effectively to identify and resist unreasonable demands on them. Others are beyond the scope of this paper but include being comfortable with face-to-face interaction with other human beings (something which I believe has become more of a problem in recent years) and the "old chestnuts" like basic English grammar, clear drafting skills and attention to detail.

Life as a lawyer can be tough. The hours can be long. And it can be challenging to meet client demands. For many, those are the very reasons for choosing the profession – why they find it so fulfilling. But for others, they are major contributors to their failure to achieve their potential. Many believe that is due at least in part to their not knowing how to keep themselves well so that they can meet those demands and thrive on the challenges. Some also argue that it is the profession, or at least many of its members, that needs to change – structurally and culturally. I agree with them. This is not about making "weak" people "stronger". It is about both individuals and the profession adjusting expectations, and learning from each other for mutual benefit.

[24]Examples include the need to comply with regulatory requirements, finding time in the curriculum, dealing with NSS feedback, meeting tight budgets, and difficulties in assessing the effectiveness of "soft skills" training (which in turn influences levels of staff interest and student attendance).

What could/should change?

So what in practice might those changes look like? Here are a few ideas for discussion.

First, increasing recognition that those attracted to law can be at a higher risk than others,[25] and developing support and educational interventions accordingly – learning, perhaps, from the experience at Bristol University which I understand has established a bespoke counselling service for those at law schools, both students and faculty.

Secondly, providing students with a clearer understanding of what life is like as a practising lawyer. Many law school faculty members have relevant experience, but may not have the time or the incentive to share it with students. Considerable benefits should result from enabling them to overcome whatever barriers they perceive, justifying the investment required in effecting the necessary changes. Based on what was said during the York Law School discussion, not only about their activities, but also about those of others, this is already happening in some law schools and generating positive results. Sharing those success stories should help others follow suit.

Thirdly, adding an appropriate form of resilience training to the syllabus, or modifying any existing programmes to make them more relevant and effective. That might require something else to be dropped from the syllabus – a task which might be challenging but which, in the current environment, ought to have the backing of the profession's regulatory bodies and may be easier when the new SQE comes in. Guidance is already available through the charities referred to above on what form that training could take, and their representatives would no doubt be delighted to be asked to help develop structures, materials and training to suit the profession's needs.

And lastly, the focus of this paper, greater collaboration with employers, including in relation to these suggestions.

What might employer/educator collaboration look like?

Making the profession healthier is the task of all of its stakeholders. No one group can achieve that goal alone. Collaboration is key.

When it comes to collaboration between educators and employers, the following may be worth considering.

First, employers being more open and honest about what life in their organisation is like. Recruitment initiatives, glossy brochures and fancy websites have their place. But they seldom provide students with opportunities to get a sense of what it will really be like – what opportunities and challenges they will face – if they choose firm X, chambers Y or in-house legal department in organisation Z as their first step into the world of work as a lawyer.

Why not invite representatives of local employers – including those at the junior end with whom students are more likely to engage – to participate more often in the life of law schools by sharing their day-to-day experiences of working life: their likes and dislikes; the highs and the lows; and what they wish they had known before choosing to work in this profession? That should increase the chances of students choosing career paths in which they will be able to thrive rather than struggle, helping them to "gain sound awareness of what their future professional environment will be".[26] It might also

[25]Supported by some of the studies carried out by Martin Seligman.

give students greater confidence to resist pressure from schools, career advisers, parents or others in their social network to do what they, rather than the students themselves, think will be most fulfilling, and as a result, reduce the risk of their becoming square pegs trying to find their place in round holes.

Secondly, shared training on resilience.[27] Many employers and educators[28] already provide some form of training in this area. Some use external providers, others internal facilitators. But is anyone considering whether they are consistent between the two stakeholder groups, and most importantly whether they raise false expectations? It would be unfortunate, for example, if a programme offered by a law school were to encourage students to push back too quickly or too forcefully on work allocation procedures of their future employer if that would, in that context, be considered a career limiting move. That is not to say students should be discouraged from challenging the status quo. Far from it. But they are more likely to achieve success if they have had an opportunity to learn more about the employer context and perspective, and to approach their challenges in ways which are likely to achieve positive change rather than their losing their job.

Sharing different approaches to this form of training should not be difficult, time-consuming or expensive. On the contrary, it is likely to save time and cost. How about starting by encouraging law schools and employers to invite each other's representatives to participate in their resilience training sessions (even easier to do when they are being run virtually), and being genuinely open to constructive mutual feedback afterwards? Each would learn from the other, and might even conclude that future events should be combined – avoiding duplication, achieving consistency, saving cost and possibly also helping with recruitment. If examples already exist, let's hear about them, let's find out what the impacts were, and let's develop and scale mutually beneficial programmes based on that experience.[29]

Thirdly, committing to joint, long-term, longitudinal studies on the impact of early interventions on people's careers – for example providing a resilience training session in the first year of law school and monitoring that cohort's performance in later studies and in their legal careers over the following few decades.[30] This would obviously require careful planning and long-term commitment, and would not be straightforward. But the benefits ought to justify the investment required.

And lastly, all stakeholders talking more about successful, thriving and healthy lawyers, rather than focusing so much on those whose health suffers, or lives come to a premature end, while working in the profession. Those "bad news" stories are important: for raising awareness, and to understand what didn't have the desired effects and to learn from that. But there is a danger in spending too much time focusing on the negative, grey and rainy skies and not enough on the big, blue sunny alternative which is the reality for many.

[26]A phrase used by Ben Waters of Canterbury Christ Church University in concluding his review of the opportunities and challenges presented by the introduction of the SQE: Ben Waters, "The Solicitors Qualification Examination: Something for All? Some Challenges Facing Law Schools in England and Wales" (2018) 52 The Law Teacher 519, page 3.

[27]See n 8 for a discussion of the meaning of this term in this context.

[28]Some of which have based their approaches on the work of Sheldon and Krieger on self-determination theory – see for example the paper by these authors cited in n 5 above.

[29]More collaboration between different faculties within the same educational establishment may also help, for example between the faculties of law, business and medicine.

[30]As suggested, for example, by Caroline Strevens, building in part on her co-edited book Caroline Strevens and Rachael Field (eds), *Educating for Well-Being in Law: Positive Professional Identities and Practice* (Routledge 2019).

Conclusion

If things don't change, the profession risks decline: in its reputation,[31] in its ability to attract and retain good people, and in its financial performance. That could deprive future generations of the opportunity to benefit from working in the profession in the way so many of us have in the past. And I believe all of its stakeholders, including those who educate and employ its members, owe it to those future generations to work together to avoid that happening.

I also believe that our profession can lead a broader change in attitudes to mental health in the wider community,[32] helping to focus on people's abilities rather than their needs and on rebuilding communities that have become fragmented.[33] In doing so, the profession would regain some of the respect many believe it has lost in recent years. It would be a shame to let that opportunity go to waste.

Disclosure statement

The author was a co-founder of the City Mental Health Alliance and has served as Chair both of its main Board and its Advisory Group. As stated in note 11, he is a shareholder in BetterSpace, Unmind and CorLife. He was for many years a partner of Linklaters LLP.

---

[31] For example, there is a link between wellbeing and ethical behaviour. Improving the former should help maintain high ethical standards, with consequential benefits for reputation.

[32] Through improved collaboration between employers (as is already being done to some extent – see earlier footnotes for examples), between the business and educational communities, and between different faculties within educational establishments (eg law, management and medical schools, all of whose York-based stakeholders participated in the discussion on 20 November 2019, for which the initial version of this paper was prepared).

[33] As advocated so persuasively by Cottam in her recent book: Hilary Cottam, *Radical Help: How We Can Remake the Relationships between Us and Revolutionise the Welfare State* (Virago Press 2018). See also Jonathan Freedland, "There's an Idea That Could Transform Britain – but Brexit Won't Let It Be Heard" *The Guardian* (London, 16 August 2019) <www.theguardian.com/commentisfree/2019/aug/16/britain-brexit-public-services-whitehall>.

Harnessing the winds of change

Anne Macduff and Vivien Holmes

ABSTRACT

Emerging scholarship demonstrates that the curriculum can have a positive impact on student wellbeing. Indeed, a well-designed and delivered curriculum may serve a protective function, bolstering the wellbeing of students in the classroom when life outside is full of pressures and stressors. This is good news. It suggests that educators concerned about student wellbeing can make a positive difference by focusing on educational design principles and developing sound teaching practices. There are already a number of high-quality, web-based resources designed to assist educators in this task. One important issue yet to be explored concerns the barriers teachers experience in implementing curriculum change and how to overcome them. This article evaluates the effectiveness of a "Wellbeing in the Curriculum Tool" at an Australian law school. We argue that if we wish to improve law student wellbeing, the way that the message of change is delivered needs to be as enhancing of wellbeing as the content.

Introduction

Teachers in many educational settings, from primary schools to universities, now recognise the importance of student wellbeing for effective learning. Various reforms have been devised and implemented, from health and counselling programmes targeting individual students to structural changes in the learning environment. The issue of student wellbeing and need for effective programmes has become all the more acute since 2019, when Covid-19 prompted a sudden and significant change to educational practice around the globe.[1] Many students remained "at home" and interacted with their teachers and classmates online. The impacts on student wellbeing of studying in this environment, both positive and negative, are still being observed and are yet to be analysed.

Scholarship demonstrates that whether students are online or in the classroom, an important aspect of the learning environment is the curriculum.[2] Course

[1]See, eg, George Marinoni, Hilligje van't Land and Trine Jensen, *The Impact of COVID-19 on Higher Education around the World* (IAU Global Survey Report, International Association of Universities 2020).

[2]Wendy Larcombe, Chi Baik and Sue Finch, "Exploring Course Experiences That Predict Psychological Distress and Mental Wellbeing in Australian Undergraduate and Graduate Coursework Students" (2021) HERD 1.

design can have a positive impact on student wellbeing.[3] Indeed, a well-designed and delivered curriculum may serve a protective function, bolstering the wellbeing of students when life is full of pressures and stressors. This is good news. It suggests that educators concerned about student wellbeing can make a positive difference by focusing on educational design principles and developing sound teaching practices, as appropriate for online, in-person or hybrid teaching.[4] There are a number of high-quality, web-based resources that have been designed to assist educators in this task.[5]

One preliminary and important issue yet to be explored concerns how to motivate teachers to make these changes. Part of this investigation involves identifying the barriers to implementing curriculum change and working out strategies to overcome them. As Larcombe, Baik and Finch note, there have been few university-wide curriculum interventions to support student wellbeing. They suggest that one barrier to the adoption of such interventions is the lack of specific evidence about which aspects of university experience make a difference to the student experience.[6] Their recent research addresses that gap by investigating the effects of six common coursework experiences on student wellbeing – "academic workload, assessment pressures, teaching style, sense of belonging, engagement with other students, and intellectual motivation".[7] The effects of these six experiences on student wellbeing, they found, were "significant and substantial".[8]

We hypothesise that another barrier to curriculum change in higher education may be difficulty in engaging teachers. Academic articles and web resources are limited in their ability to successfully engage teachers who are busy, unaware, or perhaps even suspicious, of "purported" links between student wellbeing and their curriculum.[9] Even if teachers are aware of the links between student wellbeing and the curriculum, teachers may also feel overwhelmed by the size of the student wellbeing issue and feel unable to take action.

Finding effective ways to engage and support teachers in good curriculum design is all the more important in the present climate. Covid-19 has generated a number of challenges for teachers. The sudden and significant changes required in course delivery, reduced ability to plan and lack of job certainty in the higher education sector have depleted the energy and capacity of many teachers to embark on curriculum

---

[3]Stuart Slavin, Debra Schindler and John T Chibnall, "Medical Student Mental Health 3.0: Improving Student Wellness through Curricular Changes" (2014) 89 Academic Medicine 573; Stephen Tang and Anneka Ferguson, "The Possibility of Wellbeing: Preliminary Results from Surveys of Australian Professional Legal Education Students" (2014) 14(1) QUT Law Review 27; Rachael Field, James Duffy, and Colin James (eds), *Promoting Law Student and Lawyer Well-Being in Australia and Beyond* (Routledge 2016); Chi Baik, Wendy Larcombe and Abi Brooker, "How Universities Can Enhance Student Mental Wellbeing: The Student Perspective" (2019) 38 HERD 674.

[4]Anneka Ferguson and Stephen Tang, "Determined to Be Professional, Ethical and Well" in Caroline Strevens and Rachael Field (eds), *Educating for Well-Being in Law: Positive Professional Identities and Practice* (Routledge 2019).

[5]<http://unistudentwellbeing.edu.au/curriculum-design/>; <www.wellbeinginhighereducation.com/resources.html> last accessed 30 November 2021.

[6]Larcombe, Baik and Finch (n 2) 2.

[7]ibid 12.

[8]ibid.

[9]See Nigel Duncan, Rachael Field and Caroline Strevens, "Ethical Imperatives for Legal Educators to Promote Law Student Wellbeing" (2020) 23 Legal Ethics 65, 69–70. Duncan and others note resistance amongst legal educators to the idea that they have an obligation to design curricula to promote wellbeing.

innovation and change. Nonetheless, raising the issue of student wellbeing with academic staff remains an important task, which needs to be done with sensitivity, delivering practical help and a realistic sense of hope.

In this article, we report on the piloting of a "Wellbeing in the Curriculum Tool" (the "Tool") at an Australian law school.[10] The Tool aims to engage teachers by raising awareness about the student wellbeing issue in an accessible, supportive way. The pilot results, while small, are encouraging; and we hope that, with some modifications, the Tool will achieve this aim. Once it has been more thoroughly tested, we plan to release the Tool more widely.

Wellbeing and the curriculum – the current research

A growing body of empirical research across Australia, the UK and US points to concerning levels of mental distress amongst university students, levels that are disproportionately high when compared with the same age group in the general population.[11] It appears that university education environments share common features that can erode student wellbeing, including the six common elements of coursework programmes mentioned above.[12]

Evidence of the effect of *legal* education on law student wellbeing is longstanding, international and extensive.[13] US scholar Lawrence Krieger's work on law students, lawyers and wellbeing has been influential over several decades, both in the US and elsewhere.[14] Australian scholars have developed a significant body of work addressing similar issues.[15] In the UK, the focus on the effects of legal education (as distinct from general university education) has grown in recent years.[16] Reviewing this body of work, Duncan, Field and Strevens conclude that:

> there is now a solid base of empirical evidence that establishes that the psychological wellbeing levels of law students are the same or higher than the general population when they begin their university study, but about a third of students are experiencing psychological distress by the end of their first year of legal education.[17]

---

[10]In Australia, the law degree is taught at both undergraduate level (Bachelor of Laws, usually combined with another undergraduate degree, the combined degree being five years) and postgraduate level (Juris Doctor, three years).

[11]Baik, Larcombe and Brooker (n 3) 674–75.

[12]Larcombe, Baik and Finch (n 2).

[13]Duncan, Field and Strevens (n 9) 68.

[14]See, for example, Lawrence S Krieger, "What We're Not Telling Law Students – and Lawyers – That They Really Need to Know: Some Thoughts-in-Action toward Revitalizing the Profession from Its Roots" (1998) 13 Journal of Law and Health 1; Lawrence S Krieger, "The Inseparability of Professionalism and Personal Satisfaction: Perspectives on Values, Integrity and Happiness" (2004) 11 Clinical Law Review 425; Lawrence S Krieger, "The Most Ethical of People, the Least Ethical of People: Proposing Self-Determination Theory to Measure Professional Character Formation" (2011) 8 University of St Thomas LJ 168; Lawrence S Krieger and Kennon M Sheldon, "What Makes Lawyers Happy? : A Data Driven Prescription to Redefine Professional Success" (2015) 83 George Washington Law Review 554.

[15]See, for example, Judy Allen and Paula Baron, "Buttercup Goes to Law School: Student Wellbeing in Stressed Law Schools" (2004) 29 Alternative Law Journal 285; Molly Townes O'Brien, Stephen Tang and Kath Hall, "Changing Our Thinking: Empirical Research on Law Student Wellbeing, Thinking Styles and the Law Curriculum" (2011) 21 LER 149; Caroline Strevens and Rachael Field (eds), *Educating for Well-Being in Law: Positive Professional Identities and Practice* (1st edn, Routledge 2019) <www.taylorfrancis.com/books/9781351104395> accessed 29 January 2021.

[16]Duncan, Field and Strevens (n 9) 67.

[17]ibid 68.

This leads them to argue forcefully that the evidence is strong enough to engender a collective moral obligation in legal academics to design curricula, teaching and assessment approaches that support student wellbeing.[18] We concur.

Approaches to curricula, teaching and assessment that support student wellbeing were the focus of The Enhancing Student Mental Wellbeing Project[19] undertaken by several Australian academics and funded by the former Australian Government Office for Learning and Teaching. The Project developed five principles for enhancing student wellbeing in line with the framework provided by self-determination theory (SDT).[20] SDT is a theory of human motivation originating from the work of Deci and Ryan and now well established by research.[21] SDT posits that humans flourish when we are "autonomously" motivated to do things because they are "intrinsically interesting or satisfying, or ... will facilitate valued goals".[22] In contrast, if we feel that others are pressuring us to act, or are somehow controlling what we do, our wellbeing suffers. Thus, if we are *autonomously motivated*, we do what we are interested in and what is important to us. "Controlled" motivation, on the other hand, sees us acting in a certain way because we feel pressured or controlled by others.[23]

SDT recognises three basic psychological needs as antecedents to psychological wellbeing: autonomy, competence and relatedness.[24] When our need for *autonomy* is met, we feel that we are able to live in a way that reflects our true self. If our *competence* need is met, we feel capable of mastering tasks and meeting challenges. And when we feel *relatedness* to others, we feel closely connected to the important people in our lives and have a *sense of belonging* in social groups.[25]

It is worth noting that SDT recognises the importance of context and social environment for wellbeing. Indeed, research on SDT has focused on understanding the "social environments that optimize people's development, performance, and wellbeing".[26] The call to address curriculum design should be understood in this context, and as a rejection of the idea that mental ill-health is predominantly an individual and clinical concern,[27] and consequently, not part of the core business of academics. Further, it is also worth being explicit about the values that underpin a curriculum that enhances wellbeing. The basic psychological needs recognised by SDT (autonomy, competence and relatedness) are more likely to be met if we hold to the pro-social values of self-understanding, good relationships with others, helping others and building community.[28] These are the values

---

[18]ibid.

[19]Chi Baik and others, *Enhancing Student Mental Wellbeing: A Handbook for Academic Educators* <http://unistudentwellbeing.edu.au/curriculum-design/> accessed 29 November 2021.

[20]ibid 13.

[21]Richard M Ryan and Edward L Deci, *Self-Determination Theory: Basic Psychological Needs in Motivation, Development, and Wellness* (Guilford Publications 2017) 3–8.

[22]Baik and others (n 19) 8.

[23]ibid 9.

[24]Ryan and Deci (n 21) 10–11.

[25]Baik and others (n 19) 8–9. A Guide for Lawyers (2016), 36 <https://www.lawsociety.com.au/sites/default/files/2018-08/Being%20Well%20in%20the%20Law%20Guide.pdf> accessed 30 November 2021.

[26]Richard M Ryan and Edward L Deci, "Self-Determination Theory and the Facilitation of Intrinsic Motivation, Social Development, and Well-Being" (2000) 55 American Psychologist 68, 68.

[27]Christine Parker rightly rejects this idea in Christine Parker, "The 'Moral Panic' over Psychological Wellbeing in the Legal Profession: A Personal or Political Ethical Response?" (2014) 37 UNSWLJ 1103; see also Paula Baron, "Sleight of Hand: Lawyer Distress and the Attribution of Responsibility" (2014) 23 Griffith Law Review 261.

[28]Krieger (n 14, 2011) 172.

that underpin the five principles of curriculum design developed by Baik and colleagues.[29] Such values are in opposition to the individualised, neoliberal and managerial approach to education and wellbeing critiqued by others.[30]

The "Wellbeing in the Curriculum" Tool: designing in line with SDT principles and trauma-informed practice (TIP)

The five principles of curriculum design for enhancing student mental wellbeing through learning and teaching developed by Baik and colleagues are as follows:[31]

(1) Foster students' autonomous **MOTIVATION**, and sense of meaning and purpose
- Highlight the social value of discipline practitioners' knowledge and skills
- Support students to develop learning goals in line with their intrinsic values and emerging interests and capabilities
- Demonstrate that you value students' learning and understand their perspectives

(2) Promote inclusion and **BELONGING**
- Know your students' diverse needs and interests
- Value diversity and practice social inclusion
- Induct students into your discipline's values and professional standards

(3) Promote inclusion and **RELATIONSHIPS**
- Facilitate student-faculty and peer social interactions
- Foster collaborative (not competitive) learning
- Express interest in and care and concern for others

(4) Enable **AUTONOMY**
- Justify required tasks and knowledge, and teaching and assessment methods
- Within the constraints of the curriculum, give students choice and ensure variety in learning activities and assessment tasks
- Support students to make informed choices aligned with their interests, values or goals

(5) Scaffold **COMPETENCE**
- Use informational (rather than controlling) language
- Ensure an appropriate level of challenge and support at each program level
- Provide meaningful feedback on student learning and performance

It is these five principles that inform the questions in the Tool about wellbeing and the teacher's course. The Tool helps teachers to reflect on their course design and evaluate the extent to which their teaching approach and practices implement these principles. However, these principles not only create the framework through which teachers can evaluate their courses (the content of the Tool), but they inform the design of the Tool itself. That is, rather than create yet another "task to do", the form and structure of the Tool seek to enhance wellbeing as staff engage with it.

---

[29] Baik and others (n 19).

[30] Parker (n 27); Baron (n 29); Richard Collier, "Wellbeing in the Legal Profession: Reflections on Recent Developments (or, What Do We Talk about, When We Talk about Wellbeing?)" (2016) 23 International Journal of the Legal Profession 41; Richard Pring, "Introduction" in Terence Lovat, Neville Clement and Ron Toomey, *International Research Handbook on Values Education and Student Wellbeing* (Springer 2010) xx–xxi.

[31] Baik and others (n 19) 13.

Design of the Tool was therefore also informed by principles of trauma-informed practice (TIP). This aspect of the Tool is unique. It ensures that the Tool not only promotes student wellbeing, but enhances teacher wellbeing. As explained below, while not all teachers experience symptoms of trauma, an activity that is "trauma informed" is more inclusive, engaging and empowering for participants than one that is not.

Why TIP? Trauma, traumatic events and PTSD

Studies indicate that community exposure to traumatic events is relatively common. One US study found that 44% of the general population had been exposed to at least one traumatic or "adverse life" event.[32] Figures in Australia are similar, with 57–75% of Australians experiencing a potentially traumatic event in their lifetime.[33] The figures in the published research vary between countries and over time, depending on breadth of the definition of "traumatic event". While a "traumatic event" was initially defined as a reaction to an "unusual" event, such as experiencing or witnessing serious injury or a threat to physical integrity,[34] more recent studies recognise the potentially traumatic impact of more common experiences such as the death or illness of a friend or relative.[35]

Although increased exposure to the number and severity of traumatic events increases the risk of experiencing trauma symptoms,[36] individual outcomes differ considerably. Some individuals may not experience any distress after exposure to a traumatic event, while others can develop PTSD, anxiety and depression.[37] Figures in Australia indicate that 12% of the population will experience PTSD at some point in their lifetime.[38] Some of the current criteria for PTSD include; exposure to a traumatic event,[39] an experience of feeling overwhelmed by the event, and one of a number of effects lasting a month or more such as flashbacks, nightmares and avoidance of similar situations.[40] The high threshold for PTSD has prompted some to argue that partial PTSD ought to be recognised.[41]

---

[32] Naomi Breslau and others, "Trauma and Posttraumatic Stress Disorder in the Community the 1996 Detroit area survey of trauma" (1998) 55 Archives of General Psychiatry 626.

[33] Stephen Rosenman, "Trauma and Posttraumatic Stress Disorder in Australia: Findings in the Population Sample of the Australian National Survey of Mental Health and Wellbeing" (2002) 36 Australian and New Zealand Journal of Psychiatry 515.

[34] Patricia Frazier and others, "Traumatic Events among Undergraduate Students" (2009) 56 Journal of Counseling Psychology 450, 450.

[35] ibid.

[36] Dean Lauterbach and Scott Vrana, "The Relationship among Personality Variables, Exposure to Traumatic Events, and Severity of Posttraumatic Stress Symptoms" (2001) 14 Journal of Traumatic Stress 29; Fran H Norris, "Epidemiology of Trauma: Frequency and Impact of Different Potentially Traumatic Events on Different Demographic Groups" (1992) 60 Journal of Consulting and Clinical Psychology 409.

[37] Naomi Breslau, "Epidemiologic Studies of Trauma, Posttraumatic Stress Disorder, and Other Psychiatric Disorders" (2002) 47 Canadian Journal of Psychiatry 923; Jacques Mylle and Michael Maes, "Partial Posttraumatic Stress Disorder Revisited" (2004) 78 Journal of Affective Disorders 37.

[38] Rosenman (n 33).

[39] Post traumatic stress disorder is defined in the DSM-5 as 'the development of characteristic symptoms following exposure to one or more traumatic events'. Exposure can be direct or indirect, and includes exposure to, witnesses, or is confronted with actual or threatened death or serious injury, or sexual violence. American Psychiatric Association, *The Diagnostic and Statistical Manual of Mental Disorders* (5th edn, 2013, p 271-272).

[40] Brian Borsari, Jennifer P Read and James F Campbell, "Posttraumatic Stress Disorder and Substance Use Disorders in College Students" (2008) 22 Journal of College Student Psychotherapy 61.

[41] Mylle and Maes (n 37).

The high rates of exposure to trauma suggest that this issue and its impact on sections of the population ought to be more frequently considered. In the absence of studies about the prevalence of exposure to trauma and/or PTSD in university law teachers, we suspect that levels will be at least comparable with those in the community.

Further, it is possible that the prevalence of trauma amongst university law teachers might be higher than in the community, particularly if one takes into account the impact of vicarious trauma. Pearlman and Mac Ian define vicarious trauma as the cumulative effect of 'empathatic engagement with clients' trauma experiences' and 'is an occupational hazard for those who work with trauma survivors'.[42] Although the experience of the traumatic event is indirect, shared through accounts or images, the symptoms of vicarious trauma can be just as severe as the original trauma.[43]

Law teachers might be more likely to experience vicarious trauma than the general population due to their experiences with either university students or legal clients, or both. Studies in the US confirm that college (university) students are more likely to be exposed to traumatic events than the general population.[44] A number of US studies indicate that the prevalence of traumatic events (whether or not the events resulted in PTSD) for college students is between 66%[45] and 94%.[46] Although, to our knowledge, similar studies have not been undertaken in Australia, given the similarities in rates of trauma exposure, university student ages, and rates of interpersonal violence (physical and sexual) in Australia and the US, we might guess that the rates are comparable.[47] Further, law teachers may also have been exposed to vicarious trauma as a legal practitioner,[48] particularly if they are/were practising law in areas with clients from high-risk sub-groups such as victims of crime and sexual assault.[49]

---

[42]Laurie Anne Pearlman and Paula S Mac Ian, "Vicarious Traumatization: An Empirical Study of the Effects of Trauma Work on Trauma Therapists" (1995) 26 Professional Psychology: Research and Practice, 558.

[43]ibid. Jason M Newell and Gordon A MacNeil, "Professional Burnout, Vicarious Trauma, Secondary Traumatic Stress, and Compassion Fatigue" (2010) 6(2) Best Practices in Mental Health 57.

[44]Frazier and others (n 36); Jennifer P Read and others, "Rates of DSM–IV–TR Trauma Exposure and Posttraumatic Stress Disorder among Newly Matriculated College Students" (2011) 3 Psychological Trauma: Theory, Research, Practice, and Policy 148; Jeffrey A Bernat and others, "Prevalence of Traumatic Events and Peritraumatic Predictors of Posttraumatic Stress Symptoms in a Nonclinical Sample of College Students" (1998) 11 Journal of Traumatic Stress 645; Borsari, Read and Campbell (n 42).

[45]Read and others (n 44).

[46]Scott Vrana and Dean Lauterbach, "Prevalence of Traumatic Events and Post-Traumatic Psychological Symptoms in a Non-Clinical Sample of College Students" (1994) 7 Journal of Traumatic Stress 289; Bernat and others (n 46); Borsari, Read and Campbell (n 42); Frazier and others (n 36); Joshua M Smyth and others, "Prevalence, Type, Disclosure, and Severity of Adverse Life Events in College Students" (2008) 57 Journal of American College Health 69; David G Purves and Philip G Erwin, "A Study of Posttraumatic Stress in a Student Population" (2002) 163 Journal of Genetic Psychology 89.

[47]One significant environmental differential, however, is the strict gun laws in Australia which suggests that Australians are less likely to have been fearful due to another person using a firearm. This differential was also noted in a German study of prevalence to trauma exposure in university students. A Perkonigg and others, "Traumatic Events and Post-traumatic Stress Disorder in the Community: Prevalence, Risk Factors and Comorbidity" (2000) 101 Acta Psychiatrica Scandinavica 46.

[48]Andrew P Levin and Scott Greisberg, "Vicarious Trauma in Attorneys" (2003) 24 Pace L Review 245; Lila Petar Vrklevski and John Franklin, "Vicarious Trauma: The Impact on Solicitors of Exposure to Traumatic Material" (2008) 14 Traumatology 106; Grace Maguire and Mitchell K Byrne, "The Law Is Not as Blind as It Seems: Relative Rates of Vicarious Trauma among Lawyers and Mental Health Professionals" (2017) 24 Psychiatry, Psychology and Law 233.

[49]Dean G Kilpatrick and others, "Victim and Crime Factors Associated with the Development of Crime-Related Post-Traumatic Stress Disorder" (1989) 20 Behavior Therapy 199; Dean G Kilpatrick and others, "Criminal Victimization: Lifetime Prevalence, Reporting to Police, and Psychological Impact" (1987) 33 Crime and Delinquency 479.

From "trauma-informed teaching" to "trauma-informed practice"

The increased recognition of the impacts of trauma on learners has led to reforms in teaching and, subsequently, service design more broadly.

The impacts of exposure to trauma, vicarious trauma and other adverse life events on learners, whether or not they satisfy the criteria of PTSD, are significant. Trauma can result in learners being distracted/unfocused, disengaged/unresponsive, and/or having poor self-regulation of emotions leading to outbursts, a lack of confidence, perfectionism, and/or anti-social coping mechanisms such as social distancing and rejecting relationships.[50] Studies have recognised the negative impact of childhood trauma on academic success in primary and secondary school,[51] with some further studies examining the impact on adults and college (university) students.[52]

In 2005, the Massachusetts Advocates for Children proposed three principles of "trauma-informed teaching" for children: Attachment, Regulation and Competence (ARC).[53] These principles aim to support children who have experienced trauma or adverse life events, even when they have been diagnosed with PTSD. The ARC principles do not suggest that teachers become therapists,[54] nor that the curriculum be compromised.[55] Rather, they acknowledge that a teacher can shape the learning environment to better support, rather than alienate or punish, children who have experienced trauma, broadly defined.[56]

The Australian Child and Adolescent Trauma, Loss and Grief Network (ACATLGN) has expanded and updated this research,[57] transforming the ARC principles into BRACE guidelines. To paraphrase, these include:

- Belonging – establishing a safe and secure environment, including fostering connections between students, staff and families
- Routine – consistent approach to expectations and predictable routines
- Attachment – a focus on the development of relationships, ensuring diverse needs are met
- Competence – building competence by working from strengths, capacity for mastery
- Emotions– recognition, expression and regulation emotions, including enhancing self-regulation.[58]

---

[50] Massachusetts Advocates for Children, "Helping Traumatized Children Learn: Supportive School Environments for Children Traumatized by Family Violence" (Trauma and Learning Policy Initiative in collaboration with Harvard Law School and The Task Force on Children Affected by Domestic Violence, 2005) 4, 22–41.

[51] Sue R Beers and Michael D De Bellis, "Neuropsychological Function in Children with Maltreatment-Related Posttraumatic Stress Disorder" (2002) 159 American Journal of Psychiatry 483; Susan M Shonk and Dante Cicchetti, "Maltreatment, Competency Deficits, and Risk for Academic and Behavioral Maladjustment" (2001) 37 Developmental Psychology 3; Christopher Blodgett and Jane D Lanigan, "The Association Between Adverse Childhood Experience (ACE) and School Success in Elementary School Children" (2018) 33 School Psychology Quarterly 137.

[52] Tzvi Gill and others, "Cognitive Functioning in Post-Traumatic Stress Disorder" (1990) 3 Journal of Traumatic Stress 29; Read and others (n 46).

[53] Massachusetts Advocates for Children (n 50) 44.

[54] ibid 52.

[55] ibid 54.

[56] ibid 54.

[57] Australian Child and Adolescent Trauma, Loss and Grief Network, Supporting Trust in Schools Program: ANU 3 https://earlytraumagrief.anu.edu.au/files/TRUSTBRACE_0.pdf accessed 30 November 2021.

[58] ibid.

The ARC and BRACE principles inform "trauma-informed practice" (TIP), which has the broader aim of improving the delivery of services to those who have experienced trauma.[59] There are some similarities between BRACE and the SDT principles of curriculum design developed by Baik and colleagues.[60] Belonging and Competence feature in both sets of principles. This overlap might be expected because trauma affects wellbeing, and mental health distress is an adverse event that can manifest as trauma. (We note, though, that wellbeing is a broader concept than trauma, and that mental health distress can be triggered other than through "traumatic events", even broadly defined.)

BRACE principles informed the design of the Tool in three main ways. First, the Tool seeks to enhance belonging by creating a safe and supportive space for raising the issue of student wellbeing. The Tool is designed for voluntary use, with participants able to withdraw at any time without providing an explanation. The survey results remain confidential, so that the teacher has complete control over the information that the Tool produces about their course. Teachers can choose not to answer any particular question without providing an explanation. This ensures that the teacher controls the process and the outcome, and does not feel exposed to criticism or evaluation arising from their engagement with the Tool.

Second, the Tool seeks to understand and help the teacher to articulate the feelings and emotions that arise when they engage with the issue of student wellbeing. In addition to the wellbeing survey based on the five domains of SDT, there is a preparation survey and a follow-up survey. These additional surveys are opportunities for reflection. That is, they prompt the teacher to identify their feelings and engagement with the issue of student wellbeing in order to better understand their own needs and perceptions in relation to the course, as well as the extent to which the course promoted student wellbeing.

Third, the Tool seeks to build competence. It gives teachers the opportunity to identify what was implemented well, and what they might do differently. It acknowledges strengths in teaching, and holds this focus throughout the three surveys in the Tool. The Tool allows the teacher to see, at the beginning of the course, what the results of the wellbeing survey might be at the end of the course. Thus, the Tool provides both formative and summative feedback, rather than being a purely diagnostic mechanism. These design aspects serve to build competence by turning a potentially overwhelming topic into a set of concrete and targeted ideas for curriculum changes that a teacher can later implement at their own pace.

Of course, use of a survey format for the Tool meant that full implementation of BRACE principles was not possible: individual surveys do not foster connection between participants. However, we chose a survey format because it would be widely accessible and quickly completed. Further, surveys are more interactive than journal articles and other forms of written information about wellbeing, in the sense that teachers are being asked to *do* something. Specifically, the Tool asks teachers to answer questions that apply their understanding of student wellbeing to their own course.

---

[59]Colin James, "Towards Trauma-Informed Legal Practice: A Review" (2020) 27 Psychiatry, Psychology and Law 275; Roni Berger and Laura Quiros, "Supervision for Trauma-Informed Practice" (2014) 20 Traumatology 296; Joshua M Wilson, Jenny E Fauci and Lisa A Goodman, "Bringing Trauma-Informed Practice to Domestic Violence Programs: A Qualitative Analysis of Current Approaches" (2015) 85 American Journal of Orthopsychiatry 586.

[60]Baik and others n 19.

By drawing on both SDT and trauma-informed principles, we sought to ensure that the Tool would not become just another burden on teachers, placing responsibility for student wellbeing on their shoulders and adding yet another dimension to their workload. Instead, within the limitations of the online survey format, the Tool is designed to be an empowering activity, one that respects teachers' feelings and engagement with the topic, while facilitating awareness about the links between student wellbeing and the curriculum and encouraging ideas for improvement in course design.

An alternative strategy identified in the literature to support those exposed to trauma and vicarious trauma is to develop strategies of self-care.[61] We did not adopt this strategy in designing the Tool, preferring to prioritise structural intervention in the curriculum in order to bring a pedagogical focus to the issue of wellbeing, while also building on the existing strengths of teachers.

The Tool: three surveys

The Tool comprises three surveys. The first is a preparation survey. The second (wellbeing) survey asks teachers to consider aspects of their curriculum development in line with SDT. The third survey is an evaluation survey. These three surveys are delivered through the software platform Qualtrics. They are primarily a mix of self diagnostic and self-reflective exercises about aspects of the curriculum, rather than mechanisms to gather data about the wellbeing of students enrolled in the course.

The first activity, the preparation survey, is ideally to be completed by the teacher when they are planning the course: for instance, when they are selecting content or designing activities and assessment tasks. It has five multiple-choice questions, designed to prompt the teacher to rate the degree of their existing level of knowledge about wellbeing and the curriculum. The aim is to encourage the teacher to privately reflect on their own level of knowledge, and their perceptions and attitudes towards the issue of student wellbeing in the curriculum. The survey endeavours to support the teacher to identify any barriers to change that might currently exist, and to articulate the level of control they feel they have to implement any changes. If, however, the planning window is missed, the preparation survey can be completed at any time before the second wellbeing survey is undertaken.

The preparation survey is designed not only to raise awareness about the issue of student wellbeing in the curriculum, but also to provide teachers with the conceptual framework through which they can evaluate their course design, and act immediately. To this end, the preparation survey includes a link to the second (wellbeing) survey, so that the teacher can preview how their course might rate against the five domains of SDT.

The second survey involves the teacher completing a wellbeing questionnaire, which is distributed to them at the end of their course. The wellbeing questionnaire is designed to enable teachers to self-assess their course to determine whether, and if so how, their course promoted student wellbeing. The questionnaire contains 36 questions on teaching practices that reflect the five SDT domains. The questionnaire

[61] Patricia J Shannon and others, "Developing Self-Care Practices in a Trauma Treatment Course" (2014) 50 Journal of Social Work Education 440; Douglas W Ellison, Jennifer L Walton-Fisette and Kevin Eckert, "Utilizing the Teaching Personal and Social Responsibility (TPSR) Model as a Trauma-informed Practice (TIP) Tool in Physical Education" (2019) 90(9) Journal of Physical Education, Recreation & Dance 32.

asks the participant (teacher) to rate the extent to which elements of their curriculum design (course design, activities, content, assessment, etc.) actually did address the principles of autonomy, belonging, competence, autonomous motivation and positive relationships. At this point, the Tool operates more as a diagnostic tool, enabling teachers to articulate and assess for themselves the impact of the course design on student wellbeing. After the teacher has submitted the questionnaire, a list is generated which recommends specific educational resources available online to support curriculum changes for that course. The teacher's self-evaluation of their course against each of the five areas is captured in an image, the "Wellbeing wheel". The image, available to the teacher to download, provides a visual record against which the teacher can benchmark the extent to which their course curriculum supported student wellbeing.

An optional element of the second wellbeing questionnaire is for teachers to invite student feedback. With teacher consent, students are asked to rate the course design according to the same wellbeing questions. The purpose of inviting student feedback is to help the teacher triangulate their self-evaluation with student perspectives.[62] If the teacher chooses to invite students to participate, the teacher is given an invitation text to distribute, so that it is clear that the decision to be involved (or not) will have no impact on student grades, etc. in the course. Student responses are anonymous. Other than whether or not they are enrolled in that course, no personal details about the student are collected. Student ratings on each of the five SDT domains are averaged and aggregated, and then communicated to the teacher using the image of the "Wellbeing wheel". The Wellbeing wheel, which represents the students' perspectives, can be placed alongside the teacher's self-evaluation, facilitating a comparison across the five SDT domains.

The third evaluation survey is provided to the teacher after the wellbeing questionnaire has been submitted and student feedback (if requested) has been gathered and the aggregate report (and image) sent to the teacher. This survey has 11 questions, both multiple-choice and open ended. This evaluation asks the teacher how aware and confident they feel they now are to engage with wellbeing issues in curriculum design after completing the suite of activities in the Tool.

The purpose of this evaluation survey is to encourage teachers to reflect on the process of curriculum development that they have been engaged in. They might compare how they rated their course design at the start of the course to how they have rated it at the end. If they invited student feedback, they might compare their self-evaluation with the feedback from students. An important element of the evaluation survey is to articulate what, if anything, a teacher might carry forward into the next iteration of the course. This completes the action learning cycle, which Kolb and Kolb suggest encourages action in the future.[63] Another important element is the teacher's self-identification of barriers, emotional and practical, internal and external, to the implementation of future change. Identifying these personal barriers may be the first step in addressing and resolving them. This final activity is future oriented, asking teachers how often they might consider reusing the Tool. This suggests that designing curriculum to improve student wellbeing is an ongoing project of experimentation, diagnosis and self-reflection.

---

[62] Baik, Larcombe and Brooker (n 3). Although the survey does not give students an opportunity to make suggestions on the course curriculum, the fact that their feedback is requested and considered may of itself send an empowering message to students.

[63] Alice Kolb and David Kolb, "Eight Important Things to Know about the Experiential Learning Cycle" (2018) 40(3) Australian Educational Leader 8.

This Tool does not assess the extent of teacher or student wellbeing in any course, nor whether changes in the curriculum made after engaging with the Tool promoted student wellbeing. Understanding whether there has been a positive change would be, of course, important and interesting to know, and will be the focus of future research.

To ensure that the process of enhancing student wellbeing in the curriculum also enhanced teacher wellbeing, participation in the pilot of the Tool was voluntary. This was so that engagement with the Tool could activate the teacher-participant sense of choice and autonomous motivation. To ensure that participants had real choice to engage with the Tool, we insulated the participants as much as possible from any external pressure. This external pressure might have arisen due to a perceived expectation to complete the Tool or through a perception that their course could be criticised. For this reason, the identity of the teacher participants and the outcomes from the wellbeing questionnaire remained confidential. Any student feedback gathered was provided only to the teacher.

A consequence of this voluntary approach, however, was that the participants were already likely to be interested in the issue of student wellbeing and motivated to engage with the Tool. While we attempted to make the Tool as interesting as possible for teachers with limited knowledge, time, and experience, the teachers who are most resistant to exploring the connections between student wellbeing and the curriculum are not likely to be motivated to engage with the Tool. While reaching these resistant teachers and raising their awareness is important, we felt that making the Tool compulsory would significantly erode the principles of STD and TIP. Weighing up the competing considerations, we hoped that ensuring that the Tool supported STD and TIP would not only enhance individual wellbeing of teacher participants, but that this positive outcome would generate a sense of community curiosity, that might increasingly draw in those who were less motivated.

The pilot and its (interim) results

The Tool was piloted at an Australian law school in a 12-month period from July 2020 to July 2021. Ethics approval was given by the relevant university Ethics committee. An invitation to participate in the pilot was sent to all staff responsible for teaching at the Australian law school. Eight teachers delivering courses in that 12-month period agreed to participate, with others indicating interest in future participation. Twelve courses participated in the pilot. Three were large courses (more than 200), and nine were smaller courses (less than 50). There were three undergraduate compulsory courses, four graduate compulsory courses, two elective graduate courses and three elective undergraduate courses. Nine courses were taught entirely online, and three courses in a hybrid format (both online and in person). The teachers participating were a mix of genders and their appointment levels ranged from Lecturer (Level B) to Professor (Level E). Six of the eight teacher participants opted to invite student feedback on the extent to which their course design promoted student wellbeing.

The Tool was evaluated through two surveys: a usability and an impact survey. Staff and students (if involved) were given a usability survey immediately following the wellbeing questionnaire (the second Tool activity). At the end of the evaluation survey (the third Tool activity) teacher participants were given the impact survey.

We acknowledge that data from only eight participants is a very small sample to analyse. However, the data does provide some preliminary findings. First, the data collected on the usability of the Tool suggests that, overall, the wellbeing questionnaire was appropriate and adapted to its goals. All but one of the participants reported that it was easy to use and that they did not feel that they needed special understanding or technical skills to complete it. Participants reported that they felt either very confident, or mostly confident, using the Tool. This suggests that the questions and the concepts raised in the questionnaire were mostly clear.

There was, however, one participant who indicated that they felt that it was unnecessarily long, and somewhat complex. Two other participants felt that the Tool did not provide sufficient information or detail about wellbeing, one reporting that the Tool was confusing, the other that the *online* format of the survey was unhelpful. In the next run, more specific evaluation questions will tease out issues concerning clarity, length, complexity and level of detail. It is unlikely that the online format of the Tool will change, but the benefits of its online delivery might be better explained, for example, reach, flexibility and anonymity.

While participants varied considerably in their response as to how often they would use the Tool, only the participant who did not find the online format helpful said that they would not use the Tool again. Moreover, one teacher who had not initially elected to invite student feedback indicated that they would next time. This suggests that the Tool does enhance teacher confidence.

The data collected suggests that most of the teacher participants found the Tool effective and useful. Interestingly, the degree of usefulness to a participant did not depend on either the level of the teacher participant's existing knowledge about wellbeing issues, or how important they rated the issue of student wellbeing. One participant, who described themselves as very well informed on issues relating to wellbeing and the curriculum, still found the Tool very useful. The two participants who did not find the Tool helpful also identified themselves as being very well informed on issues relating to wellbeing. This indicates that the questions and the resources provided do not detract from the issue of student wellbeing. Further, for the most part, the Tool provides a useful opportunity to reflect on a course, and generates new perspectives and insights regardless of the level of prior interest or knowledge about wellbeing.

Another outcome of the evaluation of the impact of the Tool was that although all eight teacher participants were already persuaded that there were important connections between the issue of wellbeing and the curriculum, most felt that the Tool further developed their understanding. Most teacher participants valued the fact that the survey presented the information on wellbeing in a multidimensional and detailed way. Participants mentioned that the Tool helped them to appreciate the diversity of student responses to their curriculum design and how different approaches and innovations might apply in different contexts. By contrast, two participants did not find the Tool detailed or informative enough. Interestingly, neither of these two participants accessed the educational resources that were listed at the end of the second activity (wellbeing questionnaire). See further discussion below.

These findings are, of course, inconclusive about the extent to which the Tool can help support and motivate a teacher who is sceptical about, or even rejects, the connection between student wellbeing and the curriculum. However, one teacher participant who initially did not elect to gather student input, did indicate that they would use the Tool again and when they did, would elect to gather student feedback. This suggests that the format of the Tool is confidence building. We anticipate that obtaining data from a wider cross-section of teachers will assist in further evaluating the Tool.

Most of the teacher participants commented that the Tool enhanced their capacity to identify innovations to improve their courses. This appeared to be due to the detail provided in the survey and the opportunity for the teachers to translate that detail to their specific course context and student cohort. However, two participants reported that the Tool did not provide sufficient detail about innovations that they could apply to their course. This suggests that it would be worthwhile to more explicitly flag how the outcomes of the Tool may generate specific educational innovations.

Most of the participants identified that the educational resources that appeared at the end of the second activity (wellbeing questionnaire) were helpful and well targeted, although the mechanism for viewing the list of resources (a PDF report) was not very clear or accessible. One participant reported not being able to see the list of resources. Two participants indicated that they did not access the educational resources. Interestingly, it was these same two participants who had noted that they wanted more detail from the Tool about student wellbeing. This suggests that signalling the importance of these educational resources and increasing their accessibility may be very important to enhancing a positive reception of the Tool. We will aim to ensure that the connection between the Tool and the educational resources is emphasised and accessibility is enhanced.

Conclusion

The winds of change are favourable. There is growing evidence from research that demonstrates how teachers can promote student wellbeing without needing to become either therapists or counsellors. This article reports on a new "Wellbeing in the Curriculum Tool" which raises awareness about this research and supports teachers to make appropriate curriculum changes for their context and cohort. To ensure that teachers are empowered by the process, the Tool is informed by SDT and "trauma-informed practice". The intent of the Tool is to engage teachers in an interactive and reflective way. Engagement is voluntary, information is confidential and controlled by the teachers, and the process aims to build confidence and motivation by drawing on the teachers' existing strengths and capacities. The Tool aims to create a safe place for the exploration of ideas and encouragement to change, all the while recognising that variations in teachers' context mean that what may be a great idea in one course may not work in another.

The early findings of the small pilot suggest that the Tool, with some modifications, might achieve its goals of raising awareness about student wellbeing and curricula, and supporting teachers to implement change. Certainly, most participants in the pilot reported that the Tool was useful in providing practical suggestions for how to enhance the curriculum to support student wellbeing. They also reported that this message was delivered in a manner that enhanced teacher confidence and motivation. While we do not know whether teachers translated their reflections and learning into action, the Tool will hopefully be another step forward for student wellbeing in higher education. We will continue testing and refining the Tool to better realise this aim.

Acknowledgments

We would like to acknowledge the assistance of Margaret Rowe, Anneka Ferguson, Meg Wootten and Ben Morgan.

Disclosure statement

No potential conflict of interest was reported by the authors.

Funding

This work was supported by an ANU Giving Grant (2018).

Index

Note: Figures are indicated by *italics*. Tables are indicated by **bold**.